Contents

ACKNOWLEDGEMENTS

Without the cooperation of a great many individuals and several local authorities, organizations and institutions (a few of whom prefer to remain anonymous) this study could not have been completed and I would like to thank them all most sincerely.

Many other busy people have made time to give invaluable help and advice during the course of the study and to list them all by name would probably prove tedious to the reader and risk giving offence to any whose names did not appear, but a general acknowledgement does not mean that I am less grateful.

Above all I would like to express my gratitude to the hundreds of people who agreed to be interviewed and the visually handicapped people who completed questionnaires, often with difficulty and in obvious discomfort; though in many cases they will be unable to read the results, they provided the basic data for the report and — like many of them — I can only hope that their cooperation might in some way and to some extent result in improved services for others in a similar position.

LJB

FOREWORD

It is only recently that visual problems other than blindness have been given much attention and most of that has been fixed on the able adult or student. By far the largest group of visually handicapped are the elderly and amongst them reading difficulties are commoner sources of handicap than distance. This causes surprise in some quarters which becomes astonishment when true figures are revealed. In one area it was thought by the Social Services that there were 600 handicapped, but a house to house survey uncovered 3,000.

Not only do the Social Services and medical professions bask in ignorance, but, partly owing to this, the public at large are also ignorant of what is available as visual aids, whether in print or on tape.

Mrs Bell's work, though directed at librarians, deserves to have a much wider circulation. It is a mine of information about present misinformation as to the needs and the scale of services required to meet the needs. All those concerned with the elderly and handicapped will appreciate how many quite simple measures could be taken to meet the facts she presents.

Mrs Bell herself states her professionally neutral stance became almost impossible to sustain as the research developed.

The NHS itself does not recognise the category of 'visually handicapped' who are silent sufferers of preventable deprivation with no publicity value in spite of their numbers. Complaints about the inadequacies in the NHS should be based on these sorts of shortcomings rather than on the weekly wage of hospital staff which we all hear so much about.

Such fallacies as worries about reading causing visual deterioration and fears about artificial lighting are found to be widespread. The inaccessibility of what should be simple measures because of time or distance or expense is stressed. So is the importance of objective fact finding because some of the elderly manage with very poor eyesight. Others give up active life for fear of losing their sight so that it becomes impossible for onlookers to estimate the true state of affairs.

Amongst Mrs Bell's recommendations is that wider publicity should lead to better services. This is certainly a correct view and if action were based on the facts she presents it would be a great step forward in helping the visually handicapped to lead a more active life, unhampered by fear of catastrophe.

I hope that Mrs Bell's work will get into the hands of all those who have any connection with the medical world, the social services and the voluntary organizations involved in helping the disabled or elderly.

P A Gardiner
Consultant Emeritus in Opthalmology,
Guy's Hospital

March 1980.

THE PROJECT

The interest of the Library Association and the British National Bibliography Research Fund

This report is an account of a study which was carried out between October 1977 and April 1979 and financed by a grant to the Library Association from the British National Bibliography Research Fund.

Particular attention has been paid in recent years to the needs of handicapped readers — though much remains to be done — and librarians have been made increasingly aware of the difficulties of the visually handicapped. In 1963, a Ministry of Health circular noted the need for libraries to set aside books in large print for people with defective vision, but few suitable books were available; the Public Libraries and Museums Act 1964 lays upon public library authorities the duty to 'provide a comprehensive and efficient library service for all persons desiring to make use thereof' and this provision has been generally interpreted to include the needs of the handicapped equally with those of all other sections of the community. Under the Chronically Sick and Disabled Persons Act 1970 local authorities must help 'substantially and permanently handicapped people' (including the blind and partially sighted) with radio, television, library or similar recreational activities at home and they must enable them to make use of outside recreational and educational facilities by assisting with transport if deemed necessary.

The Library Association had formed a Sub-Committee on Books for Readers with Defective Sight as long ago as 1960 (now the Panel on Reading for the Visually Handicapped) and this committee takes an active interest in large print and its use by the visually handicapped and has cooperated closely and continuously with the development of large print books. In 1964, it gave support and publicity to Mr Thorpe's experimental work on the first Ulverscroft books produced on a non-profit making basis and support was also given to the National Library for the Blind's plans for the Austin books, a loan collection of more serious large print titles intended to supplement those in the Ulverscroft series. In 1965, the Library Association published a special subject list 'Large and Clear' of

available publishers' titles in acceptably large print and in 1966 with
the help of a grant from the Viscount Nuffield Auxiliary Fund it
initiated a specialized and systematic investigation into the design of
reading material for the partially sighted, resulting in the publication
of the report 'Print for Partial Sight' by Alison Shaw in 1969.

The Library Association has acted as an informal coordinating
body for organizations concerned with the reading needs of the
visually handicapped; it has held several conferences designed to
draw public attention to various problems involved and has dis-
seminated widely. the published proceedings. It is continuously
engaged in giving advice in this area, has produced several booklists
and leaflets, notably 'Reading for the Visually Handicapped', now in
its third edition and from the start of its Large Print User Study
in October, 1977, members of the Panel have maintained a continu-
ing interest by meeting to receive and discuss interim reports.

Representatives of the British National Bibliography Research
Fund, the funding body of the project, have also monitored its
progress. The committee of the fund, which was founded as a permanent memorial to the earlier united efforts of the libraries, the
book trade and the learned societies, began its work in 1975, after
the assets of BNB Ltd were transferred in 1974 following the British
Library Act 1972 (which resulted in the BNB being absorbed into
the British Library.) The organizations involved are Aslib, BA/British
Council, British Library, Copyright Libraries, Library Association,
NBL, Publishers Association and the Royal Society; the objects of
the fund are to promote bibliographic activities and related research
and all concerned are grateful that the Large Print User Study came
within its scope.

The need for the study

Until the 1940s effort was concentrated on the provision of reading
material for people considered blind rather than on reading material
in print for the partially sighted or the elderly with failing vision.
Interest in the reading problems of the elderly and of the partially
sighted was, however, a feature of the 1960s, prompted by the
Younghusband Report and subsequent circulars and reports issued
by what was then the Ministry of Health. Large print reading
material for the partially sighted has been available in Britain since
1964 and a number of publishers have now increased the range available by entering the market pioneered by the Ulverscroft Founda-

tion. In the same period there has been a growing awareness of the importance of services to old people, among whom the greatest incidence of visual handicap is found, and in an ageing society one would expect these factors to lead to a steadily increasing provision. In 1951, for instance, there were fewer than eight million people aged 60 or more in the United Kingdom, whereas by 1981 it is estimated that there will be over 11 million (Social Trends, 1970). As public libraries are still almost the only outlet for large print book sales, provision is known to be very unevenly spread across the country, however, and loans from the National Library for the Blind also vary considerably from one area to another; the differences are apparently unrelated to population and to fundamental differences in the distribution of potential users, therefore even if one assumed that demands were being met entirely satisfactorily in some areas it was unlikely that they were being met in others; thus more information was needed in this respect.

The sales figures that were available have also shown that purchases by libraries levelled off prior to inflation in 1972 and seemed to have remained fairly static during recent years despite the introduction of Ulverscroft's smaller octavo format in 1969 and the visual appeal of the newer large print publishers' books — yet as there are still only about 2000 titles in existence for all the visually handicapped readers in the country, no library's stock of large print can even begin to compare in size with its normal stock. Should a Government Department be funding or subsidizing the publication of more large print, should librarians be buying more of the books which are available, or ought we to concentrate on reading machines or technical methods and aids to help partially sighted people to read 'normal' print — and if these were further developed, would people with even less vision then be likely to read large print? Questions such as these needed answers and because the original large print books resulted in divergent and sometimes contradictory reactions, a great deal of fact-finding about reader needs, opinions and satisfaction also needed to be done.

There has also been evidence of a lack of knowledge among the handicapped about the availability of large print and other services, typical of all kinds of aid for the disabled, according to surveys carried out in some of the London boroughs and in other areas. For example 40% of the disabled in Kensington and Chelsea were unknown to the Social Services and 78% of those who were known were not receiving some service they would have liked; of 201 people

selected for interview as being the most disabled identified in a
Tower Hamlets survey (Physical Disability and Community Care)
only 32 or 16% were registered with the local authority welfare
department and 138 or 69% of the sample were not registered with
any agency; in Greenwich half of the elderly people who said that
they did not use library services because they had difficulty in reading did not know of the existence of large print books. Similar
examples can be quoted from many other parts of the country — for
example, in Liverpool, where the corporation distributed a leaflet to
all 222,000 households in the city, the result was that the numbers
of Registered Disabled rose from 4,700 to 11,000 according to
Morris (1972), and the Isle of Wight, the first county to carry out a
house to house survey of the disabled, found not 600 as previously
assumed, but 3,000. This raises important questions about the
adequacy of statistics, about the degree of user satisfaction, about
the promotion, use and non-use of the material that does exist, and
about the most effective ways of reaching potential users, and it was
as an attempt to provide answers to questions such as these that the
Large Print User Study was needed.

No detailed investigation into the use and users of the existing
large print material in Britain had been completed, and such a study
would follow up the Association's work on the design of print for
the visually handicapped, undertaken by Alison Shaw in 1966, as a
result of which this particular area was suggested as being in need of
investigation — especially since the partially sighted as a group had
been neglected by the library user studies which proliferated and as
so few of these had looked at the problems of non-users. (The
programme evaluation being undertaken by the Division for the Blind
and Physically Handicapped at the Library of Congress and the Large
Print User Survey at Baruch College in New York are also likely to
provide useful data, but the American population is not entirely
comparable with the British population and these were regarded as a
complement to a British study rather than obviating the need for
one.) At present most of the limited information available about
large print is the result of work, publicity or evaluation carried out
by the publishers or the libraries and the procedures adopted often
only compare the achievements with the original intentions. Large
print books could now be said to have reached the evaluation stage,
where we needed to make definite statements about the extent of
use, potential use and usefulness. We needed to isolate the reasons

for non-use in particular and to be able to provide agencies with adequate information.

A good deal of progress has been made by some public libraries in making special provision for handicapped readers, including the visually handicapped, but much remains to be done and substantial further progress is often impeded by factors beyond the control of the libraries, for example the existence of suitable material and the lack of public knowledge of services available. The Library Advisory Council for England, which was set up under the 1964 Act, is very conscious of the difficulties in this area; in the summer of 1975 a Working Party under the chairmanship of Mrs Anne Corbett was formed specially to look at the provision made for those who suffer from disadvantage in relation to library services, and to advise the Secretary of State (DES, 1978). The Working Party's remit was, of course, very much wider than the problems of the partially sighted, but it was hoped that research such as this would be a valuable complement and follow-up to the Working Party's study, extending its depth considerably in one area and that it would be possible to draw conclusions from the findings of such a study about future developments in British library services for the visually handicapped reader.

Objectives

The main objectives of the study were to establish whether or not the present provision of large print reading material meets the real needs of the visually handicapped, and if it does not, to make recommendations for action. Other aims were to help librarians in regard to purchases, accessibility and the promotion of special material for the group and to collect reliable information of use to the Library Association Panel on Reading for the Visually Handicapped, the welfare services, Government Departments and publishers, though some of the facts which emerged will also be of interest to many of the 'link-men' represented in the final survey — ophthalmologists and opticians, schools, agencies and societies for the blind and partially sighted, social workers, health visitors and those who work with old people.

The study attempted to answer the following specific questions:

Who (in terms of age, education, social background and visual ability) reads large print books at present, from public library counters or messengers, via housebound or mobile services, in old people's Homes, schools for the partially sighted and blind, hospital libraries and prison libraries, together with some indication of their degree of satisfaction with the books available?

What is the size and composition of the *potential* large print reading community amongst the visually handicapped; who act, or ought to act, as 'link-men' in passing on information about services, and are *they* aware of what is available (family doctors, ophthalmologists and other specialists, opticians, hospitals and institutions, local authority welfare workers for the disabled, geriatric visitors, Home Helps, Meals on Wheels, health visitors, clergymen, citizens' advice bureaux, voluntary welfare organizations, Home wardens, ordinary library users and neighbours); how did present users get to know about large print books?

What is the effect of differing 'housekeeping' attitudes to large print books (special shelving, position within the library, publicity inside and outside the library, relationship of library services to other departments and 'link-men', availability of other aids and specialized staff such as stock editors and welfare librarians, restrictions on borrowing, reserve stocks and the allocation of funds); how do present large print book/issue rates compare with normal book/issue rates in public libraries?

What are the reasons for people *not* using services, for example ignorance of services available, lack of interest in reading, physical inability to get to the library or reach shelves or carry books home, lack of titles, inadequate print or use of other recreational material such as radio, television or talking books?

Compared with the specialized subjects of other recent research such as Aslib's survey of the production of information guides and work undertaken at the Royal College of Art recently to study ways in which the information on library labelling should be presented for maximum legibility and comprehension, the scope of this Large Print User Study would have to be considered broad rather than specific; in a general study of this nature it was recognized at the outset that it would not be possible to answer every question equally well or to provide equally valid statistics on every aspect of the varied subjects under investigation, but it was hoped that a detailed and accurate overall picture of the situation would emerge, supported wherever possible by statistics and giving clear indications of future needs.

Definitions and statistics — the existing situation at the time of the study

A logical way to begin a description of the situation existing at the time of the study would be to give straightforward definitions of large print and of potential users, each followed by tidy, basic statistics. In the case of large print books this is feasible, but in spite of a considerable amount of background reading and some consultation with experts in the field, no entirely satisfactory definition of blindness or of partial sightedness has been found.

Blindness is not darkness, for only about 5% of the adult blind can see no light at all. According to Cullinan (1977) there are at least 67 different definitions of 'blindness' in use round the world. Although most countries can agree a definition of *total* blindness as 'an inability to perceive light in either eye' they have not agreed a definition of the much more common blindness which is less than total and which affects at least 30 million people in the world with a visual disability profound enough to amount to 'economic', 'social' or 'legal' blindness.

For registration purposes in this country, normally to have greatly constricted visual fields and to be incapable of any work for which eyesight is essential, or to have a *distance* visual acuity of less than 3/60 (Snellen) is seen as the criterion. (This latter means that the person with 3/60 vision can see at a distance of 3ft. what a person with normal sight can see at a distance of 60ft.) To be registered as blind does not necessarily mean that a person is totally blind or even likely to become totally blind. About 90-97% (according to differing sources) of the registered blind — 101056 people *in England only* at 31 March 1976 (Local Authority Statistical Returns) — can at least perceive light and point out the windows in a room; about one third have visual acuity of better than 3/60 and can see such things as hand movements or the outline of a face, and the number having visual acuity of better than 3/60 is estimated to be twice the combined total of those who are totally blind or have perception of light only; well over 50% are considered to have some degree of useful residual vision and according to the Government Social Survey (1968) 24% of the registered blind between the ages of 16 and 64 and 16% of those over 65 could read large print and 11% and 7% respectively read some ordinary print, so most could more accurately be described as people with extremely bad sight. Registration as blind depends on an inability to perform any *work* for which sight is essential, but does not take into account an inability to undertake *leisure* activities such as reading or the fact that one is past employment age, on the other hand. In any case registration is a voluntary matter in which the wishes of the patient and the possible benefits or disadvantages of registration play an informal part and consequently the register cannot show the complete picture.

For registration as partially sighted in England and Wales 6/60 is officially the appropriate stage on the Snellen chart and some people classified as partially sighted in some other countries would not qualify for registration here, but other considerations such as age, the need for special education and/or aids, occupation, general health and visual field may be taken into account. Varying estimates from local authorities are that from 0.1 to 11.9 per thousand of the total population are visually handicapped and about three in every thousand of England's population is actually *registered* either as blind or as partially sighted. The World Health Organization defines visual impairment as having less than 6/18 (Snellen) visual acuity in the better eye (and only 71% of Cullinan's recent sample came within that definition) whereas for registration as partially sighted in this country 'to be substantially and *permanently* handicapped by defective vision caused by congenital defect or illness or injury' is seen as the criterion. The main causes of partial sight — or perhaps we should be thinking in terms of partial blindness — in the largest group, the elderly, are macular lesion, cataract and glaucoma, and among other adults the main causes are retinal conditions such as retinopathy and choroidal atrophy.

Our specialists, social workers and laymen agree that it is often difficult to distinguish between the two groups. Robert Greenhalgh (1978) wrote that a great deal of confusion resulted when the Partially Sighted Society attempted to establish the difference between blindness and partial sight for survey purposes, i.e. where one ended and the other began. (A similar situation seems to exist in America, for Genensky (1973) tells us that in the USA Randsight research indicated that about 70% of the legally blind were partially sighted and not functionally blind.) There seems to be a considerable overlap between the two groups at most levels of visual acuity here, for there are partially sighted people who could or should be registered as blind and blind people who could or should be registered as partially sighted (a group for whom there are no financial incentives) — one significant result being that many people with the ability to read print are routinely taught to read braille instead.

The dividing line between normal vision and partial sight is also often difficult to define and Michael Wolffe (1980) points out that it is more meaningful to define partial sight as a condition that exists when conventional optical aids (i.e. spectacles) will no longer correct vision to the level required for the continuation of the individual's life style than to relate it to levels of vision and the state of the visual field. Registration provides a record of identification or discovery rather than of incidence and when the layman seeks statistics of the actual extent of visual handicap he is confronted by a bewildering variety of estimates and statistics from reliable sources — the inevitable outcome of a lack of consistent standards for measurement and definitions which depend upon where and how the lines are drawn. Furthermore there is the varying *nature* of visual impairment to take into consideration, in addition to the varying estimates of the extent. Some visually handicapped people with an impaired field of vision can read even small print while being unable to perceive large objects like cars off-centre; others have unimpaired peripheral vision while being unable to read large print. Some people (for whom glare control is important) suffer dazzle; others have blurred vision, double vision, poor night vision or blind patches only in parts of the visual field. Some eye functions begin to diminish in middle age, some diseases cause a very gradual loss of visual acuity which can often pass unnoticed until the inability to read print draws attention to the deterioration and others strike very suddenly.

Potential large print users

Throughout the world it is commonly estimated that there are at least 30 million partially sighted people and in Britain most estimates range from 180,000 to 225,000, though according to the Optical Information Council (1973) 'there are around 300,000 people in this country registered as partially sighted and a further 300,000 registered as blind — though many of these still possess a useful degree of vision, however slight'. According to the actual Register of Partially Sighted Persons for 1976, however, *in England only* there were 42,915 people *registered* as partially sighted, though 46,000 people were newly registered between 1969 and 1976 (the average time spent on the register before leaving it or transferring to the Blind Register being only around six years.) Almost all of these can read print of some sort, but the number of people with defective vision who could regularly make use of specially legible reading material in print is known to be many times greater than this. There are the undiagnosed, the impermanently affected and the unregistered, and including only the 'registerable' the last group alone is estimated to be twice as large by the Department of Health and Social Security (1979) — 'studies indicate that registration considerably under-estimates the prevalence of visual impairment especially for the partially sighted' — and to be four or five times the size by other experts.

In addition to the registered and unregistered partially sighted (and not only those in England) potential large print users include the estimated 24-25% of the registered blind with sufficient residual vision to read print with or without aids and the much greater, growing and unknown numbers of elderly people whose sight has failed to the extent that difficulty in reading 'normal' print is experienced. For all these reasons the term 'visually handicapped' is preferred to the term 'partially sighted'.

Though estimates of numbers and incidence rates vary according to where lines are drawn, it is generally agreed that the majority of visually handicapped people in Britain as in other countries are over retirement age. Eighty per cent of the visually impaired adults in Cullinan's very recent sample were in their retirement years as were 80% of the registered blind people in England and Wales in the 1960s (Ministry of Health 1966) and 73% of the registered blind and 65% of the registered partially sighted in England in 1976 were aged 65 or over. This is understandable considering that two major causes of defective vision — macular degeneration and cataract — are really part of the ageing process. Other main eye problems of those over 65 are small pupils, obscure lenses, absence of accommodation and reduced adaptation to dark, in addition to the effects of possible systemic diseases such as diabetes. As people now live longer the proportion of the population in the higher age groups is already growing and is likely to increase further. Statisticians predict that the proportion of persons of 65 years and over in the United Kingdom will be 14.1% in 1981 compared with 12.9% in 1971 (Harris, 1968) and that by 2001 the population of the very aged is expected to be nearly two-thirds as large again as it is at present (Central Statistical Office, 1970). Inability to read is reckoned to be the biggest visual trouble among the elderly, many of whom have low expectations and accept the inevitability of failing sight. There are far greater numbers of unrecorded elderly people with failing sight, many of whom have very real visual problems though they do not actually qualify for registration, than the already disproportionate number of people in their retirement years on the register. It is important to remember that the group is predominantly elderly when assessing their library needs, for whereas education and employment are likely to be considered more important for the young and for those of working age, the very limited leisure activities available to them are of major importance to the elderly; it is also worthwhile noting when assessing their needs that over 60% of the registered blind and 63% of the registered partially sighted are female.

In addition to these potential *regular* users of reading material in large print, there are many other groups of people who could benefit by making temporary or occasional use of such material: large groups of often unrecorded proportions, including those with only temporary eye complaints; readers awaiting spectacles or new lenses; people whose eyes are tired; post-operative cataract patients; some of the estimated two million adult illiterates or new readers — and a wide variety of hospital patients, since about 120 drugs in common use are known to affect the eye.

All these groups, then, are the *potential* users of large print to some as yet unknown extent. Only a proportion of them are likely to be readers or are likely to read books, however, and by the nature of the disability one would expect that a smaller proportion of these groups would be regular library users than the one-third which is usually estimated to be the proportion of library users among the general public. What a person is potentially capable of seeing will probably differ frequently from the practical use he actually makes of his vision and although 65% of the adults tested by Alison Shaw (1975) were capable of reading 12-point print, nearly half of them read only newspaper headlines or nothing at all. On the other hand a quarter of the people whose vision was so bad that they could see only large 20-24 point print still did some reading even though this often required the use of special magnifying aids — a high proportion of these being the people who regarded themselves as 'serious' readers rather than as 'average' or 'uninterested' readers. Seventy-five per cent of the registered 'blind' people in Cullinan's sample said that they could read a newspaper and 25% did so daily — only 40% of the entire group and 11% of the older group could read braille. Thirty-one per cent of the partially sighted in a Hillingdon survey (1973) could read normal print and 52% could read large print; for the blind the corresponding figures were 7% and 22% — a significant difference.

Large Print Books

It is, of course, much easier to give a definition and statistics of the large print books in existence at the time of the study than it is to estimate the numbers and kinds of potential users. Type faces differ in size as well as in design, but in order to generalize 10-12 point type faces can unfortunately be regarded as fairly usual sizes in 'normal' books whereas most specially produced large print books for the visually handicapped are printed in much blacker ink and on lightweight yet absorbent paper in 18-20 point type faces, with letters of approximately 1/8 in. high in lower case. Shaw's research (1969) has shown that boldness, type face design and spacing are very significant in making printed material legible and the publishers of large print books do take these and other factors such as weight, margins and the colour and opacity of paper into consideration to a varying degree when producing them.

Enlargement of print for the benefit of the visually handicapped is not a new idea. Nearly a hundred years ago in Germany special large print books were being published 'for children with weak sight, whose eyes must be spared', though development of this facility was hindered by economic factors and also by the fact that medical opinion discouraged people with poor sight from using their vision for close tasks like reading in those days. As a result of recent research, however, medical opinion now encourages the use of residual vision in most cases of defective sight and registration of the partially sighted (no matter how inadequate statistically) has helped in drawing attention to the difference between partial sight and blindness, with the resulting development of special education and welfare services for the partially sighted over a period during which there have also been significant developments in printing technology (Yelland, 1980.) Macmillan and Heinemann published special clearly printed editions from 1897 to 1926 and from 1931 to 1954 respectively, but 'The Large Type Revolution' (as it has been called) in American and British publishing did not begin until the 1960s.

Large print reading material for the visually handicapped has been available in this country since 1964, when the Ulverscroft Foundation's books were first produced in large format and Mr Thorpe received over 4000 letters in the initial period from the elderly and visually handicapped, hailing the books as 'life-savers' for their social, therapeutic and psychological value (Thorpe, 1972.) In 1965/6 the National Library for the Blind initiated a loan collection of enlarged reproductions of the original editions of selected classical titles produced in conjunction with University Microfilms and known as Austin books, to complement the Ulverscroft series, but almost the only outlet for large print books was and still is by direct sale to public libraries in order to keep prices down. Later in the 1960s several other publishers entered the market (particularly in America) for short periods, but presumably found it unremunerative and until recent years only the Ulverscroft series survived — produced in the smaller octavo format since 1969 and totalling about 1200 volumes at the time of writing — together with the 300 Austin books which are available on loan from the National Library for the Blind.

In the 1970s large print publishing in this country developed considerably and several other publishers entered and have remained active in the field. Probably the best known in library circles is Cedric Chivers, who first produced large print books in 1972 under the imprint of the Lythway Press and followed the launching of this series by the introduction of the New Portway Reprints in conjunction with the London and Home Counties Branch of the Library Association in 1974 and the Firecrest imprint for contemporary books in 1977. At the present time there is a steady output between them of about 120 titles each year, with a total of about 400 titles available in all, in addition to the books of other British and American publishers distributed by Chivers. Other large print book publishers whose books are available in this country are Magnaprint, who began large print publishing in 1974 (and through them, John Curley — together producing about 120 titles each year and with about 400 titles already to their credit), George Prior — about 200 titles available (and through them, G K Hall), Harrap, The British and Foreign Bible Society and, until recently, Franklin Watts. Many other publishers and organizations have published smaller amounts of material in large print and the books of publishers in Italian, Spanish, French, Welsh, Swedish, German, Danish and Dutch can also be obtained in this country.

'What is available in large print publishing today is a good range of frankly recreational reading, together with a certain number of standard works of literature and a growing number of basic manuals on crafts and hobbies. What is not available is the wide range of knowledge and literature available to the normally sighted person. It is estimated that 2,000 large print titles are in print, but more than 30,000 new titles are pubished in the United Kingdom *each year.* To produce in large print even a sizeable fraction of the range of literature available to the normally sighted person would be neither economic nor sensible, so the visually handicapped person is always going to be at a disadvantage although his or her range of interests may be just as great' (Yelland, 1980).

METHODOLOGY

Origins

The methodology of the study derived from several sources and if one were to think of the project as a tree then undoubtedly Alison Shaw was mainly responsible for the roots, having recommended such further research in her report (1969). In defining the direction, objectives, scope and timetable of the project in detail, in stipulating that the four main surveys should provide the basis of the study and later in nurturing it, the Research and Development Department of the Library Association developed the trunk and the four main limbs (in the form of the four surveys) from the original recommendations. The researcher was then appointed, briefed, orientated and allowed to translate the plans into practical detail — symbolically to develop the branches of the four limbs, the leaves on the branches and — hopefully — the fruit, in consultation with the Panel on Reading for the Visually Handicapped.

The researcher, although a Chartered Librarian (who could therefore be expected to appreciate the administrative problems and the possibilities of libraries and their services to visually handicapped readers) had been deeply involved in educational, social and other research for several years prior to the commencement of the study and therefore found it easy to start work on the project with an open mind and from a nil hypothesis.

The four main surveys planned by the Library Association were a) of librarians and libraries b) of large print readers c) of the community and d) of link-men. The first two surveys were primarily intended to provide information about the use and users of the material, while the third and fourth were primarily expected to provide information about the non-use and non-users. It was expected that the major part of the information required from the first three surveys would be collected by personal visits to libraries and other establishments in representative West Midlands areas, by interview, discussion and observation, whereas it was recognized that the major part of the information required from the fourth survey would need to be collected from a wider area by questionnaire.

The boundaries and the timetable

It was anticipated that a period of eighteen months full-time work by one researcher backed up by part-time secretarial assistance at the Library Association would be the appropriate period of time to be funded and consequently the project was officially commenced on 10 October 1977 and ended on 13 April 1979.

In all research of any worthwhile depth it is, of course, necessary to impose and clearly define boundaries at the outset and to specify the major dimensions to be considered in detail, no matter how unwillingly, because obviously the alternatives are to get really to the heart of a limited number of specific situations or to spread the available time more thinly over a wider area — and this particular study was already a broadly based one at the outset. In these circumstances it was regretfully considered necessary for the study to concentrate on the situation and the material only in this country, on only English-speaking readers and on books in the English language, on the visually handicapped rather than on the multi-handicapped and on adults rather than on readers of under 16. Shaw (1969) had demonstrated that for children the size of type was of less statistical significance than for adults; that children could achieve a larger image by using their powers of accommodation and convergence to read easily at close distances and 'the reading needs of partially sighted children are now generally considered to be less urgent in so far as large type is concerned, since ordinary texts can be held much closer to the eyes than is normally possible for adults' (Munford, 1976.) In spite of the amount of previous research into sight utilization and the educational aspect, however, in view of letters received, needs expressed and comments made during the course of the study it might be worthwhile for some future piece of research to remedy this omission by concentrating on the large print leisure reading needs of young people.

Although it did prove possible to complete the work within these specified limits in the allotted 18 months, a certain amount of presssure was felt by the researcher at some stages of the project, notably in the course of the second survey when spending seven consecutive weeks in libraries for the major part of their entire opening hours, together with the travelling time involved since some were 40 to 50 miles distant from the central base.

The third survey could probably have been improved upon if more time had been available for interviewing the visually handicapped —

the people who proved to require the longest contact time — so that less reliance could have been placed on written questionnaires from this group; however, had it been possible to adhere to the Library Association's original timetable to the letter more time would probably have been available here. A little more time than envisaged was spent on the early part of the project by undertaking an unplanned and time-consuming nationwide questionnaire to obtain statistical information from Chief Librarians everywhere, in addition to the planned interviews with librarians in the West Midlands; consequently less time than estimated was spent in interviewing link-men in the fourth survey and the form devised for use as a questionnaire was used additionally for this purpose without any detriment to the study in the researcher's opinion. The four interim reports took more time to complete than was anticipated by the Library Association, because it seemed important to provide the funding body and the Panel on Reading for the Visually Handicapped with very detailed information about each survey in turn (though this did eventually save time at the end of the project by cutting down on the allocated three months for final report writing) and the only other delays were caused by writing an extra report which was required by a local authority's research department as a condition of use of its residential Homes for the elderly and the exceedingly bad weather which delayed completion of the general community interviewing.

It is absolutely true to conclude, however, that a thoroughly worthwhile project was perfectly feasible in eighteen months and that, like most research projects, the study would have expanded to utilize *whatever* period of time had been available. The timetable shown below is the one actually followed; in spite of the adjustments detailed it bears a remarkably close resemblance to the one originally devized by the Library Association's Research and Development Department and the researcher was grateful for the permitted freedom and latitude without feeling the need to make any deliberate changes.

Allocation of time

Fieldwork	interviewing, observing, posting questionnaires, travelling	27%
Reporting	references, notes, interim and final reports, extra reports	20%
Forms	preparation, coding, analysis, statistics, tables	18%

Liaison	Library Association, BNB, Panel, meetings and travel	9.5%
Contacts	correspondence, telephone calls, meetings and visits	7%
Orientation	preparation, reading, literature search, experts, exhibitions	7%
Administration	planning, records, filing	6.5%
Public Relations	talks, articles, kits, conferences, visits, visual aids, broadcasts	5%

The methods used in general

The study began with a literature search for references to large print and to the partially sighted and the reading of a relevant collection of material supplied by the Library Association's Research and Development Department, after which the literature search was extended to include reading aids, the elderly, the blind and several other related fields. Various experts were consulted at this stage and throughout the study, including experts in the spheres of blind welfare, publishing, vision and social work in addition to experts on special aspects of librarianship and the study benefited from their generous help. Names and addresses of the contacts needed for all four surveys were collected, initial contacts were made and the relevant statistics of various West Midlands areas were studied; factors such as the type of environment and library authority, the population and numbers of elderly, blind, partially sighted, immigrants, hospitals and prisons were taken into consideration before the research areas were finally decided upon, and although only those within a 60 mile radius of the researcher's central base could have been regarded as practicable because of the travelling time and expense involved, the differing areas and authorities finally selected were considered a fairly representative sample.

Whatever names are used for them, the three main methods of collecting data are basically from documentary sources, questioning and observation, and as all forms of enquiry have their advantages and weaknesses it was considered best to use a combination of methods and thus counter the bias inherent in any one method. Contrary to a saying which has been applied to statistics, 'everything counts, nothing matters', the researcher considered that in a study of this nature feelings and impressions *did* matter and therefore both the objective and subjective kinds of enquiry were as

TIMETABLE PROJECT

Periods	Survey A – Library	Survey B – Reader	Survey C – Community	Survey D – Link-men	Simultaneous work common to all surveys
10.10.77-21.11.77	Listed questions Devised questionnaire A1	Listed questions			Consulted experts, preliminary reading, literature search, prepared area statistics
22.11.77-17.1.78	Devised statistics form A2, interview form A3, observation form A4, peripheral interviews and observations	Devised observation form B1 and interview form B2	Listed questions	Listed questions	Reading, correspondence, administration, literature search, contacts made for A and B
18.1.78-18.4.78	Interviews, observation, abbreviated A1 questionnaires to non-respondents	Interviews, observation	Devised interview structures C1 and C2	Devised interview and questionnaire form D1	Reading, correspondence, administration, preliminary notes on A and B, contacts made for A
19.4.78-31.5.78	Analysed and digested interview and questionnaire results, Interim Report A	Analysed and digested interview and observation results	Pilot interviews and revised structure	Pilot interviews	Reading, correspondence, administration, contacts made for C
1.6.78-24.7.78		Interim Report B	Interviews with elderly community	Despatched questionnaires, interviews	Publicity, reading, correspondence, administration, contacts made for C and D
Holidays					
29.8.78-10.10.78			Despatched questionnaires, interviews with elderly and visually handicapped community	Despatched questionnaires, interviews	Publicity, reading, correspondence, administration, contacts made for C and D
11.10.78-24.12.78			Despatched questionnaires, interviews with visually handicapped and general community, extra report	Despatched questionnaires, interviews	Publicity, correspondence, administration
2.1.79-16.2.79			Interviews with general community, analysed and digested interview and questionnaire results, Interim Report C	Analysed and digested interview and questionnaire results	Correspondence, administration, preliminary notes on C and D
17.2.79-13.4.79				Interim Report D	Literature search completed, Final Report

necessary as national and local, written and spoken, general and specific research. 'The statistical method . . . was needed to give bearings, but personal observation to give life to statistics . . . the figures or facts may be correct enough in themselves, but they may mislead from want of these properties or from lack of colour' (Hopkins, 1973). Since both interviews and questionnaires can create attitudes as well as assess them, even the questioning method was carried out in several ways: by written questionnaire; formal structured interview; semi-structured interview and by time-consuming depth interview, whereby recorded informal conversation was unobtrusively guided around a specific list of topics in spontaneous order, to differing degrees according to the interviewee's field of interest — and findings were laboriously extracted later. Attitude testing was also required at several stages of the project to allow for a wider expression of opinion than a mere 'yes' or 'no' (responses were consistently recorded on a five point scale ranging from very positive, positive and neutral to negative and very negative in all cases) — hence the multi-method approach was used wherever time allowed.

The Panel on Reading for the Visually Handicapped was involved at fairly regular intervals throughout the study and maintained a gratifying interest. Forms prepared for use either as pilot interview or questionnaire forms were submitted at meetings for approval or comment, additional questions were sometimes suggested by members of the Panel for inclusion, interim reports were received and discussed, the researcher's queries about current library practice were promptly answered, several busy members of the Panel were also consulted as individuals in relation to their particular speciality, and their cooperation was gratefully received.

Mention should be made here of an attempt made at all stages of the project to undertake a certain amount of public relations work and to give something in return for information received; consequently the various professionals encountered throughout the study were shown or given booklists or information after their interviews, fairly comprehensive large print and reading aid 'kits' were assembled and distributed later to participating libraries, the individual statistics for their libraries were supplied, many readers and other members of the public were informed about available books, services and reading aids according to their needs, and all opportunities were taken to broadcast, include the subject on Talking Newspaper cassettes and speak at meetings and courses. Only three short articles had been written for publication by the end of the study period, however, though this was remedied later when time permitted — and it must be remembered that this almost incidental aim of the work had to be regarded as second in importance to the investigation itself.

Finally, before proceeding to detail the specific methodology of each of the four surveys, it is necessary to state that in the absence of any consistent definition of visual handicap an operational definition was used consistently throughout the project. For the purposes of a study of large print and large print users it seemed logical to consider as visually handicapped those people who were *unable to read normal print, wearing spectacles if normally worn,* even though the lay researcher had minor misgivings — not because the category then included the unregistered, but because, though based on common sense, in some cases it included the 'unregisterable'. Just past halfway through the study, however, Dr Cullinan's 'Epidemiology of Visual Disability' (1977) was read and the researcher then discovered with some relief that exactly that same definition had been used by lay interviewers satisfactorily (in addition to including people unable to recognize a friend across the street, which would have been an irrelevant extension in an investigation into reading) for the purposes of the Canterbury Survey of the Handicapped (Warren, 1974).

Survey A — Librarians and libraries

The list of information required from librarians and libraries included subjects such as allocation of funds, large print stocks, loans statistics, housekeeping and publicity methods and effectiveness, attitudes, awareness and the librarians' views on users. It was decided that whereas information on all the latter topics would emerge more fully and freely and be more assessable if obtained by depth interviewing over a wide area in the West Midlands, the hard statistical facts would be more meaningful if obtained on a national scale and would be more easily available at the librarians' own convenience and at their own speed, i.e. by means of a questionnaire.

The full version of Form A1 was prepared in order to seek as much statistical information as possible, but including a few questions in which opinions were sought — partly to serve as a cross-check on those obtained later by interview and partly to make the form more interesting and therefore more likely to be completed. Except for the fact that these forms were distributed with explanatory letters to all 166 library authorities in Great Britain the full version of Form A1 could be regarded as a pilot questionnaire; certainly it served the same purpose, revealing that large print statistics were rarely available separately and that in any case few librarians could give comparable figures for the years prior to local government reorganization. This fact that large print records were so rarely available for comparison led several librarians to express a wish for standards in connection with large print provision and led many to take up the invitation to make estimates or leave blanks on the form. Furthermore, some county and other large authorities filled in one questionnaire with amalgamated figures for the entire authority as anticipated while others sent in forms relating to central or specimen branches, sent separate forms from only those of their service points from which there had been a response and some considered large print to be the province of their mobile libraries or housebound services and sent in returns relating only to these. Consequently a modified version of the A1 questionnaire form was based upon the information common to the majority of the forms already received and this was later issued with great success to all non-respondents, resulting in a 90% response rate overall (149 of 166 authorities replying, by means of 216 forms from a variety of outlets).

The researcher needed basic information about the areas in which the depth interviewing was to take place and as this could be obtained entirely from documentary sources a short form (A2) was devized so that the West Midlands areas could be quickly compared or contrasted and any outstanding differences which needed to be borne in mind could be seen at a glance. This and all the other forms used are shown at the end of this chapter on methodology.

Survey A had started with the collection of a little information over the widest possible area, by the questionnaire issued nationally. The researcher then began to 'zoom in' like a television camera by collecting information in greater detail from a smaller area, interviewing librarians and observing facilities in a sample of two to four libraries and other outlets in each of the five counties which make up the region loosely known as 'the West Midlands', before the spotlight was finally and fully concentrated upon the seven Metropolitan boroughs that make up the much smaller and more specific area of the County of West Midlands. These were depth interviews based upon the list of topics on Form A3; most of the librarians interviewed seemed positively to enjoy them, often setting aside half a day and sometimes assembling in twos and threes for a combined effort. In some cases this suggested that there was a basic feeling of insecurity about knowledge of the subject under discussion, which was interesting in itself.

One hundred and sixteen such interviews were conducted in 63 West Midlands establishments and the roles of the people interviewed in depth were:

6 Chief Librarians based in Headquarters
4 Deputy or Assistant Chief Librarians based in Headquarters
7 Heads of Bibliographic Services, Stock Editors or Librarians
8 Principal, Area or District Librarians
1 Assistant Publicity Officer

5 Central Library based Chief Librarians
3 Central Library based Deputy or Assistant Chief Librarians
4 Central Lending Librarians
3 Readers' Advisers
6 Central Library Assistants

14 Branch Librarians
2 Deputy Branch Librarians or Senior Assistants
11 Branch Library Assistants
1 Ex-Branch Librarian
1 Visiting Student

1 Mobile Librarian
1 Driver/Assistant
1 Mobile Assistant

2 Principal Area Librarians i/c Services to the Disadvantaged
1 Area Librarian i/c Service to Adults
1 Area Special Services Librarian i/c Hospitals
1 Area Special Services Librarian i/c Prisons
2 Librarians i/c Special Services
2 Hospital Librarians
1 Prison Stock Librarian
2 Prison Officers i/c Libraries

6 Assistants i/c Housebound Services
5 WRVS Volunteers or Drivers in Housebound Services
5 Assistants i/c Services to OAP Homes
2 WRVS Volunteers in Services to OAP Homes
2 Welfare Officers/Visitors with Voluntary Service for the Elderly

1 Assistant i/c Community Library
1 Assistant i/c Service to Centre for Disabled

3 Literacy Tutor Coordinators

The scoring element intended at the preparation stage of Form A4 was disregarded because of the frequent non-existence of some of the services or facilities to be scored, though its use as a library observation form did ensure that the same characteristics were consistently observed and recorded at each of the 25 large print collections and library services assessed.

Survey B — Large Print Readers

The list of information required from large print readers included subjects such as the composition of the group in terms of age, sex, visual ability, education, interests and life-style, their degree of satisfaction with the range of material and with the books themselves, the effects upon them of differing housekeeping methods and the ways in which they found out about the existence of large print. Only two methods were considered necessary for the collection of this information — by observation at the shelves and by structured interview, for which forms B1 and B2 were prepared.

After careful consideration of the statistics obtained from documentary sources such as annual reports, local authority departments and year books — already recorded on form A2 — three authorities in the West Midlands (in its widest sense) were approached for permission to undertake this interviewing and observation in a total of six differing libraries and a variety of other large print outlets. The Chief Librarians of Birmingham, of Hereford and Worcester and of Sandwell were all willing to cooperate, for which the researcher was extremely grateful. Their areas represented city, rural and industrial environments, their library systems differed and also the libraries eventually chosen represented as wide a selection as possible; only the 'Costa Geriatrica' was missing, though one area *was* becoming popular as a retirement area and 13.7% of the county's population was over 65.

The findings are based on personal observation of 602 readers and browsers of large print and a further 200 interviews with readers or their messengers, making a total of 802 people in all. The hospitality in the six libraries used for the purpose was greatly appreciated; except for lunchtimes (and on a few occasions an additional short break for tea) they all cheerfully suffered this loss of privacy for every single opening session of an entire week. This means, therefore, that with the exception of the readers who came into those libraries during such mealtimes — probably less than 5% — *all* the people i.e. 95%, who either borrowed or browsed at the large print section in the six libraries were recorded by one or other of the two methods.

The number of observations undertaken depended entirely upon circumstances beyond the researcher's control, i.e. the degree of activity at the large print shelves, where there were some sessions with six or seven half-completed forms being shuffled desperately as readers of the same age-group and sometimes of similar appearance moved around and other sessions where almost half a day passed before the first sign of interest. Even the number of interviews obtained depended to a certain extent on this same uncontrollable factor, as the researcher was unwilling to embark upon an interview when the shelves were busy; one interview could have caused several observation forms to be missed and would in many cases have resulted in an unacceptable lack of privacy for the interviewee.

The interview subjects were almost entirely selected at random within these imposed limitations, though unfortunately they did not constitute the same proportion of the readers in each library; for example in a library where 218 people either borrowed or browsed during the week it was practicable to interview only 22 of the readers whereas in a library where only 27 people either borrowed or browsed during the week it was convenient to interview 10 of the readers, a much higher proportion and in fact almost all of those who did actually borrow. The only exceptions to the random selection of interviewees were the omission of people very obviously in a great hurry (who would have refused anyway) and an attempt to bring the sample up to 200 with the deliberate inclusion of more males on the final two days in the sixth library. This was in order that the balance of the sexes in the total sample of those interviewed would finally be comparable with that of the 802 users as a whole (i.e. as close to c 70% female and 30% male as possible); even this very minor and justifiable manipulation was often thwarted by the fact that the men approached were sometimes joined by or choosing for their wives, who were the real or joint readers.

Only one person refused to be interviewed and as she was being given a lift home it had been a mistake to make that particular approach. Just as the librarians had been cooperative and often fairly interested in being interviewed, so were the readers. Naturally, this varied in degree, but on the whole the middle-class readers enjoyed the opportunity to talk about books and to express their opinions while the less well-educated were flattered to have their opinions sought. In one very poor area in particular the old people were pathetically eager to have someone to talk to and the reluctant parting words of one old lady interviewed early in the week were 'yours'll be the last human voice I hear now until Friday night!' In all six areas it was common and somewhat embarrassing to be approached by eavesdroppers and praised or thanked for talking to the large print readers or for being employed on such worthwhile work. Several of these — in addition to many of the users — asked for messages of appreciation to be passed on to Mr Thorpe.

As many librarians had shown either by their replies or their manner of dealing with the questionnaires that they considered the services to Homes, housebound and hospitals to be major outlets for large print books, it seemed desirable to undertake some interviews with readers from these sources. It was probable that both the opinions and the people needing to borrow by these methods — in many cases receiving a more personalized delivery service — might differ significantly from those borrowing in the six libraries, no matter how varied and representative the libraries chosen. For these reasons occasional opportunities to interview a completely random sample and to observe others were taken when such visits were made during the course of the Library Survey and prisoners were later included. This sample was made up to a number comparable with one library, during a week spent with an inner zone service; unlike the six weeks in libraries, it would be wrong to assume that *this* total of 78 people interviewed and observed represented 95% of the *total* borrowing from any or all of these sources during one particular week — it was merely that the comparable equivalent of 10 library sessions was spent in seeking them.

The seven one-week samples thus represented:

A A new suburban branch library in a prosperous middle-class residential area of a large city, serving an indigenous population and situated in a flourishing community centre with its own car park and a variety of activities and classes, all well-attended.

B A very old branch library in a decaying multi-racial inner city area, situated on a difficult major road where there had been considerable outward movement by the indigenous population, including shopkeepers, and inward movement by immigrants in general and by the younger Asian community in particular.

C An old central library in an industrial Black Country town, situated fairly close to large modern shopping centres, buses and car parks, opposite a post office and serving a well-established, multi-racial population.

D A fairly new suburban branch library serving an indigenous population, in converted premises in a residential area at the junction of three conurbations, with its own car park, situated fairly close to shops and buses, but separated from them by an extremely busy major crossroads.

E An old town branch library in the heart of a country market town becoming popular as a retirement area, serving an indigenous rural population and situated close to shops, buses, car parks and all other facilities — open for only four days weekly, including Saturdays.

F An old Cathedral city central library, serving an indigenous population of city and country dwellers, situated in a central position fairly close to shops and buses.

G An assortment of 'delivery' services, including: OAP Homes, OAP centres, OAP sheltered housing, a voluntary visiting service for the elderly, a centre for the disabled, a mobile library, a housebound service, a prison (male) and a hospital (female ward).

The composition of the groups interviewed and observed is shown below:

Library	Observations (of borrowers and browsers)		Interviews (with – or on behalf of – readers only)		Total seen at shelves (borrowing or browsing)		Totals
	M	F	M	F	M	F	
A	42	112	15	19	57	131	188
B	7	10	3	7	10	17	27
C	27	44	13	32	40	76	116
D	14	56	8	23	22	79	101
E*	15	39	5	15	20	54	74
F	59	137	10	12	69	149	218
G	10	30	6	32	16	62	78
7 weeks	174	428	60	140	234	568	802
	28.9%	71.1%	30%	70%	29.2%	70.8%	100%
	602		200		802		

* Library E opened for only four days weekly.

Survey C — The Community

The list of information required from the community was primarily in connection with non-use. It included such subjects as the awareness or otherwise of the general community about libraries, reading aids and large print; the composition of the elderly and visually handicapped groups in terms of age, sex, education, interests, lifestyle and visual handicap; their knowledge of services available, their use of or their reasons for not using large print books and/or libraries and the effectiveness of different publicity methods. Above all it was hoped that some kind of picture of the total large print needs of the communities studied would be revealed.

It seemed advisable to define 'community' in its broadest sense and to look at the extreme ends of the range of visual ability, from the general community to the blind community. It was possible that a non-scientific, but nevertheless useful estimate of the numbers of potential users of large print in society would emerge. Moreover as Dr Tobin of the Research Centre for the Education of the Visually Handicapped in Birmingham pointed out — if knowledge of any subject is to be diffused throughout the whole of society and there is to be a worthwhile take-up of a service, then there should be a pyramid of familiarity, with a lot more people than seem theoretically to need the knowledge knowing a little, as well as a few people at the top knowing a great deal. This means that ideally, large print should be part of the common encyclopaedic knowledge of the general community, just as the knowledge that smoking causes cancer is known by the whole of society and not only by smokers.

For these reasons three separate approaches were planned — to 500 members of the general public, for which the very brief four-question interview form C1 was prepared; to 200 members of the elderly community and as many visually handicapped people as possible in the available time, for both of which the longer form C2 was prepared, allowing for the interviews of people who were able to read normal print to be drawn to a natural conclusion after 12 general questions common to all. Those found to be visually handicapped by the terms of the Large Print User Study definition were to continue beyond question 12 through a series of graded questions relating to increased stages of visual handicap until the point was reached where the questions had become irrelevant and might only have alarmed the respondent.

In addition to the reasons already mentioned, the brief four-question interviews with members of the general public were designed so that by extracting information regarding visual ability, the use of libraries and public awareness about large print and low vision aids, the remainder of the more specific research about awareness and non-use would be shown in its proper perspective and also so that the friends, relatives and neighbours in the general community could be assessed as 'link-men'.

To a great extent the sample was selected at random, i.e. no time-consuming scientific attempt was made to equate the proportions to the age or socio-economic groups in our society as a whole and anyone (over the age of 16) encountered as soon as the previous interview had been completed was approached, regardless of age, sex, colour, apparent visual ability or manner. Stratified sampling could not be undertaken in the time available, because this usually requires either the pre-selection of a specified sample or time consuming home visiting. However, in order to balance the sample crudely, the interviewing took place in several different locations which could be classified into five groups, as shown below:

Type of area	M	F	Total
Suburban	14	66	80
Assorted shopping	43	79	122
'Academic'	69	56	125
City inner zone	34	70	104
Rural	33	36	69
Total	193	307	500

By interviewing during working hours it had been hoped that the number of females would exceed the number of males encountered and by nothing more than a happy coincidence the sample of females was over 61%, a figure which compared well with the samples used in the more specialized surveys. From the following table it can be seen that another useful result of interviewing during working hours (because of the relevance of age in a study such as this) was that although all age groups were well-represented, over 25% of the total sample were in their 60s or were older — in other words, a cross-section of the people who were 'out and about' in the daytime.

Area	10s	20s	30s	40s	50s	60s	70s	80s	90s	Total
Suburban	2	7	6	19	21	16	8	1	—	80
Assorted shopping	3	12	16	22	22	30	17	—	—	122
'Academic'	32	51	12	13	14	1	2	—	—	125
City inner zone	9	5	14	20	29	14	9	4	—	104
Rural	7	10	8	10	9	16	8	1	—	69
Total	53	85	56	84	95	77	44	6	—	500

(Housebound service librarians — please note that no-one estimated to be in the 80s or 90s was encountered in the assorted shopping areas and note how very few were 'out and about' at all)

In order that the survey can be seen to be fairly representative of the general public at large it might also be useful to point out that incidentally it included 37 people (or over 7%) of known immigrant origin, 29 of them interviewed in the city inner zone, five in the 'academic' areas (e.g. near colleges, university and polytechnic) and three in the assorted shopping areas. The part of survey C considered to be second in importance only to the main study of the visually handicapped was the survey of the elderly community, which was undertaken in two parts. One hundred and thirty-three people of retiring age and above, living in the community, were interviewed in locations where many tend to gather, i.e. Over 60s clubs, social clubs, day centres and lunch clubs — and after lengthy negotiations the sample was made up to a total of 200 by the inclusion of a further sample of 67 elderly people living in local authority Residential Homes. Owing to the time restriction these 200 elderly people were all located in the same city, but efforts were made to ensure that differing areas were included and the local authority's Research and Development Officer carefully selected five very varying Homes; it was therefore only the more independent or isolated elderly people and the rural areas which remained unrepresented in this section of the Community Survey. It is important to remember this latter fact when considering the effects of distance from libraries and the necessary travelling involved. Unlike those living in the community and interviewed in clubs and centres, the sample interviewed in the five Homes was not — and could not have been — a random selection. Many of the residents would have been incapable of completing the interview, many were sleeping in chairs, some were in their own rooms, and a few were out. One person approached did not wish to be interviewed and her wish was respected. The researcher was entirely dependent on the Officers in Charge for direction to those lounges where potential interviewees were gathered and this selection in itself meant that the less alert residents (for whom reading and other activities would have been at an absolute minimum) were of necessity omitted. In some Homes there was the distinct impression that a high proportion of those capable of reading and/or leisure activities had been interviewed, and whereas in one of them this consisted of 57% in another where the sample was only 23% a much larger sample would probably have been difficult to find. At one Home in particular and at another to a lesser extent there was the very positive impression that more interviews could easily have been obtained and that a more random selection was made in these Homes from a larger potential sample of capable residents. These facts must be kept in mind when considering the results from Home residents and also the total results, i.e., that the 67 interviewed were among the probable 100 people for whom such an interview would be appropriate and that the 191 not interviewed would include about 150 people unlikely either to read or to undertake other leisure activities. (For the purpose of estimating the extent of visual handicap, the sample would be more likely to be representative of the group as a whole). Wherever possible, random selection within these limits was carried out, and because the helpful Officers in Charge tended to single out known readers, the people interviewed in the selected lounges were not always — and certainly not only — those to whom the researcher had been directed. The population of the five Homes at that time totalled 258 and 67 of the 258 were interviewed (26%). This sample consisted of about 23% in each of the four larger Homes and 57% in the small Home (where 23% would have been only four people). When large print readers were interviewed earlier in the study the percentage of females to males reading large print was 70% to 30%, but among the older group in residential care a larger sample of females was required and the 54 females (c 81%) to 13 males (c 19%) was satisfactory for the purposes of the study. The Table overleaf shows the classification by visual ability of this elderly group, after they had been shown specimens of Ulverscroft and standard print:

Where located	Able to read normal print	'Visually handicapped'	Total
Living in the community	102 (76.7%)	31 (23.3%)	133
Living in residential Homes	41 (61.2%)	26 (38.8%)	67
Total	143 (71.5%)	57 (28.5%)	200

NB[1] This overall figure of 28.5% of the elderly people contacted unable to read normal print was almost as high as the 32.5% of large print readers unable to do so (Survey B) and the figure of 38.8% of those in local authority Homes was even higher.

NB[2] For the purpose of this study, readers are reminded that people were considered visually handicapped if they were unable to read normal print, using spectacles if normally worn. When interviewing the elderly in communal premises, people were included who *said* they were unable to do so if this seemed likely after completion of the interview, together with those registered blind or partially sighted. Theoretically it would still have been possible for other visually handicapped people to have remained unrecorded if their particular eye complaint allowed them to read normal print and they made no mention of it, like some of the registered blind contacted specifically via institutions for the blind and partially sighted.

As anticipated, the main C survey of the visually handicapped community proved to be the most time-consuming of all the surveys undertaken, the subjects being more widely scattered and less often conveniently available in groups than the librarians, readers, elderly people and the general community had been. Small groups were located in or via colleges and schools for the blind and partially sighted, an RNIB Home and rehabilitation classes; a few individuals were contacted via the Partially Sighted Society, the Retinitis Pigmentosa Society and personal contacts with workers in the field; as can be seen from the table above, 57 of the visually handicapped interviewees were contacted during the course of the survey of the elderly community, which (in addition to providing a control group for comparison with elderly visually handicapped people) was therefore justified from this result alone. Special efforts had to be made to contact more visually handicapped people in their 30s, 40s and 50s specifically, because — as anticipated — interviewing in Homes, schools and colleges and — more unexpectedly — via organizations for the visually handicapped tended to produce mostly very young or elderly respondents; visually handicapped people in what might be termed 'the career years' seemed to have gone to ground.

Together these came to a total of only 110 visually handicapped people interviewed in most of the available time and this was regarded as an insufficient and an unbalanced sample; therefore the C2 interview form as written was re-typed *in large print* for use as a supplementary questionnaire form (referred to as C3 and distributed with the help of schools for the visually handicapped, associations of and for the blind and partially sighted, conferences, social workers, Panel members, meetings, the BBC, a Social Services Department and various personal contacts, resulting in the receipt of a further 262 replies in time for inclusion. These brought the total sample to 372 visually handicapped people from many parts of Britain.

The study has depended upon many people for help and in particular upon all the helpful people who completed and returned these forms, often with obvious difficulty, sometimes in discomfort and in some cases by getting a teacher or relative to read and complete the form on their behalf. It was necessary to circulate almost 900 forms in order to receive the 262 replies, but a 30% response rate was perfectly understandable when one considered the nature of the handicap and the added complication of a rapidly adapted form designed for personal interviewing. In these circumstances our visually handicapped respondents were invited to complete as many questions as they were able and this resulted in the submission of several partly-completed forms and many questions remaining unanswered, in addition to the fact that few were able and/or inclined to respond in such detail or at such length as the people contacted personally, where the interviewer was able to probe and record spontaneous comments.

The two sets of replies will therefore be shown separately wherever this differing approach and other factors are considered relevant. It must be borne very clearly in mind that many more of the people motivated to respond to a postal questionnaire basically related to reading and to large print books were likely to be readers and large print users than of visually handicapped people as a whole and of the sample selected very deliberately at random by the interview method, where the researcher always specifically asked to talk to non-readers as well as readers. (The researcher was in fact pleasantly surprised to find that 40 people had taken the trouble to return forms who read nothing whatsoever, and a further 34 who read only magazines and newspapers.) The postal questionnaire did, however, result in the anticipated flood of replies from delighted large print readers eager to 'further the cause' and increase the range or numbers available; these were reinforced by replies from a group of readers and ex-readers contacted by a librarian who kindly volunteered to distribute forms to all her large print readers, but was persuaded to restrict them to the visually handicapped, i.e., those unable to read normal print. One added the footnote 'I wish you every success if your aim is to get more of these large print books into the libraries!'

Undoubtedly Survey C could have been improved upon had it been possible to substitute for these questionnaires a similar sized sample of personal interviews obtained regardless of travelling time and expense and in view of the incomplete data and variables involved in this aspect of Survey C it seemed more sensible to draw general conclusions from what is a mass of significant information than to rely too heavily on statistics alone. Attention will again be drawn to this fact when certain topics are being reported upon.

The first of the Tables below shows how the 372 visually handicapped participants were located and the second Table shows that both sexes, life-styles and all age groups were well represented in the total C2/3 sample:

Where visually handicapped located	Under retiring age	Retiring age and over	Total
Interviewed in Over 60s centres	—	31	31
Interviewed in OAP Homes	—	26	26
Interviewed via VH organizations	39	14	53
VH questionnaires	146	116	262*
	185	187	372

*164 females (c 63%) and 98 males

Age	Male		Female		Totals
	Living alone	Living with others	Living alone	Living with others	
60s	3	3	9	6	21
70s	9	11	45	23	88
80s	3	9	32	38	82
90s	1	1	2	5	9
Elderly Totals	16	24	88	72	200
16-19	—	51	—	33	84
20s	2	10	2	12	26
30s	3	10	1	3	17
40s	4	11	3	15	33
50s	1	6	5	11	23
60s	3	6	11	15	35
70s	4	6	26	15	51
80s	3	6	16	15	40
90s	—	—	3	3	6
VH Community Totals	20	106	67	122	315

Survey D — The Link-Men

The information primarily required from the link-men consisted of subjects such as awareness of library services, large print and low vision aids, the effectiveness or otherwise of publicity from libraries to link-men and from link-men to potential users and the degree of contact with the latter. This fourth and final survey differed from the previous three in that it was planned to consist mainly of postal responses from a wider area than the West Midlands and that only one form was involved (questionnaire form D1 which was also considered suitable for use by the researcher for interview purposes, simplifying the later coding and analysis. (*Some* interviews had been considered necessary if only for comparison with the questionnaires returned, and in view of the very low response rate these proved useful in highlighting the tendency for mainly the *cognoscenti* to reply.)

Surveys A, B and C were also larger and more complex than Survey D; they had each dealt with many aspects of the topics of large print books, their readers and non-readers, but only with one main group of respondents, whereas Survey D was mainly concerned with one aspect — publicity and awareness — but with many very different groups of respondents. The ideal questionnaire form for such extremely diverse groups was impossible to achieve and some respondents could not believe that the 'easy' questions were intended for *them*. After much thought a compromise had been reached by incorporating two pages about information received and distributed (common to all potential respondents) with six different third pages, each designed to extract further specific information from one of six main groups of people whose work has certain factors in common. (See the Table at the end of this section on Survey D).

Unfortunately some respondents passed on forms to contacts in different fields, which meant that parts of their forms were inappropriate. With hindsight it seemed likely that in some cases this effort to extract maximum information and statistics from contacts by means of a third page was a mistake and one which probably proved a complication and/or a deterrent to completion. These third pages could not in any case be *exactly* 'tailored' for each different profession or category grouped together and named on them and some ophthalmologists who assumed that the multi-purpose form had been prepared specifically for their use objected to the collective term 'clients'; several opticians rubber-stamped their forms including the collective term 'opticians' while others pointed out that it was not approved by the Statutory Board of the General Optical Council which preferred 'optometrists and dispensing opticians'; one researcher commented that a question about encouraging the use of residual vision 'seemed an impertinent question to ask anyone concerned with visual welfare' (though unfortunately it was not) and several hospital volunteers who obviously considered it a breach of professional etiquette to answer questions about a library defeated the object of the exercise to some extent by passing on the forms to their hospital librarians. Nevertheless in many cases the third pages did provide useful additional information as had been hoped, though the quality and quantity of these written responses from such diverse groups of linkmen varied considerably and consequently the resulting statistics were in some cases of less importance than impressions, comments and response rates.

The findings are based on 48 interviews and 298 questionnaire forms received in time for inclusion, making a total of 346 responses. In order to obtain these 346 responses approximately 1,200 forms were duplicated and distributed and the disappointing overall return rate of 29% suggested non-links rather than links in many cases! The most convenient groups to interview (and therefore the groups most often interviewed) were the officers at different levels in Old Age Pensioners' Homes and centres visited during the course of Survey C and the teachers and other workers in the special schools, colleges and voluntary associations also visited. The most difficult and therefore the least represented were not unexpectedly the very busy professionals in the medical fields; whenever the alternatives of an interview or a reply by questionnaire were suggested to these groups, the latter was chosen.

Many methods of distributing questionnaire forms were used: professional associations were asked to distribute them among their members; chiefs and senior employees were asked to distribute them among their staff or helpers; personal contacts were canvassed directly, as were known experts and these were also asked to pass on extra copies to colleagues; forms were distributed with agendas or at relevant gatherings such as meetings, conferences and courses — both by the researcher in person and by helpful officials; Survey D forms were included (where appropriate) with Survey C forms issued to Panel members, special schools, societies and associations; Library and Social Services Departments were asked to distribute them to certain groups in their areas; names and addresses were obtained from press articles, conference reports, advertisements, colleagues and professional registers and random samples of these were contacted individually by post; coordinators of volunteers were asked for their help and representative West Midlands hospitals and branches of national organizations, agencies and societies were approached. Unlike the earlier C3 forms for partially-sighted groups, these forms were always sent out in small numbers — usually two together and at most five or six per organization unless more were specifically requested; in all cases an explanatory outline of the project and the exact part that it was hoped the recipient would play was included (though it was obvious that these were rarely passed on down the hierarchies or out to branches) and every form was accompanied by a prepaid addressed envelope to simplify return.

By far the most effective method of distribution was undoubtedly distribution with agendas for meetings or courses at which the researcher was to speak about the project and collect completed replies at the same time. Other effective methods were via personal contacts, via direct individual approaches on a personal basis, from lists of names and addresses, via librarians and via the people met *at* meetings and conferences. Although some seniors did kindly distribute forms conscientiously and methodically among their workers and contacts (notably a Principal Health Visitor and a Chief Librarian in touch with literacy groups), most seniors were presumably afraid of revealing the ignorance of their workers and either failed to circulate the forms at all or completed them personally, though they were administrators rather than workers with direct links with elderly or visually handicapped people (notably the Home Help and Meals on Wheels Organizers). A few people stated that they failed to see the relevance of the form in their situation, since they did not work with books and — as previously mentioned — several hospital volunteers and organizers passed their forms to hospital librarians.

The 346 responses were in the categories and proportions shown below:

General categories of link-men	Number of duplicated and circulated forms	Sub-divisions of six main categories	Number of responses received	Totals	%
1 Miscellaneous	400	a) WRVS, Books on Wheels,* other voluntary services, organizers, workers, volunteers°	49		
		b) OAP Homes/centres, wardens, matrons, officers, helpers	19		
		c) CABs, information centres, advisers	9		
		d) Age Concern, VSOP, other voluntary associations for the elderly, organizers, visitors, workers	8	103	25.75%
		e) Clergymen	7		
		f) Meals on Wheels and lunch club organizers, helpers, volunteers	7		
		g) Home helps°, organizers	4		
2 Social workers, health visitors and district nurses	200	a) Senior and junior social workers, advisers, instructors, specialists in visual handicap, administrators of allied voluntary associations	39		
		b) Health visitors, area organizers	20	65	32.5%

		c) District nurses, area and clinic nurses◊	6		
3 Doctors, Ophthalmologists and opticians	200	a) General practitioners	13	59	29.5%
		b) Ophthalmologists, surgeons, professors, consultants	15		
		c) Low vision aid specialists, opticians, optometrists	31		
4 Hospital librarians, other workers and volunteers	200	a) Hospital librarians,† assistants, volunteers	25	53	26.5%
		b) Matrons, sisters, nurses, social workers, therapists, administrators, volunteers and organizers	28		
5 Special schools colleges and voluntary associations for the VH	100	a) Teachers and workers in special schools and colleges for blind and partially sighted	10	41	41%
		b) RNIB workers	6		
		c) Officials and workers in other societies, agencies and clubs for blind and allied disabilities[o]	12		
		d) University researchers	5		
		e) Officials of Partially-Sighted Society and Partially-Sighted Students' Society	4		
		f) Officials and organizers of Talking Newspapers	4		
6 Literacy and language workers	100	a) Literacy organizers, teachers, institutions	22	25	25%
		b) English language workers with immigrants[o].	3		
Totals	1200			346	29%

* The Area Organizer for Cumbria, Durham and Cleveland kindly photocopied page 3 of the form and circulated it to all local offices

† Many hospital librarians replied that theirs were medical libraries only and that as their hospitals did not have patients' libraries the questionnaire was inapplicable.

o There were few or no replies from associations of volunteers (other than the WRVS and organizers of hospital volunteers) from Home Helps, English teachers of immigrants or Rotarians and —

perhaps more surprisingly — from some Eye Hospitals and from
some societies for the visually handicapped — though the latter as
a group did achieve the highest response rate (41%)
◊ A smaller proportion of district nurses than of the others was
initially contacted.

QUESTIONNAIRE AND INTERVIEW FORMS

All the forms mentioned in the previous chapter and used as subject lists for depth interviews, semi-structured or structured interviews, questionnaires, quick reference statistics sheets for personal use and observation forms are shown here in the order used and referred to:

A1 (Questionnaire form sent to all Chief Librarians)

NAME OF LIBRARY: TYPE OF LOCAL AUTHORITY:

1   Which is your most effective method of communicating with users and potential users
     of large print? . . . .
     . . . . '. . . . .
     . . . .
     . . . .

2   In your library, which are:-
     a) the MOST popular types of large print books? . . . .
     . . . .
     . . . .
     and b) the LEAST popular types? . . . .
     . . . .
     . . . .

3   To whom do you regularly give/send lists of large print books? . . . .
     . . . .
     . . . .

4   Approximately how many large print books are at present:-
     a) on the library shelves? . . . .
     b) out on loan? . . . .
     and c) in reserve to supplement the shelf stock? . . . .

5   If any of the ACTUAL figures required overleaf are ESTIMATED (e.g., No. 9 — 'Total
     issues of large print') please explain here HOW the estimate is made (e.g., 'Based on the
     number of boxes loaned to OAP Homes and the frequency of exchange' etc.) . . . . . .
     . . . .
     . . . .

<u>(Side 1)</u>

A1(continued)

N B Please mark 'E' if any *actual* figures required are estimated. Cross through 'F' & 'N F' headings and give joint totals if necessary	*1964-65* 1st large print available	*1967-68* After 1st impact	*1969-70* Ist octavo Ulverscroft available	*1972-73* Prior to spending cuts	*1976-77* Most recent figures
	F N F	F N F	F N F	F N F	F N F
6 Total library stock, excluding J. and Ref.					
7 Total stock of large print					
8 Total issues excluding J.					
9 Total issues of large print (see 5 overleaf)					
10 Estimated average issues p.a. per 'normal' vol.					
11 Estimated average issues p.a. per l.p. vol.					
12 No. of Austin books borrowed from NLB					
13 Total expenditure on books					
14 Total allocation of funds for large print					
15 Total no. of registered ADULT borrowers					
16 Estimated no. of l.p. users, including the visually handicapped and others					

Side 2 (full original version)

A1(continued)

Cross through 'F' and 'N F' headings and give
joint totals if necessary

1976—77
or most recent figures

	F	N F

6. Total library stock, excluding J. and Ref.

7 Estimated total stock of large print

8 Total issues, excluding J.

9 Estimated total (or weekly)
issues of large print

10 Estimated average issues p.a.
per 'normal' vol. (via date labels
if necessary)

11 Estimated average issues p.a. per l.p.
vol. (via date labels if necessary)

12 No. of Austin books borrowed from
NLB, if any

13 Total expenditure on books

14 Estimated expenditure on large
print books

15 Total no. of registered ADULT
borrowers

16 If possible, the estimated no. of
large print users, including the
visually handicapped, the elderly
and others

PLEASE RETURN YOUR FORM EVEN IF THERE ARE BLANKS OR ESTIMATES

Alternative Side 2 (modified version sent to non-respondents)

A2 (Information from documentary sources for own use throughout study)

Name of Library . . . .

Type of Authority . . . .

Population served — number & type . . . .

No. of Branches. . . . .

No. of Mobile & Travelling Libraries . . . .

Approx. area & maximum distance from a service point. . . . .

No. of staff . . . .

NLB issues for 1964 . . . . .1965 . . . . .1966 . . . . .1967 . . . .

              1968 . . . . .1969 . . . . .1970 . . . . .1971 . . . .

              1972 . . . . .1973 . . . . .1974 . . . . .1975 . . . .

              1976 . . . . .1977 . . . . .1978 . . . .

Registered Blind in area . . . .

Registered Partially Sighted in area. . . . .

No. of Adult Illiterates. . . . .

No. of Immigrants . . . .

No. of Hospitals. . . . .

No. of OAP Homes . . . .

No. of Prisons . . . .

Any special services to the community. . . . .

Librarian's Name . . . .

'Phone Number . . . .

A3 (List of topics covered during course of depth interviews with West Midlands librarians; spaces for brief comments, space overleaf for longer ones)

LARGE PRINT STOCK

Who chooses stock? . . . .

Which staff members have most contact with l.p. & elderly readers? . . . .

Which libraries have most and least l.p. stock & elderly readers? . . . .

c. Proportion bookfund spent 'normal' light reading like Ulverscroft? . . . .

On what basis were the proportions of l.p. decided upon? . . . .

Anyone ever observed the use of Ulverscroft for specified period?   Yes/No

        If Yes — Methods . . . .

                 Results . . . .

Any other l.p. stocked besdes Ulv?   Yes/No

        If Yes — Which publishers . . . .

                 What proportions . . . .

What proportion of your l.p. is N.F? . . . .

Are any publishers' l.p. books discriminated against   Yes/No

        If Yes — Which publishers . . . .

                 Reasons . . . .

Loans affected by '69 size reduction?   Yes/No

        If Yes — Increased/Decreased . . . .

Why is your l.p. stock located where it is? . . . .

Is it all kept together?   Yes/No

Has it ever been moved?   Yes/No

        If Yes — Where from and to . . . .

                 When & why . . . .

                 Effect on issues . . . .

Is there a written record of all requests for l.p. titles?   Yes/No

        If Yes — Location & Permission . . . .

Use NLB's Austin books service?   Yes/No

        If Yes — Written record kept . . . .

                 Location & Permission . . . .

                 Readers' satisfaction   (VG) — 5   4   3   2   1 — (Poor)

        If No — Reasons for non-use . . . .

Side 1

A3 *(continued)*

OTHER FACILITIES

Willing to distribute l.p. news-sheet?	Yes/No
Are l.p. catalogue cards filed separately from main sequence?	Yes/No
If Yes — Duplicated IN l.p.	Yes/No
Spare room available for meetings etc.	Yes/No
If Yes — Used by OAPs	Yes/No
Literacy classes	Yes/No
Vol. Soc. for B & P S	Yes/No
Lists, talks, publicity	Yes/No
If No — Ever invited	Yes/No

If you have:-	Approx. No. of LP & where located	Exactly who uses L P & Frequency	Satisfaction 5 4 3 2 1
Mobile libraries		. . . .	
Travelling libraries		. . . .	
Facilities for housebound		. . . .	
Books in OAP Homes/clubs		. . . .	
Service in hospitals		. . . .	
Prison/Borstal libraries		. . . .	

Will you please look at this list and mark it appropriately if you stock any of the following items, showing to what degree and by whom they are used, in your opinion?

	Number	Used by	Use Made 5 4 3 2 1
Alternative materials, e.g. braille, tapes		. . . .	
Magnifying glasses or other enlargers		. . . .	
Book-rests, stands, page turners, other aids		. . . .	
Reference works on microfiche		. . . .	
Large print reference books		. . . .	
Large print news in any form		. . . .	
Large print Bibles or hymn books		. . . .	
Large print crosswords		. . . .	
Large print knitting patterns		. . . .	
Large print music		. . . .	
Large print atlases or maps		. . . .	
Large print dictionaries		. . . .	
Large print recipe books or cards		. . . .	
Large print textbooks		. . . .	
Large print or clear print magazines		. . . .	
Large print books in foreign languages		. . . .	
Other material (give details)		. . . .	

. . . .

(Side 2)

A3 *(continued)*

PUBLICITY

Can you suggest ways of increasing   . . . .
sales/therefore range of l.p. books?

Ever encouraged other than p.s. &   Yes/No
elderly to look at l.p. books?

        If Yes —   Which people   . . . .
                                . . . .

Any ideas for future P.R. work —   . . . .
contacts — slogans — publicity?   . . . .

Have you any NLB posters?   Yes/No

        If Yes —   Where displayed   . . . .
                 When and how long   . . . .
                 Results   . . . .

Do you publicize NLB's Austin books   Yes/No
service in any other ways?

        If Yes —   In what ways   . . . .
                 Results   . . . .
        If No —   Reasons   . . . .

Ever featured l.p. books in displays,   Yes/No
exhibs. in or outside the library?

           If Yes —   Exactly where   . . . .
           When & for how long   . . . .
           Results   . . . .

Have any copies of red LA '76   Yes/No
leaflet 'Reading for the Visually
Handicapped'?

        If Yes —   Where usually located   . . . .
                Where circulated   . . . .

Do you have any l.p. lists?   Yes/No

        If Yes —   Where usually located   . . . .
                Where circulated   . . . .
                Own or published   . . . .
                Felt pen, l. or s. type   . . . .
                Results   . . . .

Any of staff publicized l.p:-   Yes/No   When & how often   Feedback

On local radio or TV   . . . .
In local newspaper or magazine   . . . .
In library report or handout   . . . .
By talk or lecture to local group   . . . .
Via Soc. Services or Vol. Assoc.   . . . .

A3 *(continued)*

ATTITUDES AND COMMUNITY LINKS

Do you have a Welfare Librarian or a specially interested member of staff?	Yes/No
If Yes – How senior	. . . .
Which duties	. . . .
% of staff with real conviction that community links/info are legit activity	. . . .
Which staff types least convinced?	. . . .
Ever had a visually handicapped member of staff or committee	Yes/No
If Yes – Any effects on stock	. . . .
Effects on service	. . . .
Any staff member attended any Conference on Visual Handicap, or been member of such organization committee?	Yes/No
If Yes – Findings applied	. . . .
Ever consciously made concessions to visually handicapped in choice of lighting or lettering on signs?	Yes/No
If Yes – Details	. . . .
Any concessions for OAPs, such as fines waived – extra tickets issued?	Yes/No
If Yes – Details	. . . .
How are l.p. books referred to?	. . . .
Should l.p. be published as a non-profit-making service as in Sweden?	Yes/No
If Yes – By whom	. . . .
Read Shaw's 'Print for Partial Sight?'	Yes/No
Ever approached a publisher re size or quality of print?	Yes/No
If Yes – Result	. . . .
Order of importance in making something easy to read?	Print – Format – Content – Ability – Motivation – Other
Any independent hospital/special libs. in area, which might stock l.p?	. . . .

If provision made for:-	Appro. No. of LP	Type of service	Satisfaction 5 4 3 2 1
Blind welfare organizations	. . . .		
Settlements	. . . .		
Voluntary organizations, elderly or handicap	. . . .		
Adult literacy schemes	. . . .		
Language centre/immigrants	. . . .		

Side 4

A3 *(continued)* **LARGE PRINT READERS**

Know of any survey of nos./needs of registered   Yes/No
P.S. Visually handicapped — New readers?

     If Yes —   When & by whom   . . . .

              Findings   . . . .

% of your readers that are elderly?   . . . .

Which sessions do they use most?   . . . .

c. No. of Visually handicapped or hard-of-
seeing library users?   . . . .

What sort of people are they mostly?   Young/old —Illiterate/Educated
                                         M/F — Indigenous/Immigrant

How did most find out about services?   . . . .

Which l.p. books are borrowed most?   . . . .

Readers' satisfaction with *range* of l.p?   (VG) — 5   4   3   2   1 — (Poor)

. . . and with l.p. *books* themselves?   5   4   3   2   1

What l.p. stock changes would *you* like?   . . . .

Any complaints & unfulfilled requests?   Yes/No

     If Yes —   Details   . . . .

Observed any *other* users of l.p?   Yes/No

        If Yes — Who are they   . . . .

              Any embarrassment   . . . .

Re l.p. loans, are other people —   Encouraged/Discouraged/Banned

     If encouraged —   Any to Literacy   Yes/No
                      teachers of pupils

                  English learners   Yes/No

          If Yes —   Which books used   . . . .

          If No —   Anyone suggested them   . . . .

Embarrassment among Visually handicapped   Yes/No
when browsing/borrowing l.p?

Calls/enquiries often by friends etc?   Yes/No

       If Yes —   What stated reasons   . . . .

Any borrowers prejudiced against l.p.   Yes/No
who could benefit from them?

         If Yes —   Who are they mostly   . . . .

                  Any ideas to overcome   . . . .

Any ideas for communicating with potential   . . . .
l.p. users in the community?   . . . .

Side 5

A4 (Used when observing stock and facilities in some Midland libraries)

5 4 3 2 1

EXTERIOR

Adequate and inexpensive parking facilities nearby?
Library close to housing areas or easily accessible by 'bus?
Locality free from dangerous or difficult main roads?
Exterior of building and approaches well-lit?
Access to lending department easy? If stairs, easy ones with rails and ramps?

INTERIOR

General lighting good?
Any special lighting, chairs or facilities for l.p./p.s./elderly's area?
L.p. shelving convenient — not much above shoulder level, or floor level?
Sufficient signs? Large, clear lettering on guides and notices?
Good spaces between shelves?

POSTERS AND LISTS

NLB or other l.p. posters? Any visible from outside?
Displays or notices referring to l.p. books? Well positioned?
L.p. lists on display? Readily available — counter, near l.p., or where?
In l.p. and easy to read?
Recent and up-to-date?

LARGE PRINT STOCK

Easily located? Exactly where shelved? Near literacy material?
'Private' place, not under embarrassingly close scrutiny from desk?
All on public shelves, or some locked away & only available on demand?
Reasonable proportion of the available N F & publishers other than Ulv?
Approx. no. of l.p. books actually on open shelves? ☐ Proportion v. 'normal'

COMPARISON OF ISSUES FOR ONE YEAR — (L P)

Random sample = first 3 of each type noticed, showing entire 1977 issues on label

OLDER F ROMANCES MYSTERIES WEST- ADVENTURE TRAVEL BIOG- OTHER
pre 1952   ERNS   N F or F   RAPHY N F

B1 (Interview form used with large print readers

1 Are you looking for a book for yourself

Yes 1
No 2

If No —	employer	1	handicapped	1	only time	1
	neighbour	2	ill health	2	occasional	2
	friend	3	busy	3	monthly	3
	relative	4	working	4	weekly	4
. . . . . .other		5	other 5		daily	5

ALL QUESTIONS NOW APPLY TO THE <u>READER</u> (NOT the borrower, if different)

2

male	1	living alone	1	under 19	1	left f/t educ.	
female	2	with others	2	20—29	2	15 or under	1
				30—39	3	16	2
				40—49	4	17	3
(former) occupation				50—59	5	18	4
				60—69	6	19 or over	5
				70—79	7		
				Over 80	8		

3 How did you first find out about large print books?

other readers	1
staff guidance	2
saw book-lists	3
found shelves	4
. . . . .other	5

Have you seen any lists of large print books in the library?

yes always	1
yes often	2
yes sometimes	3
yes once/twice	4
no never	5

If Yes — 1—4, how recently?

more than 1 year ago	1
6 months — 1 year ago	2
3 — 6 months ago	3
1 — 3 months ago	4
within past month	5

Which of the following kinds of publicity would reach you regularly?

BBC radio	1
ind. local radio	2
commercial TV	3
local press	4
via optician	5
via Social Services	6
talks in clubs	7
lists in library	8
. . . . .other	9

<u>Side 1</u>

B1 *(continued)*

4   What sort of book (content) are you looking for? [   ]

How often do you find EXACTLY what you want?   5 4 3 2 1

    If 1—4, when these are not available, how often do you adapt your reading tastes and take some other kind?

                                               5 4 3 2 1

Are there some kinds that you would NEVER take?   Yes   1

                                                   No   2

    If Yes — which are they?. . . . .

How do you think of yourself as a reader?

intellectual	1
serious	2
average	3
light	4
mostly mags/news	5

5   How many large print books would you estimate that you have read during the past 6 months (26 weeks)?

average 4 or more books weekly	— 100 plus	1
2 — 4 books weekly	— 50 — 99	2
1 — 2 books weekly	— 25 — 49	3
c. 1 each 10 days — 1 fortnight	— 15 — 24	4
c. 1 or 2 per month	— 5 — 14	5
under 1 book per month	— under 5	6

How often do you read to the very end of the books borrowed?

always	1
nearly always	2
usually	3
often	4
sometimes	5

    If 2—5, why is this ? . . . .

Does anyone else also read the books?

	Yes	1
	No	2

If Yes — who?. . . . .

how often?

	always	1
	usually	2
	often	3
	sometimes	4
	rarely	5

Do you ever BUY large print books?

	Yes	1
	No	2

If Yes — which ones?. . . . .

If No — would you be prepared to buy large print books if available
in the shops?

	Yes	1
	No	2

If Yes — which ones?

	F	!
	N F	2
	Ref.	3
	All	4

Side 2

B1 (*continued*)

6   How do you usually travel here or arrange exchange?

	walk	1
	own transport	2
	lift	3
	public transport	4
	messenger	5

How conveniently situated is the library for the reader?

5 4 3 2 1

How convenient is the access to the lending department?

5 4 3 2 1

When did you start to read large print?

If pre-1970 — which is more convenient — early large Ulverscroft   1
present octavo format   2

why is this? . . . .

Do you prefer any other publishers' large print books to Ulverscroft?   Yes 1
No 2

Do you find distinctive covers for large print —

	helpful	1
	immaterial	2
	embarrassing	3

7   How do you choose your books?

prefer staff guidance   1
use catalogue   2
from book-lists   3
jacket colours as guide   4
browsing   5
other readers' recommendations 6
other 7

How do you ask for specific requests?

assistant seen shelving   1
verbally at issue desk   2
written down at issue desk   3
verbally at enquiry counter   4
written down at enquiry counter   5
other 6

8   How satisfied are you with the RANGE of large print books available?

5 4 3 2 1

What other large print have you seen, besdies Fiction?. . . . .
. . . .
Are there any books in any of the following categories which you think ought
to be made available in large print?

Fiction . . . .

Non-fiction . . . .

Reference . . . .

How satisfied are you with the books themselves —

size of book   5 4 3 2 1
size of print   5 4 3 2 1
clarity   5 4 3 2 1
layout   5 4 3 2 1
paper   5 4 3 2 1

Have you any suggestions for improvement? . . . .

. . . .

Side 3

B1 *(continued)*

9   In your opinion, what makes something easy to read?

print	1
spacing	2
colour	3
paper	4
other	5

CAN YOU READ BOOKS IN NORMAL SIZE PRINT?

Yes	1
No	2

If Yes — do you borrow them more often than large print   1
less often than large print   2

which do you prefer reading?

large print	1
normal print	2

why is this? . . . .

why do you read large print books?

no copy in normal print	1
new reader	2
read more quickly	3
more restful	4
poor lighting	5
read in bed	6
elderly	7
eye operation pending	8
post-operative	9
temporary eye complaint	10
other	11

do you ever look through ordinary stock checking for clear or larger-than-average print?

Yes	1
No	2

do you read normal print with spectacles?

Yes	1
No	2

If No — when you read large print do you:

wear reading glasses	1
wear bi-focals	2
wear special glasses	3
use additional aid	4
other	5

If 3 — 5, what type?

special aspheric magnifying glass	1
popular magnifying glass	2
other magnifier	3
binocular	4
Optacon	5
microfilm reader	6
other	7

has aid been prescribed?	Yes	1
	No	2

how satisfactory is it?	5 4 3 2 1

Side 4

B1 *(Continued)*

10 FOR NORMAL PRINT READERS WITH READING GLASSES OR BIFOCALS —
AND/OR LARGE PRINT READERS WITH OR WITHOUT SPECTACLES, WHO
CANNOT READ NORMAL PRINT

Do you always read large print books clearly?	Yes	1
	No	2
If No — do you experience:	running together	1
	dazzle	2
	faintness of print	3
	other	4

how close to the eyes do you hold the print when
reading?. . . . .

is the library lighting adequate?	Yes	1
	No	2

at home do you: use a good reading lamp	1
rely on ceiling light	2

have you had your eyes tested and/or your spectacles changed within the past two years?	Yes	1
	No	2

11 ONLY FOR THOSE WHO CANNOT READ NORMAL PRINT AND WHO READ
LARGE PRINT WITH SPECTACLES, SPECIAL GLASSES AND/OR ADDITIONAL
AID

If you **REALLY** want to read something for its content, do you ever manage to read
normal print? Yes 1

No 2

Do you worry in case reading harms your vision? Yes 1

No 2

Did you become less interested in reading when vision deteriorated?

Yes 1

No 2

How much reading did you do beforehand?

average 4 or more books weekly — 100 plus		1
2 – 4 books weekly — 50 – 99		2
1 – 2 books weekly — 25 – 49		3
c. 1 each 10 days — 1 fortnight — 15 – 24		4
c. 1 or 2 per month — 5 – 14		5
under 1 book per month — under 5		6

Do you ever use other departments of the library besides the lending department?

                                                                    Yes 1
                                                                    No 2

If No — why not? . . . .

Have you ever asked a librarian for magnifying aids, or — if there are any — how to use them?

                                                                    Yes 1
                                                                    No 2

Do you — or would you — use a CCTV screen to enlarge print in the library?

                                                                    Yes 1
                                                                    No 2

Side 5

B1 *(continued)*

Do you read the newspapers and/or magazines in the library	Yes	1
	No	2
If No — would you read them if magnifiers were available?	Yes	1
	No	2
do you read a newspaper at home?	Yes	1
	No	2
If No — do you ever read the headlines?	Yes	1
	No	2
Do you — or would you — read a large print newspaper?	Yes	1
	No	2

Do you know your visual acuity and/or the cause of your condition?

. . . .

Do you know of the Partially Sighted Register of your local authority?

                                                        Yes — on it   1
                                                        Yes — not on   2
                                                        No   3

Has anyone ever recommended or supplied any type of low vision aid?

                                                        Yes   1
                                                        No   2

If Yes — who was this?

Low Vision Aid Clinic	1
Eye Hospital	2
Eye Dept. in gen. hosp.	3
Eye doctor outside hospital	4
Optician	5
Social worker	6
other	7

Can you read embossed literature?

Yes 1
No 2

If Yes — what kind?

braille 1
Moon 2

are you a member of a braille or Moon library?

Yes 1
No 2

Do you use the British Talking Book Service?

Yes 1
No 2

Have you ever borrowed NLB large print books (Austin books)?

Yes 1
No 2

If Yes — degree of satisfaction?

5 4 3 2 1

Do you use any other alternative materials?

Yes 1
No 2

If Yes — what are they?

radio 1
tapes 2
. . . . .other 3

To what extent is the growing use of tape likely to meet some or all of your needs?
. . . .

Side 6

B2 (Observation form used to record readers and browsers

TIME ENTERED LIBRARY . . . .

Male/Female . . . .
Age group . . . .

CONSULTED CATALOGUE . . . .
CONSULTED STAFF . . . .

VISUALLY HANDICAPPED/SPECTACLES/NONE. . . . .
SHOWN INTEREST IN MATERIAL OTHER THAN L P . . . .
INTERESTED IN LITERACY MATERIAL. . . . .
LIKELY/NOT LIKELY TO USE ENGLISH AS 1ST LANGUAGE. . . . .

BROWSING/SEARCHING . . . .
TIME SPENT AT L P . . . .
NO. OF ULVERSCROFT
 BOOKS TAKEN . . . .
JACKET COLOUR/S . . . .
NO. OF OTHERS TAKEN . . . .

DATE & TIME OF SESSION . . . .
. . . . .TIME LEFT LIBRARY . . . .

C1 (Interview form used with 500 members of the general public)

1   Can you tell me the address of the public
library or branch library nearest to your home?

. . . .

. . . .

Correct address	5
Almost correct	4
Described	3
Very wrong	2
Unknown	1

2   Can you read this print comfortably (with
reading glasses if normally worn)?

        (NORMAL SPECIMEN)

Easily, without glasses	5
Easily, with glasses	4
Could, but no glasses	3
With difficulty	2
Not possible	1

3   Which books have you ever seen with print
this size?

. . . .

. . . .

. . . .

. . . .

        (ULVERSCROFT SPECIMEN)

3 or more publishers	5
2 publishers	4
Ulverscroft only	3
Irrelevant examples	2
None at all	1
Other	0

4   When I mention low vision aids, what — or which
ones — come to mind?

. . . .

. . . .

. . . .

. . . .

— meaning optical aids to reading?

. . . .

. . . .

4 or more correct replies, before definition	5
Ditto, after definition	4
3 correct replies	3
Magnifiers & spectacles	2
Spectacles, or none	1

M/F   Age group   Location

C2 (Interview form used with members of the elderly community and the visually handicapped community — later also used as questionnaire C3 when reproduced in large print)

1
male 1	under 19 1	left f/t educ. at	no spectacles 1
female 2	20—29 2	15 or under 1	reading specs 2
	30—39 3	16 2	bi-focals 3
living alone 1	40—49 4	17 3	special specs 4
with others 2	50—59 5	18 4	other 5
	60—69 6	19 or over 5	
	70—79 7	(former) occupation	
	Over 80 8		

2   What are your main hobbies and leisure activities now? . . . .

. . . .

. . . .

3   How was reading regarded in your family? would you say it was:

discouraged   1
allowed   2
encouraged   3

4   How do you think of yourself as a reader? would you say that your reading is mostly:-

intellectual   1
professional   2
serious   3
average   4
light   5
mags and news 6

5   Do you use your public library:-

regularly   1
sometimes   2
never   3

If 1 or 2 — have you a book out now?   yes   1
no   2

what sort of books do you like to read? . . . .

. . . .

. . . .

If 3 (never) — Have you ever used a library in the past?   yes   1
(never)   no   2

If Yes — why don't you use it now? . . . .

. . . .

6   How far away is your nearest library?

under half a mile   1
a half mile to a mile   2
over a mile   3

C2/3 *(continued)*

7   Is there a convenient 'bus service between your home and the library?

yes	1
no	2

8   How do you (or would you have to) travel there?

walk	1
own transport	2
lift	3
public trans.	4
messenger	5

9   Do you (or would you have to) cross any difficult main roads?

yes	1
no	2

10   Are you in touch with any friends or relatives living nearby?

yes	1
no	2

11   Do you attend any meetings or gatherings with other people in a similar position?

yes	1
no	2

If Yes — what sort of meetings are they?. . . . .

. . . .

12   HAVE YOU EVER READ, SEEN OR HEARD OF LARGE PRINT BOOKS?

read them	1
seen them	2
heard of them	3
no	4

If $\underline{1}$ (read) how often do you read them?

regularly — no others read	1
regularly plus normal print	2
sometimes	3
rarely — less than 1 per month	4
not at all now	5

If 1—3 — how many do you read per month?. . . . .

have you any suggestions for improvement?

. . . .

how satisfied are you with the range?   5   4   3   2   1

and with the books themselves?   5   4   3   2   1

Side 2

C2/3 *(continued)*

If 4 or 5 — why is this?. . . . . [to. *]

If 2 (seen) — why havent you ever tried one of these books?

can read books in normal print	1
not interested in range	2
insufficient titles	3
books too heavy or bulky	4
unattractive covers	5
don't know	6
other	[to *]

If 4 — have you ever used a bookstand, rest or page turner?

bookstand	1
bookrest	2
page turner	3
none	4

If 3 (heard of) — can you remember who told you about them? . . . .
have you ever made any further enquiries about them?

yes	1
no	2

If Yes — what happened? . . . .

If No — why was this?. . . . .[to *]

+ If 1, 2 or 3 —
have you ever told anyone else who might need them about large
print books?

elderly or visually handicapped relatives	1
neighbours	2
friends	3
other library borrowers	4
other	5
none	6

If 4 (no) — Can you read this (STANDARD) print (with reading glasses
if usually worn)?

yes comfortably	1
yes but tiring	2
with difficulty	3
not at all	4

Can you read this (ULVERSCROFT) print more easily or less
easily

more easily	1
less easily	2
not at all	3

Side 3

C2/3 *(continued)*

If 1 — now that you know that there are books in this size of
print, will you be likely to read them?

Yes	1
No	2

If No — is this because of discomfort, slow speed, lack of
interest, or other?

discomfort	1
slow speed	2
lack of interest	3
other	4

[also those trans-
ferred from p.3
if <u>vision</u> is given
as reason]

If 3 (not at all) — have you ever tried to use a reading aid, such as a
magnifying glass, binocular, monocular, telescopic
spectacles or supplementary lens?

magnifying glass	1
binocular	2
monocular	3
telescopic spectacles	4
supplementary lens	5
other	6
none	7

what kind of print or other reading are you doing now, if
any? . . . .
. . . .

has anyone ever encouraged you to use your vision for
ink-print?

Yes	1
No	2

do you have talking books or someone who reads to you?

talking books	1
someone to read	2
neither	3

do you ever hear the weekly Radio 4 programme 'In Touch'
at 5 p.m. on Sundays?*

Yes	1
No	2

if a technical reading machine were available which could
help you to read normal print, would you use it if you could
afford it?

Yes	1
No	2

If No — why is this? . . . .
. . . .

* Programme times since changed

Side 4

D1 (Questionnaire and interview form used with all Link-men)

TYPE OF LINK, AGENCY, ROLE ETC:-. . . . .

Employer (where relevant). . . . .

Town, City or Area of operation . . . .

1   Have you seen any large print books?

Yes 1
No   2

If Yes —which publishers' books have you seen?

Ulverscroft 1
(detail) . . . . .others   2

— how did they first come to your attention?

via public library   1
via hospital library   2
via Social Services Department 3
via publishers   4
(detail) . . . . .other   5

If No — do you use your public library?

regularly 1
sometimes 2
never   3

2   Have you ever received any information about large print books, such as booklists, posters or publicity about their existence?

Yes 1
No   2

If Yes —did this come from your local library, the Social Services Department, publishers or some other source?

via public library   1
via hospital library   2
via Social Services Dept. 3
via publishers   4
(detail) . . . . .other source 5

— do you ever display or distribute it in any way?

(detail) . . . . .Yes   1
No   2

— about how many clients per annum would you estimate that you have told about them?

. . . .

— what sort of people were they mostly?. . . . .

. . . .

Age . . . . .   Sex . . . . .   Reason for Need . . . . .

Side 1 (common to all respondents)

D1 *(continued)*

     — how regularly do you receive such information?

several times per year	1
once or twice per year	2
less than once per year	3
only on odd occasions	4

If No — would you welcome such information from the library?

Yes	1
No	2

— are you aware that free lists are available from public libraries and from Ulverscroft Press?

Yes	1
No	2

— would you be able to display a poster or to distribute booklists?

display poster	1
distribute lists	2
neither	3

— what sort of clients would you be likely to be able to inform about their availability? . . . .

. . . .

Age. . . . . .   Sex. . . . . .   Reason for Need . . . . . .

3   Would you be willing to draw attention to a specimen large print volume or display it, if one could be provided for you?

Yes	1
No	2

4   Do you usually encourage visually handicapped clients to make full use of such sight as they have?

Yes	1
No	2

5   Are you aware that the National Library for the Blind has a collection of classics in large print, which are available for loan (free of charge) via public libraries?

Yes	1
No	2

6   Have you seen or read the Library Association's leaflet 'Reading for the Visually Handicapped', or Alison Shaw's book *'Print for Partial Sight'*?

Yes, both	1
Reading for the Visually Handicapped	2
Print for Partial Sight	3
No, neither	4

Side 2 (common to all respondents)

D1 *(continued)*

7   How many of your contacts are partially-sighted? . . . .

        If Any — do you know if they are on the Partially-Sighted Register which
                is kept by the local authority?

Yes — on it 1
Don't know 2
Not on it   3

8   How many of your contacts have failing sight, and difficulty in seeing normal
    print?   . . . .

9   How many of either group are large print readers, to your knowledge?

                              partially-sighted . . . .
                              difficulty reading n.p. . . . . . .

10   How many of your contacts use either a Low Vision Aid or a reading aid of some
     kind, to your knowledge?

                              Low Vision Aid . . . .
                              reading aid . . . .

11   How many of your contacts have difficulty either with the English language, or
     with reading and writing?

                              English language. . . . .
                              reading and writing . . . .

12   How many of either group read large print books, to your knowledge?

                              English language. . . . .
                              reading and writing . . . .

13   Do you know the addresses of the public libraries (including branch libraries) in your
     work areas?

Yes 1
No   2

14   How many of your contacts receive the Housebound Reader service from their public
     libraries, to your knowledge?

                           . . . .

Side 3 (for the Miscellaneous group only)

D1 *(continued)*

7   Do you know of any recent surveys of the elderly or visually handicapped in your area?

      (detail) . . . . .Yes 1

                                                            No 2

8   Is there any information in your case-notes which would be available and useful to the Study of Large Print Users and potential users?

      (detail) . . . . .Yes 1

                                                            No 2

9   Do you encourage your partially-sighted clients to register?   Yes 1

                                                            No 2

      If Yes — about what proportion of them does so? . . . .

10   How many partially-sighted clients do you have in your case-load?

      . . . .

      If Any — how many of these are large print readers, to your knowledge?

      . . . .

11   What advice is usually given to clients who could benefit from Low Vision Aids?

      . . . .

      . . . .

12   Is there a Low Vision Aid Clinic in your area?

Yes — know address	1
Yes — address unknown	2
Think so/Don't think so	3
Don't know	4
No	5

13   Does your department issue reading aids of any kind; (for example magnifiers, book-rests/stands, page-turners etc.)   Yes 1

                                                     No 2

      If Yes — types of aid available. . . . .

      . . . .

      number issued per annum to your clients . . . .

      total number available . . . .

14   Do you know the addresses of the public libraries (including branch libraries) in your work areas?

                                                           Yes 1

                                                           No 2

15   How many of your clients receive the Housebound Reader service from their public libraries, to your knowledge?

      . . . .

Side 3 (for the Social worker, health visitor and district nurse group)

D1 *(continued)* DOCTORS

7   How many patients with failing sight do you have in your practice?

. . . .

8   and how many partially-sighted patients do you have?

. . . .

9   What proportion of them is registered, in your opinion?

. . . .

10   Is there a Low Vision Aid Clinic in your Area?

Yes 1
No   2

11   About how many patients per annum would you estimate that you usually refer to an ophthalmologist for a Low Vision Aid prescription?

. . . .

OPHTHALMOLOGISTS

7   About how many patients per annum would you say are usually refereed to you for a Low Vision Aid prescription?

. . . .

OPHTHALMOLOGISTS & OPTICIANS

8   How would you define a Low Vision Aid?. . . . .
. . . .

9   Of the patients you see in a year, how many would you define as partially-sighted?

. . . .

10   What proportion of them is registered, in your opinion?

. . . .

1
11   Do you discuss registration with patients or encourage them to register?

. . . .

OPHTHALMOLOGISTS

12   Have you ever done unsolicited registration or certification with colleagues in the Welfare services, or with medical officers?

Yes 1
No   2

    If Yes — in about what proportion of the registrations would you say this method was used?

. . . .

13   In what proportion of cases do you complete the section of Form BD8 which asks whether a Low Vision Aid would be helpful?

. . . .

Side 3 (for the Doctor, ophthalmologist and optician group)

D1 *(continued)*

7   How many large print books are there in the hospital library?

. . . .

8   Is the library service provided by the Red Cross, the WRVS, the hospital itself, or the public library?

Red Cross	1
WRVS	2
hospital	3
public library	4
combination	5
don't know	6
(detail) . . . . .other	7

9   In which wards are large print books circulated?

general	1
geriatric	2
neurological	3
surgical	4
optical	5
orthopaedic	6
psychiatric	7
(detail) . . . . .other	8
all wards	9

10   Are they read by night-duty nurses at all?   Yes 1 No 2

11   ... and overseas patients using English as a second language?   Yes 1 No 2

12   Which patients are the main users? . . . .

. . . .

13   How satisfied are they with them, on the whole?   5 4 3 2 1

14   What lighting and other provision is made in the wards for reading?

individual lights above beds	1
curtains round beds	2
good general lighting	3
other	4
none	5

15   What facilities are available for patients not bed-bound to read elsewhere?

Hospital library	1
Lounge	2
(detail) . . . . .Other	3
None	4

16   When patients leave hospital, are they usually linked to the library's Housebound service if necessary?   Yes 1 No 2

Side 3 (for the Hospital librarian, other worker and volunteer groups)

D1 *(continued)*

7 How many partially-sighted members do you have?

. . . .

8 What proportion of them is registered, in your opinion?

. . . .

9 How many of them are large print readers, to your knowledge?

. . . .

10 How many of them receive house visits from either the public library's Housebound service, the Social Services Department or your organization?

Library Housebound service. . . . .
Social Services Department . . . .
own organization . . . .

11 What services do you provide for them? . . . .

. . . .

12 When and how often do they meet? . . . .

13 Does anyone organize activities, entertainments, hobbies, outings or crafts for the members?

entertainments	1
activities	2
hobbies	3
outings	4
crafts	5
other	6

14 Are blind and partially-sighted people all treated as one group, or are those who are nearly blind or likely to go blind treated differently?

alike	1
(detail) . . . . .differently	2

15 Has your organization ever provided any Low Vision Aid such as magnifiers, telescopic units, special lenses and other?

(detail) . . . . .Yes	1
No	2

16 Do you know of any recent surveys of the visually handicapped in your area?

(detail) . . . . .Yes	1
No	2

Side 3 (for the Special school, college and voluntary association group)

D1 *(continued)*

7   Have you ever used large print books in your lessons?

                                               Yes 1

                                               No   2

    If Yes — which ones have you used? . . . .

            degree of satisfaction. 5 4 3 2 1

            do you use them as a stepping-stone between textbooks and normal
            print reading?

                                     Yes 1

                                     No   2

8   What proportion of your new readers like to read large print?

                              The majority 1

                              About half   2

                              A minority   3

                              None   4

    If 1–3 — which ones do they use? . . . .

            degree of satisfaction? 5 4 3 2 1

9   How many of your pupils are partially-sighted or have difficulty in seeing normal
    print?

                     . . . .

    If Any — do you know if they are on the Partially-Sighted Register which is
            kept by the local authority?

                              Yes — on it   1

                              Don't know   2

                              Not on it   3

            How many of them use either a Low Vision Aid or a reading aid
            of some kind, to your knowledge?

                     Low Vision Aid . . . .

                     Reading Aid   . . . .

10   Do you know the addresses of the public libraries (including branch libraries) in the
    areas where your pupils live?

                                   Yes 1

                                   No   2

    If Yes — have you ever borrowed large print books on their behalf?

                                   Yes 1

                                   No   2

    If Yes — why is this? . . . .

    If No — have you ever helped them to choose their books?

                                   Yes 1

                                   No   2

Side 3 (for the Literacy and language worker group)

LARGE PRINT STOCKS

The demand as seen by librarians.

One of the main questions which led to the funding of the study was concerned with the demand for large print books, studied here only as librarians saw it since purchases of Ulverscroft books by public libraries apparently levelled off even prior to the spending cuts of recent years. On the basis of both the returned questionnaires and interviews, the definite impression gained was that any levelling off had occurred for reasons other than that librarians on the whole felt complacent about the provision. When 20 librarians in one region failed to discriminate against *any* available large print because their need was so great and when 36 people in the same region (asked what changes they would like to see) asked for either 'a wider range' or 'just *more* of them' we must look elsewhere than at general complacency about the provision. Twenty-five librarians hungry for more romances, 22 asking for more light biographies, 50 West Midlanders wanting more general non-fiction and 9 librarians whose purchases were limited by the main factor of availability did not sound like people who had lost interest in large print. One factor above all others which would have prevented complacency from becoming common in the researcher's opinion was the fact that the great majority of librarians everywhere regarded large print books as *books for elderly readers,* of whom they knew there was a tremendous and ever-increasing number, rather than as books for partially-sighted readers of whom there seemed to them to be extremely few in their libraries. This view was so common that some librarians automatically referred the interviewer to their OAP Homes, housebound services and hospitals rather than to the lending librarians and the library shelves; incredible as it might seem, one librarian and a couple of assistants had not realized until halfway through their interviews that large print books *were* intended for the visually handicapped. (In fairness to them, however, it must be pointed out here that they had been provided initially for both the elderly and the partially sighted before the horizons eventually became even wider and that of 359 authorities making a return to the Survey of public library service to hospitals, the housebound and prisons (1967) 324 had made the books available to all readers.)

Finance and the allocation of funds

Regarding the use of questionnaires there was always the possibility that the non-respondents differed significantly from the respondents, so that estimates based on the latter would be biased and the higher the non-respondent rate the greater the possible bias; however, readers are reminded that the questionnaire circulated to the 166 library authorities in Britain at the start of the Large Print User Study resulted in a 90% response rate, so that even allowing for the high proportion of 'guestimates' the resulting replies provided at least a fairly reliable picture that did not exist beforehand. Before proceeding to this valuable financial information on these questionnaire forms it is necessary to differentiate clearly between the two following types of information: during their interviews the West Midlands librarians were being asked to help identify the proportion of large print compared with similar *light reading* in 'normal' print only, whereas on the national questionnaire form Chief Librarians were asked for the amount spent during 1976/7 on large print compared with the amount of the *total bookfund* — including all fiction, non-fiction, junior, reference books and presumably audio-visual material and binding — therefore one would of course expect the large print proportions on the national questionnaire forms dealt with first to be very much smaller. (See Table 1, which demonstrates the tremendous variation)

Twenty counties (including one of the Education and Library Boards in Northern Ireland) were able to give both of these particular statistics on their forms and of these 20 highly significant spenders, the average proportion of their entire bookfunds spent on large print in 1976/7 was *3.639%*. Six of the counties spent over 5% of their bookfunds on large print with 10% being spent on large print on a special project for the disadvantaged and the next highest at 5.338%; the lowest proportion spent on large print was 0.439% by the only county to spend under 1%. (One interesting fact to emerge was that Leicestershire, the home of the Ulverscroft Press, was not only the county with the largest percentage of its existing stock in large print, but it also had the second highest percentage of large print purchased

TABLE 1

ILLUSTRATING THE VARIATIONS IN THE AMOUNT OF CASH SPENT AND THE PROPORTIONS OF ENTIRE BOOKFUNDS SPENT ON LARGE PRINT BOOKS IN BRITAIN IN 1976/77

Respondents' categories	Highest sum	Lowest sum	Highest proportion	Lowest proportion
Counties	£30,000	£1,500	10%	0.4%
Metropolitan boroughs	£15,867	£1,600	11.4%	1.3%
London boroughs	£10,000	£1,250	5.4%	0.6%
District, area and regional libraries	£7,680	£300	7.5%	1.3%

during 1976/7). In terms of hard cash, the total amount of money spent during this year on large print by the 24 counties able to supply this figure was £273,756, an average of *£11,406 – 50p;* with £30,000 being the largest sum spent and £1,500 being the smallest. Five of these 24 counties spent over £20,000 and only the last mentioned county spent under £2,000.

Twenty-nine district, area and regional libraries gave both figures on their forms and the average proportion of their entire bookfunds spent on large print in 1976/7 was *3.721%* (remarkably similar to the percentage averaged by the counties). Seven of the areas spent over 5% of their bookfunds on large print, with the highest of these being 7.5% and the lowest proportion of all being 1.25%. In money terms the total spent during 1976/7 on large print by the 29 areas was £63,074, an average of *£2,175,* with £7,680 being the largest sum spent and £300 being the smallest.

Twelve Metropolitan boroughs supplied both figures; they averaged *4.37%* (a higher proportion than the two previous groups) spent on large print, with three of the 12 spending over 5% of their bookfunds this way and the largest proportion being 11.383%. The lowest figure was 1.267%, again very similar to the lowest proportion in the previous group. The total money spent on large print by these 12 Metropolitan boroughs was £65,944, an average of £5,495 – 33p, with the largest sum of £15,867 being spent by one of those selected for the purposes of Survey B in the West Midlands and £1,600 being the smallest sum.

The ten London boroughs able to supply both figures required spent a significantly smaller proportion of their bookfunds on large print than the 12 Metropolitan boroughs discussed above and 11 of them spent less than two-thirds of the amount in money terms. They averaged only *1.974%*, with only one of them spending over 5% and two of the ten spending less than 1% on large print. The highest proportion was 5.376% and the lowest 0.612%. Eleven of the London boroughs were able to supply details of money spent on large print in 1976/7 and this amounted to £43,450 in all. £10,000 was the largest sum spent (and it must be mentioned that this was only an estimated figure) while the lowest was £1,250.

Probably owing to centralized purchasing only seven individual libraries were able to supply both figures necessary for comparison though ten were able to state the amount of money spent on large print; however, it was decided that the sample was so small and that these libraries varied so much in size and type as to render practically useless any figures produced.

In addition to supplying new information on actual purchases and proportions of large print the above figures did tend to reinforce the argument that libraries *were* still buying large quantities of large print books in spite of their strictly limited availability. This fact was further reinforced by the 12 authorities of various kinds whose forms included figures for previous years also:- in all 12 cases the money spent on large print had increased through the years, suffering minor setbacks at times in one or two cases, but nevertheless being higher in the most recent year, 1976/7, than in any previous year. In four of the 12 cases the increase was less than a doubling since 1972/3 and therefore was such that it would be likely only to keep pace with the increasing cost of the books rather than to result in the purchase of more volumes; but it is worth noting that even in one of these cases the bookfund itself had been actually reduced. In the other eight cases the increase had been much greater, ranging from two and a half times as great as in 1972/3 to more than 13 times as great (in a library where the percentage of large print purchased also quadrupled). In five of the eight authorities the proportionate increase in large print purchase had outstripped the general increase in the bookfund; in fact in one library where large print spending had increased by nine times the bookfund itself had slightly decreased.

According to the Publishers Association (Richards, 1978) turnover of books in general had increased by only 10% between 1971 and 1976. Book prices had risen less than the cost of living in recent years in spite of cutbacks in public spending and reduced orders (together with an escalation of paper, printing and wages costs) and clearly the 12 librarians able — and willing — to supply figures for earlier years had found that real improvements *were* possible. Finally, before leaving the topic of these national financial figures it might be worthwhile adding that although comments were not invited at this stage of the questionnaire, forms were dotted with such remarks as 'difficult to meet the demand', 'increasing use', 'growing interest' and 'more titles required'.

One question deliberately omitted from the written questionnaire to Chief Librarians on grounds of diplomacy was asked of 45 senior librarians during their interviews: they were asked the approximate proportion of their bookfund spent on 'normal' print light reading (of a type comparable with the Ulverscroft material), in order that some sort of comparison could be made with the large print provision. It was stressed that such a figure could only be an estimate but 10 of the 45 were unwilling to hazard a guess and four of those others who agreed to supply the figures later had failed to do so in time for the correlation of the results.

As some of the remaining 31 replied in financial terms and others in terms of the number of volumes or percentages it is only possible to quote the highest, lowest and average rates of comparison between 'normal' print light reading and large print provision:

One library's housebound service which had provided 50% of its light fiction in large print in the year 1975/6 had provided 100% in large print during 1976/7 because its' 'normal' print money had been diverted. One small library had spent £950 on large print compared with £660 on 'normal' print light fiction, a proportion of 59% on large print and 41% on 'normal' print, and the next highest proportion was 40% on large print. The two lowest proportions were only 2% spent on large print and the third lowest estimate (made by seven different people) was 5%. The average proportion for the 31 people — which only applied to 19 separate services — worked out at an estimated 16.831%, but excluding a housebound service and a prison the average for 17 *libraries* was changed to an estimated *12.811%*. It must be emphasized, however, that these were merely educated guesses from people in very different financial positions and able to buy vastly differing numbers of books, and in these circumstances the value of the information is reduced. No librarian could organize information that was not there, however, and we must be grateful to them for trying to help. One librarian voiced the opinion that the amount spent on large print was shocking and needed to be at least four times as great if the publishers were ever to be encouraged; this remark came from a member of one of the authorities with a fairly good proportion − 6.164% of a very large bookfund − as was shown by statistics on the questionnaire form later received from his Chief Librarian. (Incidentally an edition of 3,000 − 3,500 copies was considered by one leading publisher to be the viable size in order to keep prices down. Only about 2,000 were sold in Britain − about 98% of them to libraries and *only about 2%* to the hundreds of welfare agencies, special schools and individuals that it had been expected would buy them − and the remainder had to be sold abroad.)

The librarians questioned would have been entitled to consider a conversation about the supposed standstill in expansion as unrealistic if it had not taken into consideration the financial situation in recent years. One of the people mentioned above had been obliged to cancel a standing order; nine had given finance as the basis upon which their stock was chosen; finance had played a part in the reduction of six standing orders and ten people had said at a different stage of the interview that they discriminated against certain publishers' books (whose titles they would like to have) on grounds of price. However, the assumed standstill in large print sales was noted prior to these years of financial constraints and though it was undoubtedly affected more recently by finance we have been examining the *earlier* possible underlying causes.

Whether or not it was considered that overall sales *had* levelled off in the past, certainly it seemed very unlikely that they would be greatly increased until the financial situation had improved. Librarians were likely to 'rob Peter to pay Paul' even though most of them would have liked to improve the provision and will probably do so later; most of the 36 people of varying status who said that they would like to see more titles or a much wider range available were realistic enough to point out that at that present time they could not guarantee to purchase a larger *total*.

Human nature being what it is, it seemed advisable to attempt a classification of the people most involved in stock selection according to their age, sex and estimated degree of sympathy for minority groups and the handicapped; but efforts here met with little measurable success, mainly because book purchase proved to be usually a joint responsibility of management teams or area committees. Of 36 *individuals* identified as being significantly involved in the selection of large print books in the West Midlands, 20 were female and 16 male; two-thirds of them were estimated to be under 40 years of age, with the largest group (20 of them) in their 30s. Any 'spot' classification of personalities is of course fallible, being based on the subject's own self-assessment and/or a subjective judgement. However (for what it is worth) nine were considered to be very sympathetic, 18 to be sympathetic, six to be fairly unaware and three to be positively unsympathetic, one of these declaring himself to be both 'unsympathetic and cynical'. All age groups and both sexes were fairly evenly distributed among all categories, proving only the infinite variety of human nature. However, it was gratifying to note later that the librarian of the library which proved to have the largest and best collection of large print had been classified in the 'very sympathetic' category and the least sympathetic librarian (who merely accorded large print the importance of a single subject) did have the smallest large print shelf stock in an otherwise excellent library.

Methods of ordering

Undoubtedly another main reason for the apparent levelling off of orders to the Ulverscroft Foundation was the emergence of numerous commercial publishers in recent years — in particular Chivers, Lythway, Portway and to a lesser extent G K Hall, Prior and Firecrest. Magna and Watts have not been included in this context because though often mentioned they were usually not sufficiently popular. Librarians were asked which publishers' large print (other than Ulverscroft) was stocked and came to mind without reference to lists or shelves and the resulting replies were as worded:

30 Chivers
28 Magna (print)
26 Lythway
21 (Franklin) Watts (Ultratype)
17 (New) Portway
8 George Prior
8 G K Hall
7 Firecrest
6 American publishers
5 None at all
3 Lanewood

2 Thorpe *(sic)*
2 List of obscure American publishers (taken from list open
   on desk)
1 Dunn and Wilson
1 Charnwood *(sic)*

When Ulverscroft large print books were the only ones readily
available it was clearly the custom for libraries — and certainly the
large authorities and big spenders — to place a blanket order for
multiple copies, often without discrimination between the different
types because then the need was so many times greater than the
supply. With basic Ulverscroft stocks and so many other publishers'
books to choose from, a significant number of librarians — who had
by then gathered experience about large print readers' tastes and the
varying degrees of popularity of the different types of book — were
preferring to choose others personally to replace a few of the
duplicate titles and thus increase the range available to their readers.
Six of 20 standing orders discussed in the West Midlands had been
reduced in recent years.

Most people interviewed were unable to state exactly what percentage of the large print stocked was Ulverscroft and what proportion was published by others; all of them stated that the proportion
of other publishers' large print was either small or very small however, but most of it had been purchased recently during the years
since the Ulverscroft sales reached a plateau and some added that it
was now increasing steadily. For those who made an estimate of the
percentage of Ulverscroft purchased at the present time the range
was from 50% to 100% with an overall average of 87.25%, the other
publishers seeming to take only 12.75% of the market between them
— though in view of the very differing status and purchasing power
of the people interviewed, this figure can only be a very rough indication and the phrase 'cutting down on Thorpe to cover new
publishers and titles' became fairly familiar.

On the one hand there was a feeling sometimes voiced that
librarians *ought* to support the charitable Foundation and two
of them refused to increase their orders to other publishers out of
sense of fairness to Ulverscroft as pioneers, while a third would only
buy others as a last resort if a specifically required title was un-
available in that series. Two others would buy *all* Ulverscroft 'if
popular titles were available' while three more bought them *because*
they considered the list of titles to be excellent. Seven other
librarians also volunteered enthusiastic remarks about the incom-

parable quality of Ulverscroft books at this stage of their interviews and an additional five remarked that their cost was either the main or a significant factor in their favour. (20 in all).

On the other hand, six people complained that other publishers' lists or samples on approval were sent only to seniors and never filtered through to them; three librarians regarded Ulverscroft as their basic stock only and were now purchasing more of the others, stating that multiple copies were no answer to the need and two others would now meet the rising demand by taking everything available. One librarian had been deterred by the fact that demand had not justified the original purchase of vast quantities of the large format books, but conceded that the introduction of the octavo format had provided a new boost. (12 in all).

It would be necessary to know the sales figures of all large print publishers both in Britain and America before even accepting the supposition that large print sales in general *had* reached a plateau. In addition to the *actual* sales 'lost' to Ulverscroft by transfer to their competitors it was possible that changing methods of ordering large print would have disguised sales figures to some extent; certainly they could create the impression that overall sales were lower than was actually the case and depending on Ulverscroft's methods of judging the level of British sales it was even possible that their own sales figures might have been fractionally distorted.

One large authority in the West Midlands bought *all* Ulverscroft books and three bought all or almost all from Ulverscroft, but none of them purchased any longer by standing order. At least two of the 20 current standing orders in the West Midlands had been changed from a blanket policy to discriminating standing orders; one was for 17, 11 and five copies, and one was for 16, 13 and 11. The former was the West Midlands library with the largest large print shelf stock seen and seeming to give a very good large print service. After first reducing orders from 17 to 11 copies of all titles, the librarian then ordered 17 copies of each romance and mystery, 11 copies of all other fiction and five of non-fiction — incidentally a proportion seeming to coincide more closely with readers' requirements than most, as was seen later in Survey B. Some of the money saved was used for other publishers' titles, but towards the end of the financial year the remainder was used for a last-minute purchase of more Ulverscroft books. The second of these discriminating orders was for 16 copies of each romance, 13 copies of each mystery and (interestingly) non-fiction and 11 of all other types, again with the possibility of a further small Ulverscroft order at the end of March.

One library authority had standing orders for five Portway and five Lythway books in addition to its standing order for 11 Ulverscroft. One authority which had originally ordered all titles centrally by standing order then based its more discriminating local orders on a very careful survey made early in 1977, in which librarians of all service points were required to record and classify large print issues in their various categories and answer a brief questionnaire regarding supply and demand. Other authorities were also tending to de-centralize purchasing of large print to some extent, reducing the headquarters standing orders and leaving branch librarians to choose their own additions — which frequently came from Ulverscroft either out of positive choice, or because the other publishers' stock was often not seen by people at the grass roots.

When librarians involved with stock selection were asked during interview on what basis the proportions of large print were decided upon the 69 classifiable replies were as follows: Twenty librarians (the highest number) plus one who always used to do so, but had just recently been obliged to cancel his standing order for financial reasons, merely had a blanket policy and still ordered by a non-discriminatory standing order from Ulverscroft; more significantly these 21 (30.43%) included the largest libraries and the biggest spenders, in many cases the parent authorities or headquarters of the branches which mostly made up the remaining 69.57%; these basic standing orders at that time ranged from one to 38 copies of each fiction title and from one to 15 copies of each non-fiction title, though as mentioned previously six had been reduced in recent years for one reason or another.

Fourteen librarians decided on the proportions on a user basis, recorded variously as popularity, demand, usage and requests. 'Financial' was the reply given by nine librarians as the basis upon which their large print proportions were decided upon and one of these pointed out that the authority 'would rather spend £7 on a non-fiction book than on a large print reprint of ephemeral fiction'. Nine others indicated very positively that availability dictated their limit and these all said that they would buy more if more titles were available. Of the remaining minority replies four based the proportion on the number of OAP Homes, centres and housebound visits, three regarded large print as merely a *subject* to be represented (one justifying this by pointing out that there were 'probably less large print readers than photography readers') and there were two replies in each of the following categories: positive discrimination in areas of need, someone else's decision before appointment, accidental and shelving space. It was stated that one prison stock had been based on a Home Office instruction regarding provision for minority groups.

Some of the postal respondents who regretted being unable to supply the required statistics added notes about their standing orders to Ulverscroft and other publishers on their questionnaire forms and these reinforced the argument that the emergence of more publishers and the changing methods of ordering large print could lead to a false impression of the amount being sold. One such county spent £16,170 on Ulverscroft books, but could not give 'a complete figure'; another ordered between 24 and 60 of each title with numbers adjusted upwards in recent years, but had no separate record of other large print purchases; one county bought '25 plus' and another stated '80 to 100 volumes from Ulverscroft each month plus others'. Nineteen of the smaller library authorities unable to supply detailed statistics also referred to these publishers, though not always as unknown quantities — eight of them had standing orders with other publishers in addition to Ulverscroft and five mentioned reducing their orders to the latter in order to obtain more titles and less multiples. (With hindsight, it would have been advantageous to ask all the libraries which did supply statistics about their methods of ordering.)

Total large print stocks

One hundred and seven libraries of differing sizes and types from all over Britain were able to give either actual figures or estimates of both the total large print stock and the total adult lending stock in normal print, which made it possible to work out large print percentages. These are listed fully here and the percentages are also shown in Table 2 as they obviously have considerable interest value, but it must be stressed that many of the figures were based on estimated totals of large print and that in view of other figures given on other parts of the forms a few of them seemed to be a little unlikely:

Counties/	50,130 large print volumes =	4.059% of adult lending stock
Boards	27,984	3.215%
	14,500	2.973%
	11,500	2.732%
	18,450	2.681%

	9,500	2.587%
	50,000	2.500%
	25,000	2.213%
	21,139	2.087%
	31,000	2.085%
	22,000	1.806%
	7,500	1.789%
	48,000	1.729%
	4,700	1.709%
	22,302	1.529%
	15,000	1.337%
	15,000	1.217%
	10,000	1.211%
	8,184	0.970%
	7,000	0.721%
Metro-	6,740	5.779%
politan	11,000	3.590%
Boroughs/	11,000	2.540%
Districts	8,000	2.007%
	15,225	1.994%
	5,550	1.769%
	1,150	1.689%
	11,150	1.647%
	14,649	1.355%
	3,500	1.217%
	6,000	1.185%
	7,000	1.099%
	9,200	0.924%
Area/	5,300	6.625%
District	4,017	3.022%
Libraries	1,800	3.000%
	2,670	2.790%
	5,401	2.628%
	2,464	2.535%
	1,000	2.511%
	4,000	2.424%
	2,000	2.353%
	2,052	2.273%
	5,000	2.222%

	2,000	2.128%
	3,078	1.888%
	6,000	1.834%
	2,835	1.673%
	3,000	1.666%
	5,000	1.603%
	2,100	1.412%
	2,500	1.321%
	1,800	1.259%
	3,600	1.252%
	4,330	1.230%
	2,460	1.221%
	1,065	1.118%
	1,082	1.103%
	1,348	1.013%
	2,000	0.938%
	2,200	0.866%
	740	0.768%
Boroughs/	520	2.162%
Central	1,873	2.156%
Libraries	2,346	2.138%
	5,800	1.475%
	5,084	1.381%
	300	0.714%
	990	0.460%
London	15,000	3.587%
Boroughs	8,622	2.140%
	6,500	2.108%
	8,800	2.075%
	6,200	1.933%
	9,379	1.832%
	11,000	1.768%
	5,800	1.762%
	5,000	1.600%
	7,000	1.433%
	7,000	1.400%
	500	0.893%
	3,500	0.717%

Branch	425	5.666%
Libraries	400	4.418%
	143	3.601%
	3,319	3.319%
	800	3.239%
	307	3.174%
	300	3.125%
	405	2.731%
	275	2.500%
	1,500	2.288%
	370	2.233%
	292	2.128%
	1,076	2.105%
	520	2.059%
	300	1.990%
	150	1.547%
	1,400	1.530%
	700	1.530%
	750	1.165%
	343	1.124%
	112	0.864%
House-	1,354	27.420%
bound	500	15.437%
Services	1,360	11.921%
	6,000	10.000%

Non-fiction percentages

As far as the 62 librarians interviewed about stock were able to make an estimate it seemed customary for the proportion of non-fiction large print stocked to vary between 1% and 35% with an average of just under 13%, but judging by availability, shelf stocks and reading habits in the libraries visited the researcher would suggest that this figure was inaccurate and that the non-fiction percentage was much lower than this. Most librarians commented that the number of non-fiction held was either 'very small' or 'too small' and one suggested that some publisher should be brave and produce a range *just* in large print so that libraries *had* to stock large print to obtain them. Others criticized the arbitrary choice by publishers of a few odd titles with no pattern, one of them remarking that finding one of interest to any given reader would merely be a chance out of the blue.

TABLE 2

PERCENTAGE OF ADULT LENDING STOCK IN
LARGE PRINT (including some estimated figs.)

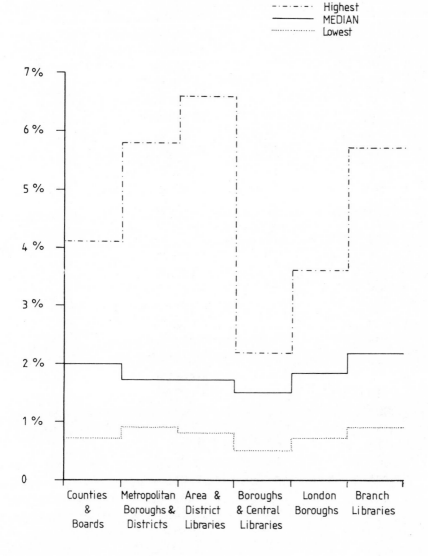

Forty-one British authorities or libraries of differing sizes were able to supply both the numbers of large print fiction and of large print non-fiction books in stock on their questionnaire forms and these are given here. (Estimates are marked 'E'.)

E	1,000	large print NF volumes = 50.000%	of the large print stock
E	1,200		37.500%
E	150		37.300%
E	2,000		33.333%
	750		33.333%
	1,560		33.191%
	1,649		31.663%
E	13,000		27.083%
	20		17.857%
	50		16.667%
E	50		16.667%
E	500		14.286%
E	200		14.286%
	192		14.243%
E	150		13.043%
	539		12.449%
	120		12.121%
E	300		12.000%
	1,065		11.356%
	264		10.714%
	353		10.636%
	45		10.588%
	208		10.136%
	270		10.112%
E	50		10.000%
E	50		10.000%
	40		9.877%
	600		9.677%
	100		9.390%
	13		9.091%
E	500		7.692%
	1,160		7.619%
	387		7.612%
E	500		7.143%
E	50		7.143%
	680		6.099%
	40		5.405%

10	3.846%
13	3.790%
41	3.789%
7	2.397%

Shelf stocks

Mention should be made here of an endeavour to provide some information upon which members of the Panel or others might be able to base the standards for provision which appeared to be needed. A very careful attempt was made to work out the average number of large print books available to readers on open shelves at service points of different kinds, using only national questionnaire forms purporting to relate to specific service points. These figures must be accepted with caution as a rough guide only, however, because the unwitting inclusion of even one reply relating to more than one outlet would slightly distort the result and in any case some of the replies had included estimated numbers (See Table 3).

a) Twelve replies related to central libraries or branches with a total adult lending stock of *over 100,000 volumes,* the kind of library buildings often not convenient for the elderly. The average large print stock to choose from on the shelves was *516.5* volumes, with the lowest at 200 and the highest at 850. (This latter served a population of 14-15,000 and estimated its large print issue at 20 per day, which — if correct — would be 1.302% of the adult issue.)

b) Eighteen replies related to central libraries or branches with a total adult lending stock of *between 50,000 and 100,000 volumes.* The average large print shelf stock to choose from in these was *514* volumes (almost the same figure as the previous one) with the lowest at 128 and the highest at 1,287. (Whether or not every one of these figures did in fact relate only to one service point, the comparative figures are exact and do certainly demonstrate the very differing views of the need — which could, of course, vary slightly from area to area.)

c) Forty-three replies related to libraries with a total adult lending stock of *between 10,000 and 50,000 volumes.* The average large print shelf stock in these was *243.5* volumes, with the lowest at 88 (in a county library branch where surprisingly the estimated large print issue made up 4.951% of the adult issue) and the three highest all with 500 volumes each on the public shelves.

d) Twenty-three replies related to small local branches and collections for housebound services with total adult lending stocks of *under 10,000 volumes*. The average shelf stock in these was 199.5 volumes, with the lowest at 30 in one branch of a London borough and the highest at 660, 482 and 397 in housebound services stocks, followed by 280 volumes (5.666% of the adult stock) in a *branch* where the large print issue was 7.413% of the total adult issue.

e) Fourteen replies related to *mobile libraries* where the average large print shelf stock (constantly changed) was *87* volumes, the lowest being 20 and the highest 160.

TABLE 3

AVERAGE NUMBERS OF LARGE PRINT BOOKS ON

OPEN SHELVES (Showing also the HIGHEST and LOWEST)

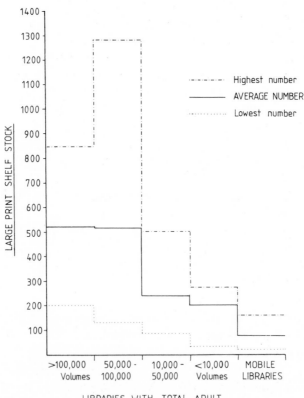

In the West Midlands central lending libraries visited personally the estimated shelf stocks averaged *361 volumes*, with the lowest at a pathetic 120 and the highest at 800. These stocks were also classified in a subjective way, from the point of view of a borrower but taking into consideration the size of the library and its stock in normal print. Four with stocks of 500, 530, 600 and 800 were considered very good indeed, three with stocks of 120, 140 and 200 were considered very unattractive and inadequate and the others in between made up 'the various shades of grey.' In the smaller West Midlands branch libraries visited personally the estimated shelf stocks averaged *251 volumes*, with the heaviest use being made of one of the smallest collections, as was also the case in the central lending libraries. Four collections, of 450 (the least used of all!) 320, 300, and 220 in a very small branch were considered very good indeed, while the lowest stocks of 120, 130 and 150 were rated 'bordering on adequate', considering the size of the libraries and before talking to readers and non-users.

It was recognized at the outset that it would be easy to be carried away in the current and become over-enthusiastic when immersed in this sort of work, nevertheless as an open-minded newcomer to the section before undertaking the study the seasoned researcher found it difficult to remain completely neutral about very inadequate collections by the end of the eighteen months.

A collection of 200 volumes seemed to be the very minimum ever recommended for small hospital collections or deposit collections in OAP Homes yet many libraries had less on the shelves for their elderly large print readers. According to the recommended standards for libraries, whose readers are constantly changing (Library Association, 1972) hospitals of 250 beds or over need at least 3,000 books, which should be continuously changed and kept up to date. Hospitals of between 300 and 600 beds need up to 5,000 books, and a recent Home Office study (Home Office, 1978) recommended that there should be ten books per head of the prison population or 5,000 books, whichever is the *larger;* therefore it seemed reasonable to suppose that visually handicapped readers and senior citizens unable to read normal print (and for whom the large print collection was, in effect, their entire library) should fare as well as was possible given the already existing limitation of the amount of material available. Integration is a popular word in social work today and large print leads to integration — no section in the library can have given more pleasure.

Reserve stocks and large format books

One main reason which emerged for the levelling off of purchases was the initial overstocking of the original large format books when large print initially appeared. These were mentioned voluntarily by many librarians on their questionnaire forms and were also introduced into the conversation by many senior librarians being interviewed. As neither the librarians nor the readers liked these books once an alternative existed they were usually referred to as dead stock, redundant stock, or more politely as reserve stock; several librarians actually bemoaned the fact that they were so well made that they lasted too long — 'too well made' as some of them worded it. Although statistics about these large format books were not asked for on the questionnaires, clearly this was an omission that with hindsight the researcher would rectify; however even the spontaneous comments might be worthy of mention —critical comments about '192 shelves', '3,000', 'a roomful' and '850' etc., recorded during interviewing. Many of these libraries donated their surplus large format books to Social Services Departments, Homes and hospitals; two commented that they were difficult to sell and one West Midlands library then agreed to liaise with local volunteers and have them distributed one to each optician's waiting room.

Only two of the libraries observed were *using* these large format books to a large extent, though unfortunately in view of the readers' unanimous opinion of them one of these was the library with by far the greatest number of large print users, while the other was one with very little use at all. (Here the librarian had placed them in an adjacent bay and had discovered that the octavo format books were borrowed about three times as often, which could of course have been partly because they were newer.)

Some librarians felt that if the demand were urgent these large format books would be used more by each new 'generation' of large print readers and of course this does happen where the already-addicted readers are desperate for material, though to a much lesser extent now that the more convenient books are known to be in existence.

There was evidence also that *planned* reserve stocks were beginning to be built up systematically in several large libraries and headquarters, with the most common method being the retention of one copy of each title and in some cases different branches sharing the alphabetical sequence. On the questionnaire forms British libraries of varying sizes gave particulars which were used:-

Fifty-three of them (32.317%) had 100% of their large print on the public shelves and no reserves at all. Most of these 53 libraries were small libraries or county branches with *shelf* stocks of 500 or less large print (i.e. 34 — or 64.151% of the 53) but there were also two countries with 2,100 and 11,000 respectively, eight Metropolitan boroughs and central libraries with shelf stocks ranging from 500 to 8,000, one London borough with 2,000 all on the shelves and eight area or district libraries with between 540 and 3,700 on open display. The remaining 111 libraries (67.683%) including most of the larger ones had some sort of reserve stock (including the unplanned redundant collections). The average % of large print stock on the public shelves in the 164 libraries overall (including those without a reserve) was 80.927%, with an average of 19.073% in reserve.

Of 62 librarians questioned about loans in 1969/70 after the introduction of the smaller format, thirty-four were positively convinced that they were increased; 23 either did not know or, while suspecting that they were increased, were unwilling to commit themselves without concrete evidence; two people felt that issues had not been affected; two were involved with a small specialized collection which still stocked only the large format books and one library did not provide a service in 1969/70.

Pleasure about the reduction in size was unanimous. In addition to the 34 with definitely increased issues, 16 of the 23 who suspected, but could not confirm increased use volunteered remarks to the effect that the smaller books were certainly more popular and the other seven pointed out that their readers preferred them and were pleased to be able to sit up in bed and read them. One of the two who did not think the issues had been affected explained 'this was because the group is grateful for everything and never complains, but the readers do prefer the octavo format'. (This reply is quoted in full because it qualifies one of the two negative responses about issues and so exactly sums up later findings about the readers.) Four librarians volunteered enthusiastic remarks about the smaller books being easier to handle, four mentioned the advantage of being able to fit them into ordinary shelves and three referred to the larger ones as dead stock since their advent. One librarian called the introduction of the smaller books 'the biggest step forward to date' and four librarians volunteered the information that their readers specifically asked for octavo, having now lost interest in the large format; as one of these worded it 'they would always find *some* excuse not to take them.'

Librarians' views on large print books

Librarians were asked if they discriminated against any publishers' large print books and if so, for what reasons. Considering that *all* large print books were needed, 20 of those interviewed about the stock did not discriminate against any of the available material, though one added 'however poor' and three from one authority commented that nevertheless the John Curley books were rejected by the *readers* 'because the print is too dark'. John Curley books were also discriminated against by 12 librarians, mainly because the typeface was considered poor and too black and their readers complained; it is interesting to note that John Curley's name did not appear at all on the list of publishers whose books were *stocked* and whose names came readily to mind [Page 85]. Magnaprint was also criticised and discriminated against for these same reasons by 16 librarians, four of whom commented that they were not borrowed and two of whom also added adverse comments regarding their price, quality, binding, appearance and lack of margins; their name *did* appear, however, near the top of the list. One librarian criticizing both these types complained that 'these readers can't read elongated and funny print' and another said that 'it was an insult to expect elderly people to learn new tricks in order to be able to read'. (At this point it ought to be mentioned that by the time this report is available all Magna and Curley books — both hardcase and softback — will be sewn, and that later surveys among the readers and the linkmen did not reveal similar discrimination, as will be shown later.)

One librarian considered the large format Ulverscroft books expensive to bind and both Magna and Lythway books unlikely to rebind; five discriminated on grounds of high price — three considering Lythway to be 'pricey' and two referring to George Prior, G K Hall and Watts, though admitting that they would like to have the titles. Price was a criticism generally levelled at all large print and five others said here that they discriminated against all except Ulverscroft on this account alone. Three discriminated against American publishers whose names they were unable to recall and another criticized Watts because some readers objected to the American spelling; six were against all large format or cumbersome books in general, including both Watts and the old format Ulverscroft.

The fact that the newer publishers' books were not easily identifiable as large print worried four librarians; it led to 'wrong shelving on Saturdays' and doubts as to whether they *should* perhaps be integrated with normal stocks. One person objected only to spiral-bound Gospels and three objected to softbacks 'because the elderly cannot hold them open'. In spite of a straggling list of complaints, however, it was necessary to keep a sense of proportion and recognize that only the more numerous comments regarding Curley and Magna (on account of their typeface) and — to a lesser extent — Watts (on account of the format) would have been likely to affect sales, or potential sales of these publishers' large print books to any significant extent.

Many of the librarians interviewed in the West Midlands were *unaware of the availability* of most of these 'other' large print publishers' books, incidentally, and it is possible that a significant number of these people might in future discriminate against Ulverscroft books when knowledge of their availability becomes more widespread (for example the 19 who, at a different stage of the interview, said that they would prefer to see illustrations and/or illustrated jackets, the nine who would welcome the introduction of paperbacks and the two who referred to them as 'institutionalized books'.) Members of the Panel considered this to be a very significant finding, as did some of the publishers.

Perhaps at this stage it would be useful to refer the reader to the replies given by West Midlands librarians when asked 'what makes something easy to read?'. After classifying their responses three different arbitrary methods of scoring were tried out in an effort to arrive at an order of importance. These were a) 6-5-4-3-2-1 for all or any of six factors per person b) 3-2-1 for only the first three factors named by each *group* of people seen together and expressing a group named by each group of people seen together and expressing a group view. It was not possible to reach a definite conclusion as to which method of scoring was most fair or accurate, but that is of little importance since the following two main facts emerged without becoming too technical:- a) that librarians placed size of print surprisingly low in their order of importance and b) that the order was remarkably similar whichever method of scoring was used. (See Table 4a)

TABLE 4(a)

GROUPED REPLIES GIVEN BY WEST MIDLANDS LIBRARIANS WHEN ASKED
'WHAT MAKES SOMETHING EASY TO READ?' – SCORED BY THREE DIFFERENT
METHODS

		Method 1	Method 2	Method 3
1	Print quality, type-face, clarity	183	81	54
2	Spacing	94	37	22
3	Paper	88	35	22
4	Print size	64	25	22
5	Print colour, density, boldness, blackness	71	23	11
6	Format	51	19	12
7	Contrast	51	19	10
8	Content, style, punctuation	27	8	8
9	Margins	30	4	2

Note that print size came only fourth in the librarians' order of importance.

TABLE 4(b)

192 READERS' ANSWERS TO THE QUESTION 'HOW SATISFIED ARE YOU WITH
THE BOOKS THEMSELVES?' FOLLOWED BY MENTION OF THE FIVE FEATURES
LISTED

	5	*4*	*3*	*2*	*1*	*?*
Size of book	35	95	42	8	2	10
Size of print	115	65	5	3	1	3
Clarity	73	74	10	1	1	33
Layout	63	81	8	1	1	38
Paper	50	86	14	—	1	41

Key
5 = Highly satisfied
4 = Satisfied

3 = Average
2 = Dissatisfied
1 = Highly dissatisfied

Note how pleased the readers were with the size of print and
how many had failed to consider such things as clarity, layout and paper

Housekeeping methods

The very definite impression gained was that the most effective method of housekeeping was to *'keep a well-stocked larder'*, though it is necessary not only to point out that this was an impression rather than a fact supported by statistics, but also that several examples had been noted to the contrary.

From the use made of stocks of differing sizes both on a national and local scale it was seen that no logical pattern could be proved. Where people knew about the books and *were* already borrowing them, it had been noted in the West Midlands that they would borrow from small stocks with inadequate lighting and inconvenient locations, returning repeatedly until something was found — even the unpopular large format books which had probably been on the shelves since before 1969. Where they were *not* already borrowing them it seemed to make little difference that the collection was good, well-illuminated and situated close to chairs and other attractions for the elderly, as was shown quite clearly again in the Reader Survey. Perhaps the key to the puzzle lies in the statement repeated several times by assistants that 'once people start reading large print they become addicted', or words to that effect, in which case a *prominent location* must surely be a very significant factor in their use, together with adequate *publicity* and personal recommendation. Many branch librarians and assistants had noticed that pensioners made heavy use of shopping mornings, pension days and market days to change their books and it did emerge later in the Reader Survey that unless shopping or pensions drew elderly people to the vicinity of the central libraries with their larger stocks many preferred to choose from pitifully small collections nearer home. Even in this there were exceptions, however, and both the librarians and the researcher knew of pensioners travelling the rounds of three or four libraries in order to find something to read.

What one obviously did *not* want to see were the unguided collections in obscure anterooms and *any* collections without guiding or without adequate guiding (no matter how temporary) — the collections on the first floor or with the Z end of the alphabetical sequence ending at the unguarded top of a flight of stairs — the collections so far above eye level that bifocal users had almost to dislocate their necks in order to read the titles through the lower (reading) lens — or the collections at floor level which obliged old people to make joints bend which had not bent for years or to get down on their hands and knees; usually because of sheer thoughtlessness they existed, however, and in other cases libraries with miles of shelving had 'run out of space'.

Librarians in the West Midlands were asked during the course of their interviews about the reasons for the existing location of their large print collections. Because some were not directly responsible for a specific library's bookstock and others gave more than one reason, 68 reasons were put forward for choice of location. These were as follows:

Fifteen (the largest number) opted for locations of prominence and conspicuousness and five of these were specifically placed very close to the entrance or desk; two sited the collections in positions which were deliberately inconspicuous in order to combat self-consciousness. One treated the collection as a minority interest and 'therefore not in the first place you see'.

Twelve located the books with other aspects of their elderly readers' convenience very much in mind, four of them deliberately choosing an area that was quiet and one choosing a well-lit area, while two others had chosen the location for their own convenience.

Shelving dictated the choice in nine cases; three opting for low shelves, four for eye level shelves and two having to accommodate special bookcases where they could.

Nine librarians wanted their large print to be close to the fiction shelves and one of these (a small collection) was sometimes integrated with them; two others deliberately chose to place their large print close to the literacy material to allow for cross-use.

Seven had no special policy and the remaining nine choices were dictated entirely by limited space.

All but three of the collections seen or referred to were shelved together, to provide a special compact unit or 'library' for the hard-of-seeing people for whom they were originally intended; in fact in one of these libraries each book was carefully marked 'for the use of partially-sighted readers only,' which probably had a deterrent effect on many of the potential readers.

Two of the three with integrated stocks were small allocations in OAP Homes, but in the third case the authority stated that the policy varied, with only two-thirds of its branch libraries keeping large print together. However, although all the others did state that all their large print was shelved together one qualified the reply by adding 'the Ulverscroft', which implied that others were not always shelved with them; one added 'except for shelving errors with the illustrated jackets' and one had not kept the collection together until the month prior to its research week.

At this point it might be advisable to remind the reader of the people who had not fully realized the *purpose* of a large print collection — that the books had been produced for people who could not *see* very well and that for those who could not read normal print this was their total *library* (not merely one section of books from which to alternate when they felt inclined.) Bearing this in mind the researcher felt extremely sorry for these borrowers in some of the libraries whose stocks were examined: shelf stocks had varied in number from 800 (the best collection, in an industrial area's busy central library with 3,500 out on loan) to 120 (in a well-stocked and otherwise excellent central library in a popular retirement area) and of course as few as 60 in such establishments as OAP Homes.

Twenty-seven of the librarians reported large print stock moves when asked. Some of them had moved stock once only and others more frequently, but it was not possible to prove that varying housekeeping methods affected the issue, though later some readers commented on the difficulty in finding the section again when this had happened.

Thirteen of the moves were made merely to make more space for the catalogue, cassettes, paperbacks, additional junior books, and in three cases actually for the large print itself; in 12 cases there had been no noticeable effects on the large print issues and in one case it was considered too early to know.

Five librarians had moved their large print so that it was more noticeable and situated where pensioners could be seen and helped; four of these considered that the issues had increased or probably increased and the other that it was too soon to know. Two had changed the shelving system from integrated fiction to separate shelves; in one case it was too early to reach any conclusion and in the other case (where the move had been in response to *users' outcry!*) it was presumed, but could not be proved, that issues had increased. One librarian had stored large print in an inaccessible bay in an effort to limit its use to those *needing* it, but as it was not visible only the 'regulars' ever found it and in this case 'the issues picked up' when it was moved to a more conspicuous place. Four librarians reported moving the Magnaprint non-fiction series into the general non-fiction sequence in an effort to have it used more and this proved effective, though these loans were then not made to the elderly or visually handicapped. Finally, two librarians had moved the large print stock onto lower shelves, one of them because she noticed more people using it; but she considered that the method of approach to borrowers was a much more significant factor than the position of the stock. The researcher watched lame and elderly readers getting down onto their hands and knees on the floor in order to reach the floor-level shelf, and was obliged to agree. (Incidentally this librarian — who was very short of space — was eager to discover how the readers felt about this; many needed no encouragement to voice their opinions.)

Without being able to prove it, the definite conclusion reached was that a conspicuous and convenient place was best, but that those in real need who knew of the existence of a large print collection would borrow books however they were housed. It is probable that in many libraries not enough consideration was given to the problems of the handicapped when training staff, who should ideally be able to appreciate the difficulties experienced, look at situations from the users' viewpoints, anticipate potential problems and deal with them before they arose.

Incidentally, although some librarians integrated the large print with their normal stock in their eagerness to get it used by a large variety of people, overlooking the fact that the visually handicapped were then unable to find it, by no means all librarians encouraged the use of large print books by people who were not elderly or visually handicapped. Such use was positively discouraged in ten of 84 establishments (12%), in one of which each book was carefully marked 'for the use of the partially sighted only' and in another of which the librarian flatly announced that they were 'bad for eyesight'! Of the remaining 74 establishments, 39 of the librarians (46%) could only bring themselves to say that they 'allowed' such borrowing and 35 (42%) did positively encourage it. One can understand why — with the British sense of justice — so many librarians failed to encourage other groups to make use of the section, especially when one saw and heard of the difficulties in finding something new to read which existed in some of the libraries; however, it would seem to be a more sensible policy to make adequate provision, thereby encouraging further expansion in publication with a consequent increase in the range available and then (without integration) to encourage maximum use of the section by all who could benefit. Since most librarians *were* aware of the short-comings of their large print stock one hopes and believes that in most cases they intended to rectify this when possible and that then perhaps these other groups would be universally introduced to large print.

Issues and investigations into use

Quantifying output provides a standard against which progress can be measured and statistical records of issues are usually suitable for aggregation, are simple to analyse and are an indication of demand. Nevertheless, it emerged that the keeping of separate statistics for large print issues was unusual and that completing the questionnaire forms caused a great deal of extra work in many cases. It seemed to the researcher that the increasing use of expensive computers for the simple charging process could more easily be justified if the capacity of the computer were utilized to a greater extent for obtaining such meaningful information as the use of large print books and other special items by the allocation of special symbols.

By eliminating all questionnaire statistics which were not either factual or considered on the basis of other figures given to be fairly reliable estimates, however, a comparison was made of a) the percentage of large print issues of total adult issues and b) the percentage of large print stock of total adult lending stock. From this method based on 70 forms only the resulting supposition was that nationally *3.109% of the issues came from 1.981% of the stock* and the definite information that in 47 cases the percentage of large print issues exceeded the percentage of large print stock, whereas in 23 cases the percentage of stock exceeded the issues.

On the questionnaire form authorities were asked to give comparative figures of the average annual issues of large print volumes and normal print volumes and 99 forms included this information. Taking fiction and non-fiction books together (as 44 of the librarians did) the overall result of all 99 libraries or systems was 9.682 issues per annum per average large print book and 12.541 issues per annum per average normal print book. In other words, the average large print volume got *77.203%* as much annual use as the average comparable normal print volume, though librarians were agreed that the large print books lasted much longer.

Of the 44 combining fiction and non-fiction the authority getting most issues from its large print was getting 28 issues per annum per average large print volume (compared with 26 per annum for its normal print) and the library getting least was getting five issues per annum (compared with three for its average normal print volume.) Twenty-five authorities or libraries were getting less use from the average large print volume than from normal print, two were getting equal use and 17 were actually getting more issues from large print volumes. Ten authorities unable to supply figures or make reliable estimates offered comments: nine of these considered themselves well satisfied with the use made of their large print and one said that it was only occasional. It seemed probable that the 44 authorities or libraries giving a combined figure for fiction and non-fiction gave less carefully considered replies than the 55 who differentiated between the two; certainly their figures when taken alone worked out slightly differently, with the large print book averaging 10.472 issues, or 84.25% of the average normal print book with 12.43 issues.

Working only with the 55 forms which separated fiction and non-fiction figures the statistics for *fiction* came out as follows:
An average of 11.655 issues per annum per large print fiction volume compared with 16.133 issues per annum per normal print. fiction volume. In other words the average large print fiction book got 72.242% as much use as its normal print counterpart. Of these 55 the authority getting most issues from its large print fiction was averaging 26 issues per annum (compared with 29 issues per average normal print fiction book) and the library getting least use was getting only 2.4 issues per annum (compared with 9.6 for normal print fiction.) In the case of fiction issues from these 55 authorities or libraries, only seven were getting more use from large print volumes than from normal print, three were getting equal use and 45 were getting less use.

Fifty-four of these 55 establishments were able to give an actual figure or a reliable estimate for *non-fiction* use and the results were as follows:
An average of 6.920 issues per annum per large print non-fiction book compared with 9.060 issues per normal print non-fiction book, which is 76.379%. Of these 54, the two getting most issues per annum from their large print non-fiction were each getting 16 (compared with 12 and 31 per annum respectively from their normal print non-fiction) and the library getting least was getting only one issue per annum (compared with three per normal print non-fiction book.) In the case of non-fiction issues from these 54 authorities or libraries, 11 were getting more use from large print volumes than from normal print (one of them pointing out that large print non-

fiction books were all popular reading) seven were getting equal use
and 36 were getting less use.

Only four of 62 West Midlands librarians questioned about the
stock had ever attempted any sort of observation or investigation of
the use of large print. One of these had done so only in a non-scientific way by careful watching over an unspecified period, but had
noticed the increasing social need as the area grew in popularity as
a retirement area and new elderly readers were drawn in. This Branch
Librarian then kept and submitted a record of all large print issues
for the following two months, which showed that large print
accounted for 3.87% of the total issues — from a shelf stock of
approximately 150 volumes, some of which were stored at floor level
in order to house the collection in a prominent and otherwise convenient location.

One Central Librarian had counted all books returned to the desk
during one week 'within the past three years' and this had shown
that 65 of 9820 returned books were in large print, a percentage of
only 0.662%. This was in a full-time library with approximately
250 large print books on the shelves, but less than moderately well-
situated from the point of view of the elderly shopper. Both of these
libraries were in the West Midlands county with the highest percentage of residents over the age of 65 years (13.7%).

The other two librarians, both from an authority with only 10.3%
of its population over 65 years of age, quoted the very careful
researching of large print use for a month (one year previously) at all
service points, upon which the existing proportions of large print
were based. This showed a weekly issue of 224.5 from a shelf stock
of slightly less than that number in the central lending library and
this piece of research also divided the books into different categories and quoted each librarian's assessment of adequacy. (The
results were kindly made available to the researcher and these
revealed that at 14 service points the collections were kept separate,
at three they were integrated and at two others only the romances
were integrated and all the others kept separate. The demand at most
service points was considered by the branch librarians to be moderate
to heavy, with the mysteries and romances coming most often into
the latter category and the stocks were all assessed as 'adequate'
(just under half) or 'inadequate' (just over half) with none at all
assessed as 'surplus to demand'.)

A fifth librarian referred to some earlier questionnaires upon
which a talk had been based and given at a staff residential course on

services to the disadvantaged. This was in a county with only 11.7% of its population over 65 years of age and where a large print booklist had been found; the topics covered had included large print books, library access, special collections, sound recordings and staff training.

Regarding the degree of usage of large print an interesting rule of thumb seemed to emerge almost by accident. When visiting libraries with date labels these were examined in order to establish the comparative use of the different categories of large print books. After a while it became noticeable that it was possible to forecast the degree of use in any given library by the annual issue of the romances (the most consistently used category) so the theory was then tested by listing the libraries in order of these recorded totals. When the library code numbers were replaced later by their names they were exactly in the order which would have been suggested by other statistics, so perhaps it might be worthwhile mentioning this very rough but rapid guide for the use of any librarians who do not have the time or resources to embark on proper research:- it seemed that if the average number of issues of a good sample of romances which had been on the shelves (and not out on bulk loan etc.) for a complete year was above 20 in that year then there must have been an extremely high level of activity at the large print section; it seemed that an average of 12 to 20 issues in a year denoted good to very good use and that under 12 suggested below average use. Of course this was tried out only in a small number of libraries open for four or more days weekly and might not have been applicable everywhere.

Finally, before leaving the topic of large print stocks in general and large print issues in particular it might be worthwhile reminding readers (if only to demonstrate that the researcher was aware of the fact) that just as registration by automatic meters of the number of radio or television sets switched on is not necessarily a reliable guide to the numbers of people actually listening or watching, the number of books on loan does not necessarily indicate the numbers of people actually reading. When measuring achievement the observations of the staff, the comments of users and their letters of appreciation should also be taken into consideration in conjunction with issues statistics.

OTHER FACILITIES

TAPES, CASSETTES, NEWSPAPERS, PERIODICALS,
INFORMATION LEAFLETS AND BOOKLISTS, ETC.

NLB Austin books

Of the two hundred large print readers interviewed in West Midlands libraries and other establishments during the course of Survey B, the forms of 69 were eventually separated from the others because they were unable to read normal print. It emerged that none of the 69 had borrowed Austin books from the National Library for the Blind and it was obvious that the vast majority were unaware of their availability. Two offered the additional information that they would be unlikely to do so because they had read all the classics at or after school and two would possibly do so now that they were aware of the service.

One of the Midland library surveys already quoted had referred to the lack of use of the NLB's large print in all but one of the authority's libraries and a question had been included about the *staff's* awareness of the existence of the service. In the West Midlands area which came under close scrutiny, of 55 librarians in a position to borrow or have borrowed Austin books for their readers from the National Library for the Blind, only 12 said that they had ever done so. In four cases there had been no feedback and in three other cases only one specifically requested classic had been obtained. Two of the 12 had borrowed them in the past but did not do so now and two borrowed regularly for one reader each, both of whom were extremely grateful and satisfied with the books. The remaining librarian had borrowed on several occasions and her readers were well-satisfied; only one had commented on but had not criticized the method of production and one had mentioned the weight of the three volumes needed for one work.

The main reason given for non-use by the remaining 43 librarians was unawareness of the service, with 21 of them never having heard of the National Library for the Blind's large print books, though one of these mentioned its braille library and one had once referred to that library regarding books in Moon.

Of the remainder of the non-users seven people stated that they never had any demand for classics, six considered that dealings with the National Library for the Blind were now the business of the Welfare Department or Social Services, four librarians (one of whom had bought up a collection of remaindered large print classics) considered that their own stocks then made it unnecessary for them to take the trouble to borrow others, two decided to refer people direct to the NLB, two from one authority were irritated by that library's pro-rata subscriptions geared to population rather than to use and termed as 'donations' and one reported unfortunate dealings with the library in the distant past, remarking finally that 'the National Library for the Blind could do with a PRO'.

Only three of 50 people asked had seen NLB posters (or remembered having seen them) and these all belonged to the same authority, which did not stock any at the time of its visit. There was a booklist of Austin books, however, in this library and the only library publicizing them in any other way was mentioning them in talks.

It seemed possible (without any factual evidence) that the increased postal charges for returning the books might have been a hidden reason for some of the librarians who *were* aware of them failing either to use, publicize or be involved with the service, therefore further enquiries were made and very generous cooperation was forthcoming from the Public Relations Officer for the GPO and from the people working with the NLB's lending records. The latter showed that all five counties and all except one of the seven Metropolitan boroughs being studied *had* in fact borrowed Austin books for their readers occasionally throughout the past ten years and that three of the rural counties had made relatively heavy use of them. The two Metropolitan boroughs making most use of the Austin books were the two with the largest large print stocks on the shelves of at least their central libraries and again one of these was the library quoted previously as having a good service and a 'very sympathetic' lending librarian who had reported borrowing them on several occasions. This surely suggested that use of the supplementary postal service depended more on having a caring librarian than on having inadequate stocks. (It also suggested, as did other unrelated factors, that since librarians might be expected to have above-average memories, there had been a great deal of mobility of staff between authorities and between particular posts.)

For all authorities nationwide the degree of use of these sets of 300 Austin titles rose steadily each year from their inception until it reached a peak in 1968-1969. In 1969 the smaller octavo format Ulverscroft books appeared, with a resulting boost both to their sales and to libraries' own stocks and this must have been one very significant factor in the declining use from that year on. However, it would have been unrealistic to suppose that in some cases increased postal charges had not influenced attitudes and even decisions. During the four years in which borrowing was steadily rising (1964-1968) the relevant fairly low parcel postage rates were only steadily rising also — by a total of 50% between 1963 and 1968. Having increased by another 40% in 1972 (by which time borrowing from the NLB was lower) postal charges then rocketed by a remarkable 214% in the years between 1972 and 1976, which meant that a parcel in the 2lbs/1 kilo range more than trebled in price from 21p to 66p. (The weight of 2lbs or later one kilo had been selected for comparison because one or the other was the only suitable weight used constantly in the scale of charges over the 13 years.) Judging by the NLB records all but three of the 11 West Midlands authorities seemed to have opted out by that time (27.27%)! Dr Munford himself felt that postal charges had a significant effect upon the use of the service and he had tried unsuccessfully to persuade the GPO to treat the partially sighted in the same way as the blind; at the time of writing this report the use of inter-library transport was being considered in the London area.

Nationally the situation was not dissimilar in its use of this supplementary collection of classics in 1976/7. Altogether 167 libraries of differing sizes completed this part of the questionnaire form and 36 of them had borrowed from the NLB during the year in question — 1976/7. This was only 21.56%; but supposing that the reason why all the small branch libraries had failed to use the service was because of a *centralized* policy, then it would be logical to remove the forms of these 21 small non-users and we would then have got a figure of 36 out of only 146, which is 24.66% — fairly similar to the 27.27% in the West Midlands that same year. Remembering that this is merely a useful back-up service, it would be interesting to compare it with the use made of inter-library lending schemes for normal print books. The total number borrowed from the NLB in 1976/7 was the all-time low of only 620 books, compared with 2,354 in 1968/9.

If we drew circles of ever-increasing sizes on a map of Britain with London as the central point, then (as one might expect) use of the NLB decreased almost regularly as one moved further and further out towards the circumference of the outer circle. The users included ten of the responding London boroughs and a further 13 authorities in what could loosely be termed the southern 'half' of England, only ten in the northern 'half' and three outside of England. Usage varied between one and 40 borrowings per annum (if one excluded one stated total of 236 which must presumably have included those of earlier years) and the average was 14.33 books borrowed during the year.

One hundred and sixty of 333 responding *link-men* who replied to the question in Survey D (48%) were already aware that the NLB had large print classics for loan via libraries, however, and 173 (or 52% of the respondents) were unaware of the service. This was as high a percentage as the percentage of awareness existing among the librarians and the readers, even allowing for the non-respondents, which was very interesting. It presumably stemmed from the fact that in many local authorities all dealings with the NLB either were (or were now thought to be) the province of Social Services Departments rather than of Library Departments. Understandably, the workers in the Literacy Group 6 (for whom the information was fairly irrelevant) were the least aware, followed by Groups 1 and 3, the miscellaneous and the medical categories.

According to the Survey of public library service to hospitals, the housebound and prisons (1967) 184 of 359 authorities (44.9%) who made a return for the survey of public library service to hospitals, the housebound and prisons advertized the NLB's large print scheme at that time and 140 of them (34.2%) reported some use made of the service. Mention was still being made of the service in *some* of the leaflets and booklists produced for the use of the visually handicapped and submitted by librarians with their questionnaire forms for this study, but as supermarket magnates are well aware, advertisements — useful as they are — do not attract consumers in the same way as seeing the actual material attracts them, and this aspect of the system probably accounts for the low take-up to some extent.

Reference materials, information and alternative materials

'The literature on the information needs of the blind or deaf person is minute. Unlike other disadvantages, blindness or deafness consists wholly of impairment of a communcation channel . . . the blind and deaf need information about devices that compensate for their disability — where to get them and how to finance them. Secondly, they need information on the public and private services that are available specially for them. Other than these, the information needs of the blind and deaf, *per se,* are similar to the information needs of the general population; the sparse literature supports this assertion' (Childers, 1975.) The situation is not unique to America, however: 'Each week in the "In Touch" office we receive dozens of letters from blind listeners, and over the eight years I have produced the programme it has become increasingly obvious that what blind people have in common, apart from their visual handicap, is a great lack of information' (British Broadcasting Corporation, 1973).

A mere handful of leaflets and booklets were received during the course of the Large Print User Study which showed that in some libraries steps were being taken to remedy this lack of information. A few authorities issued library booklets in conjunction with the Social Services Department, listing all the local services for the blind and and partially sighted together — ranging from library services for books, tapes and braille to low vision aids and a variety of other aids, classes and courses, services and concessions, with lists of useful addresses. A few libraries produced their own handouts in varying detail, but none of the libraries visited mentioned or produced anything of this nature and no embossed maps of the library layout, the local 'bus service or the nearby shopping centres were noticed anywhere — nor were collections of large print information leaflets such as those produced by Lloyds Bank on such topics as retirement, house buying, mortgages, improvement grants and the management of money, or others produced by the Health Education Council or the Gas Boards — all very relevant information for elderly people. No-one mentioned holding a register or list of available readers for the visually handicapped.

Forty-eight interviewees in West Midlands libraries were shown the list below and asked to indicate which of the items were stocked and used:

1 Alternative materials, e.g. braille, tapes
2 Magnifying glasses or other enlargers
3 Book-rests, stands, page turners, other aids
4 Reference works on microfiche
5 Large print reference books

6   Large print news in any form
7   Large print Bibles, parts of the Bible or hymn books
8   Large print crosswords
9   Large print knitting patterns
10   Large print music, including song books
11   Large print atlases or maps
12   Large print dictionaries
13   Large print recipe books or cards
14   Large print textbooks
15   Large print or clear print magazines
16   Large print books in foreign languages
17   Other material (give details)

Excluding items 1 and 2 (which will be discussed in later sections) and excluding the hospitals in the case of item 3, many had not even heard of the existence of the majority of the items listed. Seven of 26 libraries — including some belonging to large authorities — had none of them at all. Two had only one item each or multiples of the same one item and four libraries had only two different items. Eight libraries had three different items, three each had four items, one library had five and the library with most had seven different items mentioned on the list.

The most common items were the dictionaries and Bibles. Fourteen of the libraries had one or more copies of the dictionary, but though one library reported average use, mostly by OAPs, all the others reported very little use by anyone. Ten libraries had Bibles and another four had parts of the Bible in large print; here the use was slightly higher, with heavy use in one library, average use in two more and little or unknown use in the remainder — in all cases by the elderly and in one case additionally by those in a local blind establishment with a little residual vision.

There were cookery or recipe books (a category often requested by other librarians at different stages of the interviews) in six libraries; these seemed to receive a very mixed degree of use — 'very popular' in one library, average use, mainly by the elderly, in two others and little use in the remaining three. The large print hymn books stocked in five libraries got between poor and average use, entirely by the elderly and blind; the knitting patterns in three libraries were rarely used by anyone; the reference works on microfiche in two libraries were reasonably well-used but mostly by researchers and not by large print readers and the one library with a large print song book reported average use.

Only three of the 69 most visually handicapped large print readers interviewed used departments other than the lending department of the library, however, and the three did so only very occasionally. One was a first visit and the remaining 65 never used other departments at all, though some did so in the past when they were employed. Excluding the 30 who did not visit the library personally (17 of them housebound) reasons given by the remaining 35 able to do so were: 'No need now' (14) — 'Reading only for pleasure/pastime now' (7) — 'Too busy' (4) — 'Lighting/normal print/stairs impossible/ a strain' (3) — 'In a hurry' (2) — 'Not interested' (2) — and then 'Have shopping with me', — 'Never have done' and 'Didn't know of others' (one each) — not very encouraging findings for reference librarians.

The lack of demand for an inadequate reference service would not necessarily indicate a similar lack of demand for any *possible* service. However, even though the majority of the potential users were elderly and home-orientated, there were the younger people to be considered and the exceptions among the older ones. There *was* relevance for libraries in the field of visual handicap and it was possible to attract new readers even where there was little tradition of use, if librarians found out what was needed and positively encouraged its use rather than just providing what seemed appropriate; this much had been demonstrated by those few libraries venturing into the field.

One of the Welsh counties had included services to the visually handicapped in a project under the Job Creation Scheme, of which the object was to assess the needs and to attempt to satisfy those needs; a full-time liaison officer between the library and the Social Services Departments was then to be appointed to enable the work to continue at the end of the special project. An English county also reported a fairly comprehensive service for the visually handicapped, with booklists distributed by the Social Services Department, a permanent collection of local Talking Newspapers, the free issue of music cassettes to recipients of the latter and an information service whereby the Talking Newspaper users (who had special recording machines in addition to playback machines) recorded their queries and information requests on the cassettes, which were then returned to Talking Newspapers and passed on to the reference department which recorded the replies for distribution.

Few of the 119 librarians interviewed knew of any surveys in their areas of the numbers or needs of the registered partially sighted or of the visually handicapped, though one authority cited a proposed WRVS survey prior to its Books on Wheels provision, another mentioned a local scheme to coordinate all local services to the blind, a branch librarian said that one of the local schools was contemplating a survey and a fourth supplied a report of the library's own survey of extra-curricular activities in its area, including the potential for large print distribution.

With the availability of about 350,000 volumes of braille literature in addition to Moon, a Students' Braille Library, a Tape Library for Students, a tape transcription service for students, over 3,000 talking books and weekly tape versions of about 200 local newspapers from voluntary organizations, the expectation of help from libraries in fulfilling the information needs of the visually handicapped — and especially those absolutely unable to read print — was found to be understandably low. Some workers in the field considered that the blind should be less dependent on voluntary bodies for their services and that the supply of braille books was not adequate for the more advanced stages of education, however; some of the younger braille readers interviewed would have preferred to obtain books from their local libraries 'like everyone else', though it seemed unrealistic to suggest duplication of existing services at a time of financial constraint, and small local collections — even if practicable — could in any case only be a supplementary source of supply.

Many of the respondents in the Community Survey were able to read braille, as will be shown later in the report, and a considerable number of both library users and library non-users used two or more methods of reading or obtaining information, such as the use of low vision aids and print plus braille, large print and embossed print, or talking books and braille, etc. Fewer than initially expected of the visually handicapped — or even of the registered blind — could in fact read braille, however, and of the 69 large print readers who were found not to be able to read normal print only two could read embossed literature; one was an ex-private nurse in her 80s with double cataract who had learned Moon earlier when her mother went blind and the other was a diabetic in her 60s with problems of the retina who was learning braille. (Neither were members of a braille or Moon library.)

Only 16 of the 359 responding libraries in the survey mentioned previously (1967) held samples of braille or Moon literature at that time (13 of them advertised the service to the blind) and none were noticed during visits to West Midlands libraries. What *could* reasonably have been expected, however, were prominently placed large print lists of the addresses and telephone numbers of all the above mentioned suppliers and other relevant organizations which might be helpful to the visually handicapped, together with some indication of the presence of any relevant books or information held. Several librarians mentioned either Agnes Cameron's bibliography which had just then been published (Cameron, 1977) or Bowker's recent international catalogue *Large type books in print* (1978) but it should be mentioned that the latter concentrates on books published in the USA, giving only the American address for Ulverscroft and does not include Chivers or Magna.

It seemed to the researcher that two minimum requirements in communication should be the liberal, carefully-chosen distribution of the Library Association's large, eye-catching leaflet 'Reading for the Visually Handicapped' at £1 for 20 copies (Library Association, 1978) and that all notices and large print booklists should be produced *in* large print and aimed at independent readers as well as at link-men and agencies.

Tapes, cassettes and records

At the time of the Large Print User Study about 140 of the 166 library authorities in Britain possessed record and cassette libraries according to the Libraries, Museums and Art Galleries Year Book 1976 and these included all the Midland areas investigated, though, of course, this applied only to selected service points and the service was not always free. The records in some cases included not only all kinds of worthwhile music, but also drama, poetry, language, documentary and other items. In one library over 300 were issued in one year to 13 partially sighted users and the postage was paid by a local blind society. In the Welsh county already mentioned the use of spoken word cassettes both commercially produced and produced by the library staff (particularly in Welsh) was being actively promoted. Another county was considering the wider provision of cassette collections in an effort to increase the libraries' value to the blind. Seven of the West Midland libraries had collections of tapes ranging in number from two to 100 and their use was very much higher than that of the other items listed on page 115-6. Two collections were extremely well-used and three others got average use.

The users included the general public, the elderly, adult literacy students, the blind and 'one or two visually handicapped'.

None of the 69 people unable to read normal print (interviewed in the course of Survey B) had made use of the Talking Book Service, though four were likely to do so after hearing about its existence — all would have been eligible. The replies to another question on the use of alternative materials proved to be inconsistent and therefore of reduced value because of ambiguity in the wording (some people including radio if used at all and others including it only when plays, books and stories were listened to as an alternative to reading books.) It was clear, however, that radio and — to a lesser extent — television were the main alternatives used, though by no means used universally, and that only three of the 69 were known to use tapes. (One person named a special typewriter and one named her own imagination as alternative materials used!)

Seventy-five readers considered to be visually handicapped because they found normal print reading very difficult or impossible were asked to what extent the growing use of tape would be likely to meet some or all of their needs. As already stated, three people already used tapes and a further six gave replies which suggested that they were not averse to the idea and might be likely to do so (three of these would try them if their sight deteriorated further, two elderly professional people said that they were always happy to learn something new and one would probably try them as long as the recorder was made available free of charge) making a total of nine in all. The remaining 66 people (many of them elderly) were averse to the idea, some of them very positively so, and the following additional information was volunteered: 27 'preferred to read a book' — 22 'were not interested or wouldn't bother' — seven 'disliked technical things/ gadgets' — one mentioned limited means and nine didn't expand on their replies. Comments typifying their attitudes were 'you can't beat remaining in control of your own speed and repetition and the sheer pleasure of handling a well-produced book' and 'I've always been a bookworm and nothing will replace a book for me'.

When the visually handicapped non-library users encountered in the Community Survey were questioned, it emerged that a few people would use their libraries if tapes and records were available. One blind career man wrote, 'I feel that a cassette book department in libraries would be an excellent service to the blind and also the handicapped. The existing Talking Book Service is excellent, but many people are unwilling to take it because there is a stigma. To be able to take cassettes at the public library to play on one's own machine at home would be a great innovation, also talking magazines would be stimulating . . .' Several *main* reasons emerged later for the non-use of libraries, but additional reasons included poor reading ability, apprehension about going into a library building and the lack of records or tapes: 'the library I used to use had records and tapes but this one only has books' — 'I can't read any longer and my library doesn't get cassettes, which is a great pity' and 'what I would like to see in a library is a closed circuit TV, more books on cassette tapes, or someone who would read for me'. A listener asked 'In Touch' whether a service of books on cassette as well as in large print could be provided in public libraries to supplement the Talking Book Service, and the reply given was that 'though a few public libraries do now stock some recorded books this kind of service is not as yet very widespread. Libraries can however borrow from each other, so if a particular book is not available in the required form it is always worth asking the librarian if it can be obtained elsewhere' (*Public Library Services,* 1979.)

There was evidence of the popularity of cassettes in some housebound services also, in spite of the fact that many elderly people were unfamiliar with tape recorders and technical equipment. One family with three visually handicapped members had discontinued the Talking Book Service because tapes were usually tangled when received and there was no-one near to help, and a housebound service librarian commented 'I am asked about cassettes and players constantly and can never keep up with these demands. It is obvious that this vision problem of the elderly is escalating all the time. There is trouble too with the players as elderly people are not used to tape recorders — and as they can't see at all well anyway, we get many mangled tapes returned.'

Libraries have been known to meet individual membership costs of the British Talking Book service under the terms of the 1964 Act and they are now also being urged to consider providing the new variable speed machines which bring blind readers closer to the faster reading speed enjoyed by the seeing (Sturt, 1977.) The addresses of the National Listening Library and of the British Library of Tape Recordings for Hospital Patients are included in the list at the end of this report and also that of the Foundation for Audio Research which is currently working on highly condensed cassette tape which will give at least twelve hours of material (or an average novel) on a C90 cassette.

Newspapers and magazines

Britain lags behind some other countries in that there is still no large print newspaper printed here, mainly because a massive circulation would be needed to cover the cost involved. If one were to be produced, however (perhaps as a sponsored service by a well-endowed voluntary association) it is probable that librarians would be happy to help with distribution. Forty-eight persons were questioned about other aids, facilities, services and alternative materials in a total of 27 separate libraries or authorities in the West Midlands. Forty-five of them declared themselves willing to distribute a large print news-sheet if one could be produced free of charge and 'distributed' merely by being placed near the large print books, on the counter, or circulated at the same frequency as mobile library or housebound visits. The remaining three all belonged to the same county authority which believed in circulating only official circulars regarding council matters, etc.

When the 69 most visually handicapped of 200 existing large print readers were interviewed, however, their replies to a question about the likely readership of such a paper were less enthusiastic than other results of the study would have suggested. Not one of this home-orientated group read the magazines or newspapers in the library and not one of them would do so if magnifiers were available. Twenty-six of them read newspapers or parts of newspapers with magnifying glasses at home and a further 15 managed to read the headlines only. Twenty-five did not read a newspaper at all and in three cases the respondent was unable to answer. Somewhat surprisingly, only 16 of the 69 said that they would be likely to read a large print newspaper if one were available, eight were undecided or unable to answer for someone else and 45 replied in the negative, some adding reasons such as 'I like the news up-to-date' (8) — 'I get the news on the radio' (7) and 'I get the TV news' (7). In view of the popularity of newspaper reading among the elderly and visually handicapped respondents discussed at later stages of the report, however, it should probably be borne in mind that this was a small, predominantly elderly group which *might* have replied differently if specimen large print newspapers had been available for inspection and if it had been certain that no extra expenditure would be involved.

No question was specifically asked about *Talking* Newspapers, but these were spontaneously mentioned by some of the readers interviewed, by the elderly and visually handicapped people interviewed and by some of the visually handicapped postal respondents. Well over 200 of these are now in existence and most parts of the United Kingdom are covered to some extent, which means that the emphasis can be on the local news which keeps recipients in touch with their own communities. As the movement seems to be accelerating it is probable that Talking Newspapers are likely to become a permanent feature and some libraries were already responding at the time of the survey by storing past copies of the cassettes not only so that absentees at college or on holiday could 'catch-up' on local events, but also for their local history value. P R Craddock, speaking at the Annual Joint Conference of the Library Association of Ireland and the Northern Ireland Branch of the Library Association, suggested that libraries should go further: 'If we see libraries as activity centres for the transmission of information, then the implications for Talking Newspapers will be self evident — there is little difference between providing a photocopier for transcribing information and providing a tape recorder and microphone . . . we provide a photo-copier in a library because it is relevant to print media. We should provide a tape recorder because it is relevant to another medium in which we deal — sound.' (Craddock, 1978.)

No specific question was asked about large print magazines and these were not deliberately sought, but odd copies of 'Yours' (the national monthly paper published for the elderly in clear, large print by Help the Aged) were noticed in two Midland libraries and on a voluntary association's housebound library service, and a copy of 'Oculus' (the official magazine of the Partially Sighted Society) was seen in one library; no copies of 'Look Forward', 'World Contact' or the large print version of the BBC's 'In Touch' were seen in any of the libraries visited and at that time neither the 'Reader's Digest' nor the 'National Geographic' were available in this country in large print, though the 'Reader's Digest' was available at the time on talk-ing book cassettes and the matter of production of a large print edition of the radio programmes section of the 'Radio Times' was still being pursued by the Partially Sighted Society. A women's maga-zine would be popular, but none existed at the time of the study.

Closed-circuit television, reading machines, magnifiers and other aids.

A wide variety of reading aids for the visually handicapped are now in use in a wide variety of locations, but few were encountered in the libraries visited and where CCTV existed it was regarded as a reference tool and not mentioned by the staff in the context of service to the visually handicapped. The available equipment includes rear projectors which allow viewers to sit close to the screen without blocking the picture, a computer which reads printed material aloud and which was being tested by the National Federation for the Blind in America, listening rooms or carrels for the use of aural aids, audio materials and braille or large print typewriters, keyboard braille writers, talking book machines and tape recorders, the Optacon (a device which converts print into a tactile sensation) the variable speed tape recorders and highly condensed cassette tape previously mentioned, and various adaptations of CCTV which all show a magnified image on a monitor screen, with magnifications from X5 to X100 being possible.

Sixty-nine large print readers were asked if they used − or would use − a CCTV screen to enlarge print in the library. In 60 cases the answer was 'no', in six cases it was 'yes' and three people did not know. This was a very disappointing result in view of the potential of the equipment, but it must be remembered that 30 of these respondents were either housebound or did not go into the library and almost all of them belonged to an age-group which is unfamiliar and uneasy with most modern technical equipment. This situation is likely to change considerably as the next generation reaches retirement age, though the group is always likely to remain home-orientated. Apart from the 30 not using the library itself, the main reasons offered for not using such equipment were a liking to get back home to read in comfort, perhaps in bed; the love of books themselves; haste to catch buses or 'lifts' or do shopping at the same time as making the library visit; inability to stand or sit comfortably, or inability to watch TV or use artificial light. Those who would use a CCTV screen added such remarks as 'that would be a wonderful thing for me' − 'especially if the quality of the artwork were not reduced by magnification' and 'I'd find that *very* useful − to be able to look at all the tiny print non-fiction books as well'.

The final question asked of all the elderly and the visually handicapped respondents both by interview and by questionnaire in Community Survey C was 'if a technical reading machine were available which could help you to read normal print, would you use it if you could afford it?' One hundred and sixty-nine of the 324 respondents who answered this question would do so (52% overall) and 155 of them would not do so. One hundred and twenty (71%) of the 169 potential users were young or middle-aged people and only 39 (25%)

of the negative responses were from the younger people; 49 (29%) of the affirmatives and 116 (75%) of the negatives were from people of retiring age and over. Only one of the 26 OAP Home residents and two of the 31 elderly people interviewed in OAP clubs and centres would use a machine (one of them a retired teacher of 90!) mainly because of lack of interest in reading, a dislike of change, or lack of confidence or mechanical skill in using machines and fear of intricacy. 'It's not that I wouldn't like it — I'm scared of misusing anything new' — 'most of the time you just want to sit' — 'I don't like gadgets and I can't get to the library' — 'I'm not interested in a machine, but I *would* like a spy-glass and a new pair of spectacles' — 'just wait 'till *you're* ninety-two and you'll know then why I couldn't be bothered!' — 'too much trouble — I'm on my way out' — 'old people don't like change and machinery' — I'd rather have my knitting even if I could only knit dishcloths by feel; I don't want to be a special case — I believe in making the best of things' and in one case the situation was assessed by a 'kindly' colleague, who replied, 'she wouldn't know how to use it — she's past it!'

Several expressed a positive preference for large print, actual books or other alternatives (one pointing out that she could read braille in bed in the dark) and others considered themselves too old. One old lady said that she 'only read for pleasure and there'd be no pleasure in a machine' and another replied, 'what, at ninety-four next month? No, I'll not use any machines! Tell them they can *keep* them, but I'll try those books you've been showing me now'.

The reason offered by most of the younger people who said that they would not use such a machine differed from those given by older people — it was almost exclusively the ability to read normal print with LVAs. There were a few interesting exceptions, however, such as, 'I'm always tense when I'm reading braille so I don't expect I'd be relaxed struggling with a machine' — ' I don't think it would help me — it would be like all the magnifiers and just blur' — 'I don't *need* one — that might sound bold when I'm registered blind, but I honestly believe it' and 'they're only superior to an individually prescribed LVA if the subject matter is incomprehensible without the diagrams'.

User requirements could be fairly closely estimated from the additional comments — 18 of the 169 who answered 'yes' qualified their replies with remarks like 'if more efficient than present aids' — 'if easily portable' — 'if easy to learn' — 'if audio' — 'as long as you didn't have to wear it' — 'if faster than an LVA' — 'if it wasn't as laborious as braille' — 'as long as it was simple' — 'as long as it didn't make you feel too different from everyone else' and 'as long as it doesn't give me a headache'.

Sharing his children's books and helping them with homework would have given great pleasure to one man. Many others added such remarks as 'without the slightest doubt' — 'I certainly would' — 'definitely' — 'I'd certainly try' — 'I've tried one out at Moorfields' — 'it'd be lovely if you could read your own Christmas cards and letters' and several underlined the word 'yes' or added 'please'. Five mentioned that they found CCTV helpful and another added, 'with CCTV I can read normal print at about 20X magnification and the smallest print at 30X magnification'. Bearing in mind the fact that few such machines were likely to be readily available in time to help the elderly groups and that the findings for their groups were at variance with the findings among the people contacted via visually handicapped organizations, it seemed sensible to show the totals separately and this has been done in Table 5.

TABLE 5

REPLIES GIVEN BY 324 ELDERLY AND/OR VISUALLY HANDICAPPED RESPONDENTS TO THE QUESTION 'IF A TECHNICAL READING MACHINE WERE AVAILABLE WHICH COULD HELP YOU TO READ NORMAL PRINT, WOULD YOU USE IT IF YOU COULD AFFORD IT?'

Potential use of machines

Method	Yes	No	Unanswered
VH interviewed in *OAP* clubs and centres	2	26	3
VH interviewed in *OAP* Homes	1	25	—
Totals	3 (c5%)	51	3
VH interviewed via *VH* establishments	35	17	1
VH questionnaires	* 131	87	44
Totals	166 (c61%)	104	45

Avid large print readers were over-represented in this sample.

In terms of education, independence and pleasure for visually handicapped people unable to read even their own private correspondence and financial matter, this existing proportion of potential users would probably already have justified such provision at central points when equipment had been fully developed and tried out. In a technical society making increasing use of microchips and with today's young blind people being educated in special schools to make use of the low vision aids which are available, the potential use of such machines is likely to increase in the future and possibly even develop into a demand. (Note the 61% of *existing* potential users among those of all ages contacted via organizations for the visually handicapped.) As one octogenarian commented, 'I'm too old, but what wonderful things there are these days for the ones that are young enough to use them!'

'While, if there is a considerable visual deficit, relatively few will continue to read for pleasure, the ability to read for information can be sustained [by optical devices]' (Silver, 1978.) Several forms of magnifier are available and though some experts would prefer these always to be individually prescribed, others would be pleased to see a range available for use in libraries. One of the latter mentioned that a range of four magnifiers would probably cover the different magnifications required and that in some of our older library buildings it would be useful if illuminated magnifiers were provided.

Surprisingly, only six of the libraries visited had magnifiers available, in some cases only one or two in all and in other cases at least one in each branch. These seemed to receive about average use in most places in spite of the fact that no mention of their availability was seen, but this was in five cases by reference library users, in one case by children and not in any of these libraries by large print readers. In view of the popularity of hand-held magnifiers among the elderly large print readers and the elderly visually handicapped respondents, this must have been mainly due to lack of knowledge about their availability coupled with the group's unwillingness to 'trouble the staff', though it was probable that those absolutely dependent upon magnifiers carried their own. One large print reader expressed a wish for magnifiers to be stocked in her branch, because her own magnifier was too large to fit into her handbag and another user encountered during the course of the general community survey commented that he'd 'read somewhere that the man who created *The Times* didn't make any money out of *The Times* print, but he made a fortune out of the sale of spy-glasses'!

Thirty-nine of the 65 Midland large print readers unable to read normal print used magnifying glasses regularly; these consisted of 26 merely defined as 'popular' glasses, seven special aspheric magnifiers, three stand magnifiers, two 'coil' (Combined Optical Industries Limited), one rolling rod and one supplied free of charge with a directory. Two readers used a stand aspheric magnifier and also wore spectacles with thick lenses. One-third of these aids had been prescribed, almost all in an Eye Hospital or in the Eye Department of a General Hospital — only one 'by an eye doctor outside a hospital' and the remaining one by an optician — but the difference in their users' degree of satisfaction between these and the magnifiers bought or inherited was so small as to be immeasurable. It seemed that some readers hated the magnifiers they used; none considered them to be in the 'highly satisfactory' category and knowledge about the range available was non-existent. Several readers without magnifiers were interested in purchasing one and others with glasses described as 'popular' sometimes asked where they could buy 'a good one'. Many of these latter were not even aware that they could be purchased from opticians. Users' opinions of their aids were divided fairly evenly between the remaining four categories: satisfactory, average, unsatisfactory and highly unsatisfactory and those which had been prescribed were well represented in all these categories as were the others. Not one of these readers had ever asked a librarian for the loan of a magnifying aid in the library, including the woman who expressed the wish for one to the interviewer.

Magnifying glasses were also by far the most common aid used by the elderly and visually handicapped respondents in Survey C, with 175 users among 329 people, as will be seen later in the section on the visual ability of the non-users of large print. The aids named by this group included only five LVAs and one 'LVA spectacles', three 'special spectacles' and one 'cataract spectacles,' four CCTV, three special typewriters, one anglepoise lamp, one Opsec cataract glass, one illuminated reader and one 'old opera glasses', in addition to the more numerous telescopic spectacles, monocular, binocular and supplementary lenses.

In addition to the many types of stand and hand magnifiers, there are of course other reading aids such as those which support books and magazines, those which enable pages to be turned mechanically and prismatic spectacles for reading when lying in a horizontal position — aids more familiar in hospital libraries than in public libraries, and which are fully described by Joy Lewis in Going's 'Hospital

Libraries' (Lewis, 1973.) These are usually supplied by Social Services Departments for use in the home but as they could be relevant in housebound services librarians were questioned about them; excluding the hospital librarians some had not heard of their existence, however, and none of the libraries stocked them, evidently considering that these items did not come within their province. (Only ten of 359 responding libraries in the survey a decade earlier has stocked these aids. Survey of public library service to hospitals, the housebound and prisons (1967) and in fact only 65 of them had known of such aids being held by local welfare services.)

Of the 65 Survey B readers unable to read normal print, 41 used aids other than spectacles, but only one of these was a bookstand. Several of the elderly or visually handicapped respondents in the community survey mentioned being unable to hold a book, usually because of arthritis, but only one used a stand and most had never heard of such things; one said that 'being on the pension he just rested his book on the table'. Group 1 respondents (the miscellaneous category of contact which included OAP Home wardens and workers with old people, in the link-men survey) were asked how many of their contacts used a reading aid other than a low vision aid and only one bookrest and one unnamed aid (in addition to magnifiers) were mentioned — which tallied with the replies of the visually handicapped in Survey C.

Group 2 respondents were asked whether or not their department issued such aids, together with a request for information about the numbers and types available and the number issued per annum; these were the social workers, health visitors and district nurses and only 20 of the 59 (from all parts of the country) who answered the question replied that their department did issue such aids and the remaining 39 replied in the negative; as might have been expected, 17 of the 20 were social workers. In 12 cases bookrests or bookstands were available, in seven cases page turners, in five cases magnifiers (one adding that these were to try out only), in one case anglepoise lamps, in one. case 'phone dials and in one case (a hospital) simple spectacles and telescopes to try out. Some gave evasive answers, such as 'any, as appropriate', 'all listed' or 'none so far but would be considered if requested under the 1970 CS and DP Act.' Except in the case of the hospital social worker who recorded 323 such issues and 58 returns in the previous year it seemed that extremely small numbers of such appliances were involved. The numbers quoted ranged from one to five per annum being issued mostly to the social workers' contacts (in particular, to the contacts of the specialist social workers for the visually handicapped) and averaging only 2½ each per annum. Most of the Social Services Departments which were represented in the survey purchased such aids 'as needed', 'as required', or 'as requested', rather than holding a basic stock. Bearing in mind, however, how few interviewees and postal respondents even knew of the existence of such aids and how many of the former expressed a wish for one or other of them when they were informed during the course of their interviews, it was highly likely that the respondent who answered 'all needs met' was being unduly optimistic.

Catalogues, booklists and requests

When the 200 large print readers were interviewed, it was established that the group made little use of catalogues and 'didn't like to trouble the staff' on the whole. When the 602 borrowers and browsers were observed as unobtrusively as possible this became even more apparent and it was highly likely that those readers who stated that they did make use of catalogues only did so on rare occasions and not habitually. (Table 6 shows the number of the large print borrowers and browsers observed who either consulted the catalogue or the staff during one whole week in each of the libraries.) Except for the readers served by the various delivery services few of them *ever* consulted the staff. Readers receiving their books literally at the hands of librarians in housebound services and on mobile libraries etc. were at a disadvantage in having limited time and choice, but they did have the compensation of being in closer contact with members of the staff and these always seemed to ensure that something fairly appropriate was produced.

The readers were questioned as to how they asked for specific requests, with these results: 118 of 167 people questioned had never asked anyone for anything; they 'didn't like to be any trouble', 'didn't like to ask', or 'didn't want to reserve them and *pay*'. Of the remaining 49 who had ever made specific requests, 29 (many of them in the suburban libraries) had had their requests written down at the issue desk; 10 had made verbal requests at the issue desk, four had relied on a messenger, three had made verbal requests at an enquiry counter, two had had them written down at an enquiry counter and one was related to a member of staff. None of the 62 librarians questioned about large print requests kept a register or retained any permanent written record, though five readily produced current lists

TABLE 6

THE NUMBER OF THE LARGE PRINT BORROWERS AND BROWSERS (OBSERVED
ONLY) WHO EITHER CONSULTED THE CATALOGUE OR THE STAFF DURING ONE
ENTIRE WEEK IN EACH OF SIX LIBRARIES AND WITH VARIOUS DELIVERY
SERVICES (200 ADDITIONAL READERS WERE ALSO INTERVIEWED)

602 borrowers and browsers observed

Library	Consulted catalogue		Consulted staff		Total observed
	M	F	M	F	
A	1	1	4	3	154
B	—	—	—	—	17
C	1	1	2	5	71
D	1	—	2	5	70
E	—*	—*	3	2	54
F	—	—	3†	4†	196
Delivered G	—*	—*	6	17	40
Totals	3	2	20	36	602

*There was no catalogue in Library E and no catalogue at most delivery points
  – G
† it was possible but not probable that a few other readers consulted a Readers'
  Adviser whose desk was situated out of sight of the researcher

which had been marked by readers and were to form the basis of the
next delivery for the housebound service or to OAP Homes.

Not one of the 27 libraries or services examined in this respect
had large print catalogue cards filed separately from the main
sequence, many mentioning their computerized catalogues. One
library had no catalogue at all, one mentioned that *all* entries were
in clear type, one had entries under 'large print books' and two
libraries which did at one time maintain separate entries for large
print had by then discontinued the practice (one because it was
seldom used, though they later regretted having done so because they
would have found it useful and the other merely because the
sequence had been under 'Ulverscroft' which was no longer entirely
appropriate.) One library had tried to maintain a list of all large print
published, but had given up the struggle two years previously owing

to lack of time; it is possible that this might be updated by a member of staff and published for general use by the Library Association as a result of the study. Specific questions were not asked, but during lengthy conversations which included the subjects of catalogues and booklists no-one mentioned reference to the large print card index held by the Disabled Living Foundation's information service, though perhaps this would have happened had the interviewing taken place in London.

Readers' Advisers were available in most of the central libraries visited, including the one used for the purpose of interviewing and observing large print readers and browsers, but none were encountered in branches and smaller libraries and none were suggested by the librarians as interviewees. Members of the Panel considered that probably more reader guidance was needed to develop tastes and to make elderly people feel at home in libraries, though judging by the researcher's findings and impressions these would need to have outgoing personalities and be willing to make the first approach to their elderly readers in all but the middle-class areas.

And what of booklists? A quarter of a million readers' lists are printed annually by one major publisher alone and issued free of charge. In 25 public libraries whose facilities were examined, only nine had any lists on display at all. (Three published their own lists, like some of the well-produced examples which a few librarians posted with their national questionnaires; two of these were *in* large print and one included large print on the same list as normal print — the remaining six libraries had Ulverscroft printed lists only on display.) Incidentally all 25 libraries *possessed* this publisher's lists, but in all the remaining cases they were either kept for staff use only or distributed to OAP Homes and via the housebound service. Sixteen librarians *thought* that they were displayed, but the researcher failed to locate them in the other seven libraries when working with the large print books. Even the word 'displayed' was misleading when describing the odd few copies flopping about on and underneath the large print shelves and out of sight on top of the book-stacks, or neatly piled up with other leaflets on or near to the issue desks. Only in one library where a box-like container had been constructed and fastened to the end of the large print stack could the lists really be considered to be displayed and displayed conspicuously.

It seemed that librarians in all five counties tended to underestimate the usefulness of these booklists. No librarian interviewed suggested that they might have led readers to learn about the existence of large print books and indeed it did seem reasonable to suppose that prominently displayed collections of books were much more noticeable than a few booklists, yet three readers — presumably already members — first found the books this way. It will be shown when considering non-fiction books, that the readers had a marked tendency to see only what they were seeking and no doubt the same applied to booklists. Nevertheless, no less than 145 of the 194 readers asked had *never* seen a large print booklist of any kind. (The groups in which the highest percentage had done so were the groups which did not come into libraries. These were obviously the readers most in need of them since they never saw the collections, being served by the various delivery services — Homes, housebound, etc.) Furthermore, with the large print lists looking rather colourful and expensive to produce, with the group in general being so undemanding and also fearing charges of any sort and with the numbers of booklists left around usually being so minute, even some of those who did notice them had not realized that they would have been welcome to take one home free of charge. Of the 49 readers who did know of their existence (30 of them in the delivery schemes, although these readers were not specifically asked) only nine had seen them 'often' or 'always', 21 had seen them 'sometimes', and the remaining 19 answered 'once or twice'. Some of the readers had only ever seen lists immediately prior to the research visit, others had seen them at regular intervals and some estimated that it was either 'six to twelve months ago' or 'over a year ago' — it was not possible to reach any helpful conclusion about the regularity of such provision as did exist.

In one local authority, owing to the initiative of a member of staff who had links with the Talking Newspaper, the Social Services Department undertook distribution of booklists for the Libraries Department. Most, but not all of the link-men circulated did display or distribute lists and/or other material to some extent, or pass on the information received in some way. For example, 73 publicized the material either by placing it on notice-boards, referring to it in their own publications or reading lists, or by mentioning it verbally; 44 retained it for their own use or information; 35 passed the material on to the actual readers and ten used it in staff/student or volunteer training. One hospital social worker remarked that in her opinion 'those who haven't heard of them are people who aren't interested in reading anyway'; similar remarks had been made by WRVS ladies, particularly in suburban areas and at other stages of the study, but although true to a limited extent, Survey B had shown that this happy state of affairs had not yet been completely reached, nor was it likely to be achieved with a constantly changing pool of potential users.

From Table 6 and from earlier findings about the non-use of other facilities and library departments it was proved to the researcher's satisfaction that very few of the *existing* large print readers used their libraries for any other purpose than to choose books as quickly as possible to read at home and therefore the easiest and most effective way of serving *this* large, existing majority group to its own satisfaction in most libraries (and certainly at branch level) would simply be to make adequate shelf provision of a variety of large print books according to the need and in a separate collection, to advertise them effectively and whenever possible to locate them at service points close to post offices, local shops or housing for the elderly. A small minority group − mostly professional people − among the existing readers, together with a much larger number of the potential readers would have appreciated a much wider range of books in large print and/or aids to enable them to have access to entire library stocks. If after experimentation it is considered that their numbers justified the provision of such items as CCTV sets then these would obviously need to be made available in quiet libraries, well-served by public transport and with fairly easy access − and to achieve a reasonable degree of use the facilities would need to be regularly advertised through all the most appropriate channels.

The following is an excerpt from a talk given at an Open Forum Seminar in 1977: '. . .might perhaps convert themselves into resource centres which blind people would enjoy visiting, and which might provide, on long or short loans, such things as tape recorders, braille machines, talking calculators and perhaps even the Optacon. The centres could also provide information, not only through Talking Newspapers but also by offering advice on a variety of subjects ranging from buying a house to filling in a tax form . . .' − but the speaker was referring to voluntary associations and not to public libraries! (Armstrong, 1978.)

SPECIAL LIBRARY PROVISION

Housebound Services

West Midlands senior librarians were asked what percentage of their staff was estimated to have a genuine conviction that such time-consuming minority services as those to the elderly and housebound were a legitimate activity for library staffs. This was a loaded question, however it was worded unfortunately; the resulting answers and estimates were in many cases felt to be diplomatic rather than accurate and in some cases to be either accidentally or perhaps deliberately off the point. As pure research, the replies must be discounted but for their interest value they are included here:

In 17 of the 30 libraries all or most of the staff were considered to be 'convinced', 'sympathetic', 'helpful', 'dedicated' and they 'liked to see the servies used'; in fact it appeared that some of them were even 'difficult to keep in check'! Most of these workers apparently recognized that the public came before routine and there were comments about librarians' social role in addition to the educational one, librarianship being about *making* people want to read and librarians being aware that they were serving the whole community. Without being able to defend the action scientifically, the researcher isolated a second category of five libraries where vaguely similar suitable noises were made but where the answers were either cancelled by riders or contradicted by other factors in the libraries themselves or in the interviews. Here money was most likely to be at the root of the situation, with specialists considered to be desirable if they could be afforded and a division of opinion as to who should pay. (In this as in other respects the timing of the study in a period of such financial difficulty was unfortunate.) In eight libraries there was the unmistakable feeling that even the people being interviewed were not by any means convinced and that most felt that it should be the work or at least the expense of Social Services Departments. This is best illustrated by quoting some of the verbatim remarks:

'Involvement, yes — get people *into* libraries but Social Services should contribute to extra-mural activities' — 'Social Services should deal with extra-mural activities and libraries with those who can use libraries' — 'I believe in outreach but there comes a point where we're using library money to do Social Services' work' and 'most feel it's not a library priority owing to pressure on their time, but one for the Social Services.' One of the eight librarians remarked that most staff lacked a real career feeling but just accepted everything as normal and another said that the majority hadn't considered it.

None of the librarians was keen to apportion blame and both the 'most convinced' and the 'least convinced' categories of staff included a cross-section of old and young, senior and junior, male and female. One immeasurable factor which nevertheless did not escape attention was the marked effect often made on an entire staff by the attitudes of the chief and senior personnel.

Housebound services were thought by many librarians to be the basis of their large print book provision rather than the readers in the libraries themselves, yet the large print provided in these ranged from an astonishing 0% in one case where they had been offered and refused, to 100% in another where 'they never have enough' — with the majority providing between 25% and 60% to the housebound. All were agreed that their housebound services catered for almost 100% OAPs, mostly female, with either only very isolated cases of younger handicapped readers or none at all. Except for one who considered satisfaction with the range available to be 'average', all reported extreme dissatisfaction with the available range, but general satisfaction bordering on delight in some cases with the books themselves. (The readers' own opinions are discussed in the chapter on large print readers.)

Provision for the housebound seemed to be the most erratic provision of all: some senior librarians cared so much that they would take the books out themselves while others would conduct almost an inquisition on the doorstep of anyone armed with a doctor's certificate and requesting such a service. Therefore it would seem there is a need for formal standards in this area more than in any other, for at present they clearly depend upon which side of the border the house in which one is 'bound' happens to be situated. Indeed while some librarians encouraged referrals from social workers for their housebound services others were positively afraid of publicizing such a time- and petrol-consuming service in a period of financial constraint. As will be seen later among the reasons for the non-use of libraries and of large print books, the lack of such a service was very often an important reason where the elderly were concerned.

One of the five counties investigated reported a delivery service of books and gramophone records to 700 housebound readers 'in many parts of the county' and a request service was included. Others also provided a book service without specifying numbers served, though again some areas were covered and others were not. Seven hundred was also the number of housebound readers visited on the round of one of the responding London boroughs and it seemed probable from correspondence with one housebound services librarian that most of these readers fared rather better than their Midland counterparts, where often the number served was from none at all to under 200.

The Chronically Sick and Disabled Persons Act of 1970 should have eliminated the charitable aspect of such services, since it was intended to improve conditions for disabled people as a right, but it seemed that such provision was left to the discretion of local authorities and as their obligations were translated differently in different areas such services were more likely to be related to their suppliers' will or ability than to their users' needs or demands. According to 'The Libraries' Choice' (Department of Education and Science, 1978) there are no national statistics of these special library services, but the estimated provision drawn from particular surveys was an 89% coverage, in which case the library areas investigated for the Large Print User Study must have been atypical in this respect — at least when seen from the potential users' viewpoint. In some areas Social Services Departments had been known to cover the cost of petrol for such delivery services, in others voluntary bodies had been known to pay the total cost and yet another variation had been the use of Urban Aid money for the initial establishment of the service. In some areas there were transport arrangements to convey housebound people to their local libraries and judging by the amount of pleasure derived from weekly outings to such places as day centres this would seem to be an ideal solution in many cases; no-one in the study area mentioned such a service, however. Another innovation reported by a county in the south of England was a newsletter to provide a link between housebound people. This was being distributed by volunteers to 1,000 homes of people served by the Housebound Library Service.

The majority of such services depended on volunteers to deliver the books, though in some libraries this was done by staff of widely varying levels. The majority of the volunteers were WRVS but others cited included the Rotary Club, Boy Scouts, sixth formers, school pupils in community work classes and 'the Lady Bountifuls of the community who offered their services in response to advertisements'. A weakness of the service seemed to be that in most cases where volunteers were used the (often junior) staff who prepared the books never met the clients and frequently the volunteers who did know their clients were unfamiliar with (and in some cases never saw) the stock. Another difficulty experienced recently was a shortage of WRVS ladies to undertake delivery, for with more women now in full-time employment the WRVS itself was finding recruitment more difficult. Nevertheless most recipients were extremely grateful to have a service at all and were unaware of any shortcomings save the immediate shortage of romances!

In Survey D, the survey of link-men on a national basis, respondents in Groups 1, 2 and 5 were asked to estimate how many of their contacts received the housebound readers' service 'From their public libraries.' It was certainly not the researcher's intention to underestimate the valuable work being done in this respect by the WRVS but at this stage the ladies insisted that the service was theirs, with such replies as 'none — we run a Books on Wheels service with books from the local public library', or 'None — it's all done via the WRVS' (16). Regardless of the mechanics of the exercise it was clear that these volunteers were performing a very worthwhile service, with individual respondents serving numbers ranging between one and 68 housebound readers each (averaging about 30) and mention being made of seven to eight WRVS rounds in one area and the service in one county reaching 1,786 readers.

Workers and volunteers in Group 1 *other* than the Books on Wheels ladies knew of only 27 readers between them who received the service; their remaining replies were 'none' (19) and 'don't know' (25). Many of those who did not know how many of their contacts received the service also did not know of its existence and made such additional remarks as 'to tell the honest truth I didn't know there *was* such a thing' — 'I have no knowledge of it at all' — 'I didn't know about the service until you told me' and 'I wasn't aware of the service — nor did I know the library would supply books to the Home until you told me'. One added 'there isn't a mobile library from this branch — I once 'phoned up to ask' and another who was interviewed said, 'I know one of my ladies is trying to get it at present, without much success so far — he keeps saying he'll come himself and then nothing happens.'

One social worker knew of 40 contacts receiving the housebound reader service from her local library, but she was very much the exception among the workers in Group 2. Another replied 'most of the elderly housebound', but the majority of them replied 'none' or 'none at all' (24) while 22 replied that they did not know and the remainder (16) who quoted numbers knew of between one and six housebound readers. Including the 40 readers in the one social worker's case-load, only 82 readers *in all* were known by this group to be receiving the service and from previous replies it was clear that in most cases these workers were quoting actual numbers from written records. Some who answered 'none' added the following remarks: 'I asked them all recently when I knew you were coming' — 'it's available to any who need it' — 'most of the visually handicapped are not housebound — i.e. they have relatives' — 'I feel that the service may not be well-known' — 'they use talking books and the NLB's and 'none at all — this is a sore point; even a mobile library in the area would be welcomed, but — 's a Cinderella area. Some of them have requested books from the local branch but they're always 'coming' and they never come. If they lived in the inner city and were immigrants it would be a different matter'. Even in *this* important group of link-men (or more often link-women) there were two respondents who had never heard of such a service.

Most of the workers in Group 5 did not have this kind of information about their contacts. It seemed, however, that visits by Social Services Department workers were considered on the whole to be too infrequent — often only once when the clients were being 'settled in' — and one agency which had discontinued its house visiting when this role was taken over by the local authority was about to re-start the service. There was a great deal of evidence of *non*-visiting or of lack of knowledge about whether visually handicapped contacts were being visited at home, however, which suggested that if and when this one (often temporary) link was broken there would be a fairly isolated group of visually handicapped people living at home and unlikely to come into contact with *any* of the groups of link-men. (The services being provided by the respondents in Group 5 were mainly education, information, training, rehabilitation, residential care, social, assessment, research, entertainment and occasionally financial.)

Hospital libraries

According to the link-men in hospitals, when patients left hospital not a large proportion of those who would benefit by or who needed housebound library services were linked to them by hospital librarians or workers. Seventeen replied that this was done in their hospitals, ten respondents did not know (though some of these doubted it) and two said that patients were *told* about the existence of the service, but 23 merely circled the word 'no'. In one case 'very few left', in others 'if they left they were unlikely to be housebound'; one respondent pointed out that 'patients were often transferred elsewhere and more important issues were at stake', while another admitted 'there's no such service run by the Red Cross though I believe the WRVS do run such a service' and some WRVS respondents again pointed out that their organization and *not* the library was 'responsible for the housebound service'.

The numbers of large print books stocked in hospital libraries varied even more greatly than did the numbers stocked in public libraries. Most of the many non-respondents among 48 West Midlands hospital librarians contacted sent notes to the effect that theirs were medical libraries only or that the hospital did not have a patients' library, and of those who did complete forms several replied 'not enough' to the question 'how many large print books are there in the hospital library?' Apart from three libraries with none at all the lowest number of volumes quoted was two, provided by a librarian herself to start a patients' service and nine librarians gave replies of 20 volumes or less. A large 'central' hospital lending about 1,000 large print books to other institutions in the area stocked 1,350 in all, but the largest stock mentioned in one specific hospital library was 1,000 and two libraries each had 600; the average number for individual hospital patients' libraries was 169 large print volumes.

According to the West Midlands Branch of the Library Association Report (1970), of 200 hospital libraries surveyed (with 43,000 beds among them) 99 were provided by voluntary bodies, mainly the Order of St John of Jerusalem and the British Red Cross Society; 31 were provided by public libraries direct and 16 by the hospitals' own volunteers. The responding libraries (not all of them in West Midlands hospitals) were also provided by a variety of bodies – public libraries, the Red Cross and St John, the hospitals themselves and Friends of the Hospitals, WRVS, industrial firms or various combinations of these — and staffed by as wide a variety of professionals and volunteers. The largest large print stock of them all was in a library provided by the Red Cross, but in general the most consistently large stocks were in hospitals where the service was provided by public libraries, most of these being numbered in the hundreds and in one case supported by 500 additional County Library discards. Large print books were not stocked or used at all in three hospital libraries, including an Eye Hospital where 'most patients were not encouraged to read after eye surgery'.

Facilities for reading in the hospitals also varied greatly. Most, but by no means all of them had individual lights above beds and most claimed to have good general lighting; less had curtains round the beds, however, and one respondent remarked that 'the real problem was noise in the wards, not light'. Only 15 had libraries where patients could read, whereas 29 respondents stated that there were lounges available and ten answered that their patients could read in the Day Rooms attached to wards. Nine replied that there were no facilities for patients not bed-bound to read other than in the wards; one of these added that some mentally handicapped patients attempted reading via the Schools and Social Education Departments; another said that 'a patients' reading room would be very therapeutically useful' but that there was no possibility of getting one at present.

In 19 hospitals the large print books were circulated in all wards. The hospitals contacted included various specialist hospitals with a variety of wards between them, but of those who did not circulate the books in *all* wards the largest number (14) circulated them in the geriatric wards and the remainder circulated them as follows — general wards (6) psychiatric wards (6) optical wards (5) orthopaedic wards (5) surgical wards (4) neurological wards (1) and female medical wards (1).

Opinion was fairly evenly divided as to whether or not nurses read the books when on night duty, with 17 answering 'yes', 19 answering 'no' and 10 not knowing. It was possible that rather more than half would have replied in the affirmative had there not been an attitude that reading when on duty was unpardonable — three of those answering 'no' added 'as far as we know!', 'not officially' and 'I hope not!' When asked whether or not the books were used by overseas patients using English as a second language rather more answered in the negative, though the area covered was a wide one and it was probable that not all of the hospitals had many such patients. (The numbers were 'No' 24; 'Yes' - 10, and 'don't know' — 12 and one librarian added that some overseas staff used them.) To the question 'Which patients are the main users?' most respondents replied 'Geriatrics' or 'The elderly'. A variety of other answers were given by one or two respondents each — long stay patients, those with failing vision, people who experienced difficulty in reading normal print, the late middle-aged, old ladies, the introverted, the intelligent, psychiatric patients, females, the partially sighted, ophthalmic patients, those with vision temporarily affected by drugs and the disabled with poor sight, but 30 respondents named the elderly, which corresponded with findings reported later.

Rather more of the hospital readers than of the other readers were thought to be 'highly satisfied' with the books, though it was interesting to note that 10 hospital *librarians* placed their readers in this category while only four of the other hospital workers did so. The next largest group was of readers whose degree of satisfaction was thought to be 'satisfied' (8) and the remainder were classified as 'average' (7) — 'dissatisfied' (1) and 'highly dissatisfied' (1). The main cause for complaint was still the size and/or weight of the books though two people commented that more non-fiction and short stories were required.

Four West Midlands librarians interviewed on general topics during Survey A reported on service to hospitals and all four included large print books as a significant part of their provision. One commented that many more went to Geriatric Hospitals than to General Hospitals; one said that there was not a great demand so she only supplied 15% and one was buying three sets of Ulverscroft books with a Social Services grant for exchange bi-monthly by the Red Cross. Bearing in mind the size of the total stock the two collections seen seemed varied and adequate, though in the only three hospital authorities investigated at this stage there were no less than three different systems in operation: entire provision by the city libraries with professional staff; by the Red Cross with a committee and volunteers — and by the hospitals themselves with assistance from the local authority libraries.

The following are brief excerpts from one authority's informal survey of its hospital libraries, which demonstrate some of the inherent difficulties when local authority boundaries, library authority areas and health authority areas change:

'The quality of the service given in the area differs greatly. Many of the patients' services are poor but this is often due to outside factors which cannot yet be remedied. . .A had three hospitals in the area; in one the County Library is responsible for stocking and staffing the service to wards, in another the library provides the books but service to the wards is traditionally provided by the WRVS and in the third the Domestic Superintendent has responsibility for the book stock. B has three geriatric hospitals; large print books are supplied by the County Library; they are exchanged monthly from the stock of B lending library, which limits the number of books supplied . . several hospitals in C area have no service at all. . .D area has a hospital at D; the library is for both patients and staff and it opens on only two days a week. . . .E area has two hospitals. The first has a bi-annual exchange of 50 books, not provided by the area itself but by HQ and the WRVS provide the ward service. The second hospital has a tri-annual exchange provided by E area library. . . F convalescent home is visited weekly by F mobile library. . . . G area has two hospitals. At one there is a patients' library, open on Tuesday mornings and a staff medical library service provided by D; at the other there is a service one afternoon per week. . . H area has two general hospitals and a geriatric hospital — large print books are available in them all . . One is supervized by a qualified member of staff and one by a voluntary helper, while the geriatric hospital service is provided by a voluntary organization. . . J has a medical library service provided by H; this was at one time provided on a part-time basis by a nearby Borough Library, but it is now provided by the hospital at H . . .K has three small hospitals controlled by a different Area Health Authority and the matter of rationalization is still under consideration; no-one is at present providing a library service, though Friends of the Hospital circulate a trolley of donated books in the largest of the three hospitals' and so on . . .

None of the responding librarians mentioned talking books or books in braille, though specific questions had not been asked about these. It is possible that they would have been available in a few of the libraries, however, as ten of 128 surveyed hospitals as long ago as 1966 had stocked collections of braille books and three had stocked talking books when these were less common (Sanders, 1966).

It is impossible to imagine that this necessarily short and limited experience with large print in hospitals will add anything new to the facts already available in the considerable literature of hospital librarianship, but such visits and interviews as were possible in the time available did at least corroborate them. Hospital patients (like the elderly in the libraries themselves) were a cross-section of the public as a whole, but whereas in the second case reading tastes appeared only gradually to lead to books which required less effort and concentration, in the first it seemed that the change to lighter reading was more sudden and sometimes imposed, having been brought on by illness with its resulting tendency to look inward. In addition to the categories of reader using large print in the libraries themselves these hospital librarians provided them on occasions for depressed patients, multiple sclerosis sufferers, children, people temporarily without their spectacles, those affected by medicines, post-operative patients unable or disinclined to read and a small proportion of the post-cataract operation patients in ophthalmic wards, usually those fitted with special lenses. The size and weight of the books was apparently even more significant in the hospitals than in libraries, in spite of the fact that aids such as book-rests and stands, page turners and prismatic spectacles were usually available in addition to magnifiers.

Voluntary library service

Only one voluntary service providing large print books to the housebound elderly was investigated, other than the volunteers mentioned as taking part in libraries' own housebound service deliveries, but this proved to be an interesting example of practicality, cooperation and initiative: a small local charity providing a visiting service to the elderly in an inner city area had its own stock of 2,500 books including 500 large format large print books and supplemented it by obtaining specific requests from its nearest branch library. The books were housed on office shelves together with a few additions bought each time the collecting box contained enough coppers to purchase another. Volunteers such as the retired medical social worker accompanied on a round called fortnightly on the lonely clients with laundered sheets (where required) and such items as tea, sugar, tinned milk pudding and evaporated milk in solo sizes for purchase at bulk-purchase prices together with library books (in many cases large print) for exchange. Furthermore there was discreet liaison with the appropriate body if someone on the round was thought to be ill or in need of specialized help.

Mobile libraries

Fourteen librarians of mobile libraries returned questionnaires for Survey A and others discussed services in the five counties visited, but only one rural mobile library was included for the purpose of interviewing or observing readers. Among the national returns the lowest large print stock consisted of 20 volumes only and the highest number was 160, with the average at 87 volumes, usually changed fairly frequently. In the Midland counties not all the authorities provided mobile or travelling libraries. Most of those which did so provided between one and two shelves or between 20 and 100 volumes of large print (averaging 47.8 — rather less than those on the national questionnaire forms) and one provided none at all, saying that 'there's no handy space'. The large print readers were mostly OAPs, especially females, most of whom expressed satisfaction with the books themselves and great dissatisfaction with the range available. One librarian's comment was 'and no wonder!' The readers on the mobile libraries did have their large print stock changed over frequently from basic library stocks, however, and they also benefited from the personal attention of the librarian — especially where stops were of limited duration!

Most of the mobile libraries were treated administratively as branch libraries and made their visits on a weekly or on a fortnightly basis; some allowed their readers the same number of books as the libraries did, some increased the allocation and others placed no restriction on the numbers borrowed — and though the weight of the large print books often did place a restriction on the numbers borrowed it was conspicuous that the mobile library readers usually made a special library visit instead of combining it with a shopping expedition as did their counterparts in the library buildings; they also had less distance to walk and consequently they usually borrowed more books. To summarize a later section on travel to libraries, distance was a very relevant factor for many of the elderly who must walk there, as was the availability or non-availability of local bulk loans, housebound services, mobile libraries and messengers. The availability of private transport and the convenience or otherwise of travel by public transport were equally significant among the elderly and would be likely to be more so in rural areas; difficult main roads were an additional deterrent. Library use by *all* elderly people (whether or not they were visually handicapped) was likely to be affected by accessibility but the use of libraries by visually handicapped younger people seemed less likely to be affected by these factors.

In the general community section of Survey C, surprisingly 164 of the 258 non-users of libraries (of a total of 500 interviewed) did not know or could not recall either the address or the location of the library nearest to their home, but in the rural areas served by mobile libraries the non-users had at least seen the vehicles and this was the only group in which the non-users who did *not* know of its whereabouts were outnumbered by the non-users who did know. When librarians all over the country were asked about the most effective methods of communicating with users and potential users of large print, the reply 'mobile and travelling libraries' came twelfth on their list of twenty answers — above such replies as printed information, readers' advisers and voluntary associations. In a recent survey on the elderly at home (Hunt, 1978) people of 65 years and over were questioned about visits from social services and other bodies during the previous six months and 2.8% named their mobile library visits — slightly more than the 2.6% who named Meals on Wheels and the 2.7% who named a voluntary organization, but probably not enough considering that 26.8% of them named reading as an interest spontaneously and 55.4% did so after prompting.

OAP Homes, clubs and centres

Cooperation between library authorities and other authorities such as area health authorities and Social Services Departments is encouraged in Section 7 of the Public Libraries and Museums Act of 1964 and according to paragraph 60 of the IFLA (1969) Public Library Standards deposit collections should be supplied to residential Homes, day centres and clubs for the elderly on the scale of two to six books per head with an absolute minimum of 200 volumes, changed at least four times a year and additionally when requested.

According to the Large Print User Study respondents, a very wide range of large print provision existed — from '8 to 30 in each Home' to 100% large print — but the majority provided a very significant proportion. The range of material available was unanimously considered unsatisfactory by the workers responsible for providing the collections, with such exasperated phrases as 'they've *had* them all', 'can never get enough' and 'lack of titles' recurring, but the readers were considered to be very pleased with the books themselves. No national statistics regarding the provision of such services to OAP Homes were traced but a 58% coverage was estimated by the DES (1978) and of 275 Homes and/or hostels served by respondents at the time of the survey conducted by the Hospital Libraries and Handicapped Readers Group of the Library Association in 1967, 265 were sent large print books.

Interviews and observations were only carried out in the OAP Homes of three Midland areas but the work was discussed with all the Midland librarians visited. Not all of those interviewed provided services to Homes, most deposited collections of varying sizes changed at varying intervals, a few provided a trolley service to selected lounges using mainly library staff but in one case volunteers, and a few organized special activities such as story hours and singing for the residents, though the popularity of these apparently decreased as the average age of the residents increased; sometimes these different systems were operating within the same authority. It seemed that where there was a trolley service there were many more borrowers than where the books were merely deposited – and often not known about, by the residents interviewed during Survey C. It would be interesting to compare the use made of books (and of large print books in particular) by saturating one Home after pre-testing, providing a trolley service in another and leaving a third as a control group, because the increased use of the trolley service noted above was merely an impression and could not be supported by the collection of statistics in the time available.

Library authorities now have a duty to encourage use of the service and it is often left to their staff to find ways of introducing new interests to the elderly. Some took the opportunity of publicizing large print at old folks' clubs and gatherings, some undertook lectures at pre-retirement courses and some produced and distributed large print booklists. On the whole librarians were very aware of the potential for publicity about large print in OAP Homes: 39 gave such answers as 'books in OAP Homes, hostels, day centres, lunch clubs or by liaison with wardens' on the national questionnaire forms, where these methods were sixth in popularity in a list of twenty named methods of communicating with users and potential users of large print and 'OAP clubs and social centres' actually topped the list of ideas quoted by 116 interviewees in the West Midlands, for 40 of them gave this reply to the same question.

The replies received in the Linkmen Survey revealed that the workers in OAP Homes and centres had not been circulated by publishers and had been entirely dependent upon public libraries for any initial contact made with large print books, though a number of them were not library users themselves and only one of 19 had ever received any publicity material. Sixteen respondents averaged five partially sighted contacts and 27 contacts with failing vision, and when questioned about this latter category some added 'all', 'most', 'almost 100% even if they don't admit it' and 'all those over seventy'. The average percentage of *large print* readers among the considerable numbers of residents estimated by these wardens and other workers to have failing vision worked out at 34% (based on only 14 of the 19 respondents' estimates, the other five 'not knowing') and additional remarks included 'not a lot read at all', 'most of those who do read', 'they get lazy when they get to eighty' and 'a large number would if sufficient were available'.

The publicity situation among the elderly in Homes and at clubs and centres was not good in spite of librarians' replies, when one considers that 57 of the 110 visually handicapped people interviewed were located there and that those of the remainder who were readers at all could be considered as potential large print users. Forty-five per cent of those interviewed in Homes and 47% of those interviewed in clubs and centres had never read, seen nor heard of large print books. When 37 Home residents who *had* read, seen or heard of the books were asked if they had ever told anyone else about them it emerged that this was the most uncommunicative group in this respect, with only three of them having done so. However, on the other hand, when 200 large print readers were asked how they first found out about large print books 26 of them had first seen them in OAP Homes — the third most common reply even though only 40 people had been interviewed in other than library premises.

The estimated age group most commonly represented in the interviewed samples from each of the Homes individually and in the total sample from all five Homes used for Survey C was the 80s. Thirty-six of the people interviewed were estimated to be in their 80s (54%) and this was followed by the 70s (21 residents, or 31%) with six estimated to be in their 90s (9%) and only four in their 60s. (It was also likely that more of the older groups would be among those *not* interviewed). Fifty-one of the 67 (76%) were either known or estimated to have left school at 15 years of age or less and a further five who either did not remember or gave no indication of this factor or of their employment were probably also early school leavers — bringing the possible total to 56 or 84%, which tallied with the custom of their time. Six were estimated or known to have stayed in full-time education until they were 16 years, two until 17 years, two until 18 years and one until 19 years or more. The category of previous employment most commonly represented was that of unskilled workers (32) or 63% of the 51 whose earlier work was named. (In 16 cases the previous employment was not discovered, usually because it was not possible to ask the question privately or diplomatically). Six people had been employed in clerical or lower administrative work, five in skilled or semi-skilled employment, five had never been employed, and three came into the lower professional category. There was no representative of higher professional employment.

Thirty people named three or more leisure activities, which usually included radio and television as two of them; 37 people named less than three, including 20 people either with none at all or with only radio and/or television. The residents in one suburban Home seemed to have the most interests, with ten of 14 coming into the first category, whereas in another outwardly similar Home only two of 13 came into that category. TV was the most often named interest, mentioned by 41 residents. *Reading* came second with 35 mentions, though not always meaning books. Radio was third with 30, and knitting fourth with 21 (often meaning knitting only blanket squares or dishcloths.) Much lower in their 'scores' but next in order of popularity came helping in the Home (7) — sewing (7) — walking (7) — church (7) — crocheting (5) — drinking (5) — bingo (4) — talking (4) — crossword puzzles (4) — gardening or garden interests (4) — embroidery (3) — horse racing (3) — music (3) — window-shopping (3) — art (2) — mending (2) — dominoes (2) — cards (2) — draughts (2) — and handicrafts (2). There were single references to: writing letters, talks, singing hymns, politics, visiting, watching sport, concerts, cooking, travelling, riding on buses, weaving, chess and blind classes. Non-listeners to the BBC's Radio 4 programme for the visually handicapped ('In Touch') included 21 of 26 visually handicapped OAP Home residents and 25 of 31 elderly visually handicapped people interviewed in OAP clubs and centres. In many cases they had never heard of the programme, had the communal radio permanently tuned into a different channel, 'observed Sundays' or the programme coincided with tea-time in the Home, though the timing has since been changed. The leisure activities, interests and reading tastes of the elderly are discussed in much greater detail in later chapters about large print readers and non-readers.

When asked whether they attended any meetings or gatherings with other people in a similar position the gatherings most often named were: Church (15) — Home outings (11) — bing (6) — 60+ Clubs/centres (5) — pubs (5) — blind and partially sighted societies (3) — art classes (2) and concerts (2). Meetings each named once were: political party, YWCA, bridge, Rotary, family gatherings, friends and visits to old houses. These were probably not the sum total of the old people's outings, but they were the ones which came to mind when they were asked, which was in itself significant.

It is fairly obvious that service to Homes and centres is uneconomic in terms of issues and costs, but it is of value beyond such calculations and increased resources must surely be made available soon to provide the services which will be required by an ageing and a more highly educated population. At one stage of the study 140 ex-library users were asked why they no longer used their libraries; 57 of them were elderly people living in the community and interviewed in clubs and centres and 35 of the 57 gave as the reason the inability to get to the library owing to disability and the unavailability of the books in the Home or centre to which they were transported, which should be borne in mind when planning bulk loans to Homes, clubs and centres. As Joy Lewis pointed out 'Service to our elderly should not be allowed to fall behind because of the awareness of new and different needs of others. The potential voting power of the elderly may be a persuasive element in arguments for allocation of resources to this service by the local authority, but the best reason for provision is that this group makes up a very large section of most communities and has special and real needs for library provision which should be understood and met' (Lewis, 1974)

Literacy services

In a study of this nature it is easy to become immersed and to overlook the fact that the bookstock under investigation is a small one, serving a relatively small group of people. It is, however, necessary to consider this point, because the discovery of any extra potential market for the books — either of temporary or of different users — could encourage publishers and librarians and in turn aid the visually handicapped.

In some cases literacy problems are entirely unconnected with visual problems and in other cases the two are directly linked, as when visually handicapped people who have been reading braille turn to print or when illness or disability leads to both problems. The Education Officer of one well-known school for the blind wrote 'My main need is large print books suitable for residents who are just learning to read with the assistance of LVAs. The large print books assume a level of literacy which many of our folk have not reached — and many never will' and the theme was echoed by other teachers of the visually handicapped and also of the disabled who often suffered such additional difficulties. Some use was made of Ulverscroft's Trigger books, though these, like George Prior's large print books for younger readers and Margaret Marshall's list of 160 recommended books and series (Marshall, 1977) seemed to be relatively unknown in these circles. The need for books for teenagers was also frequently mentioned during Survey C.

When West Midlands librarians were asked about their large print readers and in particular about any *other* readers who had been observed in addition to the elderly and visually handicapped, the list included literacy students, literacy teachers, dyslectics, new readers and teenage boys with low reading ages; when *readers* were asked about large print one of the reasons volunteered spontaneously for reading it was that new readers felt encouraged by their progress and even average readers 'could read more quickly'. When the link-men were asked which people they informed about large print books the list of replies included young adults undergoing remedial education, adults with literacy problems, cases of poor literacy, new readers, people who found small print difficult, slow readers, near-independent readers, students of low academic level, literacy tutors and volunteers; six young people observed at the large print shelves were seen to move on to literacy material only, and in some libraries this was shelved nearby.

Most librarians had only ever observed one or two of these groups using the large print and some either did not have any such use at all or had failed to notice it; there were 28 reports in the West Midlands of the books being used by literacy teachers and/or pupils, for example. Large print books were used 'officially' in only four of 33 libraries for adult literacy schemes or classes, but they were occasionally used in others to a very limited extent. In two libraries the central stock got a small amount of use as the new readers proceeded from literacy material via the less intellectually demanding large print romances to the general stock. One library included a few large print books in the stock provided to the tutor/organizer and another included Trigger books only. The policy in some libraries of discouraging use of large print by people not visually handicapped might have accounted to a limited extent for the small degree of such additional use, but the feeling among literacy workers was that such use would be likely to decrease in general by the group, now that more specifically produced material had become available.

A total of 21 respondents in Group 1 (the miscellaneous group in the Link-men Survey) knew of contacts who had difficulty with reading and writing, though in most cases each respondent knew of only one, two, three or 'a few' people — the exceptions being a clergyman who replied 'very many in this area', two Age Concern respondents who replied '62' and 'quite a high proportion' respectively, two Books on Wheels ladies who replied 'quite a few' and 'many are semi-literate' and two OAP Home respondents who referred to 'some who've forgotten' and 'a few with failing faculties who were able in the past'. When asked how many of these contacts ever read large print books one Books on Wheels lady answered 'quite a few', but hers was a lone voice for hardly any of the other respondents knew of any at all. 'They don't ever read' was one flat reply and this seemed to be the verdict of most of the group.

The situation was different among the 22 literacy workers in Group 6a, however. Twelve of the 22 had used large print books in lessons and these had been mainly Ulverscroft and the literacy schemes' own publications. Romances, Westerns and 'simple sequential crime' were mentioned specifically, as were Magna's books 'on specialist subjects' and although some considered the vocabulary too difficult most were well satisfied with the books; seven of the 12 had also used them as a stepping stone between textbooks and small print. When asked what proportion of their new readers liked to read large print, answers varied greatly with just over half of them opting for 'a minority' or 'none' and just under half replying 'the majority' or 'about half'. Not unexpectedly 'the men liked crime and the women liked romances', though some thought that there should be more working-class writers and some used a large print dictionary only. Eight of the 22 literacy workers had borrowed large print books from the library on behalf of their students 'in order to maintain the reading habit at the end of the course' and mainly because 'they're usually reluctant to go in', 'the students are shy of libraries at first' and 'the older ones are unlikely to visit a library owing to a sense of unfamiliarity and inferiority'. It was considered likely that the earlier use of large print books in the actual lessons would decline in future as more material was being produced specifically for the adult non-reader. As one County Librarian remarked 'obviously large print is an important feature of this type of material but so too are short sentences and paragraphs, brief, direct text, etc.'

All but 13 respondents in Groups 1, 2 and 6 knew the addresses of the public libraries (including branch libraries) in the areas where their contacts lived, including everyone in Group 1d, 1e and Group 2, though no doubt more interviews (rather than questionnaires) would have led to more answers in the negative category; responses in the general community survey were an indication of this.

With an estimated two million people in need of help with reading and writing and over 100,000 having already responded to the BBC's recruitment drive, the potential market for large print could have been considerably extended, had there been more books of short stories for those unable to sustain interest for long periods, more books with simple vocabulary and structure and more deliberate linking of the two services. Instead, a glut of little-used literacy material in many libraries seemed to have dampened some librarians' enthusiasm for making generous responses to minority needs.

The psychological aspects of reading large print could not be fully investigated in a study of such a general nature, but when 97 West Midlands librarians were asked if they had ever noticed any embarrassment on the part of their large print readers 80 of them (82½%) said that they had never been aware of its existence. Seventeen of them replied in the affirmative (17½%) and when they were asked who these people were it emerged that most of them were the literacy students and new readers with a confidence problem, who were 'furtive and acutely embarrassed to use anything at all different and were even difficult to get into a library'. This study represents a first attempt to cover the whole field of large print and large print users, including peripheral information, and the researcher has been very aware of time constraints and limitations; it is to be hoped that it might stimulate further and more specialized surveys and one area might well be research into the effects of different kinds of display and publicity, including its effects on use by literacy groups and classes.

Services to ethnic minorities

One million seven hundred and forty four thousand people in the United Kingdom (3.2% of the population at the time of the study) were of New Commonwealth ethnic origin (Community Relations Commission, 1976) and according to the 1971 census there were 53,294 people in Birmingham alone with *both* parents born in the New Commonwealth. As they were an extremely young population, however, with only 7003 of them over 45 years and 400 over 65 years, the researcher was unsuccessful in finding any bulk provision which included large print to immigrant organizations, centres for English as a second language or Settlements in the entire area under investigation.

A few of the link-men contacted said that if they received any information about large print they would circulate it to Asian ladies learning English and the West Midlands librarians interviewed had observed large print books being used by 'immigrants learning English', 'male Sikhs', 'Asian ladies' and 'Bengali ladies'. Most of them had only ever observed occasional use by these groups, however, and some did not have any such use or users at all; from 116 responses there were only 15 reports of their being used occasionally by English learners. The books most often cited as being popular with these groups were the romances (which were favoured by Asian males and females alike) and to a lesser extent the Westerns and Trigger books. This was obviously only a tiny minority readership — one could accurately call it 'a minority *of* a minority' — but clearly it existed and this could be significant for those who publish and publicize.

Groups 1 and 6 (the miscellaneous workers and the language and literacy workers among the link-men) were asked about the use of large print books by people other than the visually handicapped. The 103 respondents in Group 1 had remarkably few contacts who had difficulty with the English language and it seemed that only a minute proportion of these was known to have read large print books; only one of the three workers with immigrants (6b) had borrowed such books on their behalf and the same respondent had used the Ulverscroft romances in lessons. The others stated that their pupils 'never reached the stage of using them as a stepping stone between textbooks and small print in their short sessions' and that 'the books were not really suitable' (though the sole user was highly satisfied with them).

From the observation period it became evident that large print books — even in multi-racial areas — were very little used by people of immigrant origin, even bearing in mind the use by a few Asians learning English, as stated by librarians, literacy tutors and prison officers. It was probable — though outside the scope of this study — that libraries themselves were under-used by this group and in any case relatively few immigrants had reached the ages linked with failing vision. When merely observing people it was not possible to be 100% certain about the language spoken in every case, but not one of the 200 people interviewed was of immigrant origin and not one of the 417 people observed who actually borrowed large print was considered unlikely to speak English as a first language. In four of the areas selected for the study there had been no immigrant settlement and only one person obviously of immigrant origin was seen at the large print shelves in one of these — he subsequently borrowed literacy material from a shelf nearby. Library C, on the other hand, was in a town in the centre of an area of established immigrant settlement and several Asian readers were noticed at the normal print shelves; however, although four teenagers of West Indian origin glanced through one or two large print books superficially, only one of them borrowed a romance. Even in Library B — situated right in the heart of what had then become an area of mostly Asian settlement and multi-racial schools — all the large print users were indigenous, with five children of varied immigrant origin browsing to pass the time during their school lunch hours but not with any intention of borrowing. As stated earlier in this section, the degree of use by immigrants learning English was a very small minority of a minority readership.

Prison libraries

Not all those interviewed provided services to hospitals and prisons and those who did so formulated their replies in such a variety of ways as to be statistically immeasurable, therefore it seemed best to discuss the replies in general terms. Four librarians interviewed on this topic reported on service to prisons and three of these included a few large print books in the provision. One mentioned that their 25 books were used mainly by psychiatrics being rehabilitated, but in the other prisons as well as in those visited the main use was by elderly prisoners newly-arrived without either teeth or spectacles; apparently they were loaned 'prison teeth and prison specs' until their own National Health dentures and spectacles were ready and during this period they read large print books. One prison officer mentioned two or three new readers who had initially taken large print books after a series of literacy classes, but this was apparently rare. What was more common here was for Asian prisoners learning English to borrow the romances — almost the only males encountered during the course of the study to do so.

The prison populations in the prisons visited were extremely young populations, however, with the average age in one of them being only 23 years; this should have been balanced as far as large print use was concerned by the fact that 10-25% of the prison population in general had a reading age of eleven, however, (Pearson, 1972) and one wondered what would have been the effect of more discreet borrowing arrangements among a group sometimes known to take books to 'keep up appearances' and even to discuss books which had remained unread. Mr Thorpe discussed an informal experiment staged in one such establishment and reported upon (1972). Twelve large print books and their counterparts in small print were placed side by side in the prison library and all the large print books were borrowed first. 'Borrowers appeared to be of two classes — those who could read small print but found they could get the same enjoyment with less bother by reading large print, and others who, if they did not read large print would read nothing.'

The use of large print in hospitals seemed at least to be well-established, whereas in prisons provision and therefore use was extremely patchy judging by the tremendous variation within even *this* very limited experience. The situation was likely to be improved in the near future, one suspected, with the increasing part played by professional local authority librarians as they gradually gained the confidence of the prison officers with whom they liaised, though it was likely to be some time before the prisoners dependent on large print for one reason or another had more than a shelf or two to choose from in some cases, or anything approaching the ten books per head recommended by the Home Office study for use by their counterparts who were able to read normal print.

The staffing of special library services

Seniors in local authority libraries in the West Midlands named 12 assistants responsible for services to the housebound and OAP Homes, 12 branch librarians and 11 counter assistants, six mobile librarians and five volunteers as the members of staff having most contact with large print and elderly readers. (It seemed probable that between 12 and 18 of these 46 people were professionally trained and/or qualified.) Readers' advisers, bibliographic services librarians, mobile library drivers, special services librarians and hospital librarians were each named twice and one Chief not only passed the large print questionnaire and correspondence to one of the latter, but also selected that person to be available for the authority's sole interview.

In 19 of 30 Midland libraries there was no member of staff either appointed as (or thought of as) a welfare librarian or a person having a special interest in disadvantaged groups. However one of their Chiefs wanted to have eight community services librarians when possible and two of the others had not been allowed to replace their qualified specialists when these had left. In the 11 authorities who did have such a member of staff, the person named in three cases was an unqualified assistant in charge of services to housebound and OAP Homes, whereas in the other authorities where people were doing this as part of their allotted duties they were not named here as being 'especially interested members of staff'! This tallied with experience when interviewing some of them — mainly the people moved around internally during the 'freezing' of appointments and doing work for which they would not have applied and in which they admittedly had little or no interest. One Chief Librarian named a particular branch librarian who dealt with literacy groups, OAPs and service to the housebound personally and one Chief named an administrative officer who assisted at a centre for the disabled.

A significant factor was that only in six (of 30) were there professionally qualified librarians specially appointed as librarians for special services or for the disadvantaged. In one authority these members of staff were known as Disadvantaged Teams, in two other authorities the member of staff was known as a Special Services Librarian and in the remaining three the appointments were as Principal Area Librarian; one of these three also had an Area Librarian in the field. The duties of these professional librarians included some or all of the services to hospitals, ethnic minorities, prisons, the disadvantaged, OAP Homes, the housebound and literacy groups; no specific mention was made of the physically handicapped or of the visually handicapped, but presumably these were covered by the term 'disadvantaged'.

LARGE PRINT READERS AND BROWSERS

Ages

The librarians' estimates of the percentage of *all* their readers who were of retiring age and over averaged about 30% and anyone contemplating any special experimental approach or handouts to the existing large print readers in their libraries would be well advised to plan the operation for mornings rather than later in the day and certainly within 'bus pass hours — on pension days in branches near to post offices and on market days in central libraries. With the exception of the community centre library which drew a few of its large print readers in prior to evening classes, these were the most popular borrowing times with the readers in all the areas, though obviously such local events as church coffee mornings and jumble sales had some effect.

One of the main reasons for undertaking a survey of large print readers and browsers was to discover in terms of age, sex, education and visual ability exactly who read, showed an interest in and was aware of the existence of the large print books available at the time. Most West Midlands librarians clearly considered them as books used by elderly readers rather than as books for the partially sighted and though it is known that most of the visually handicapped *are* elderly, the assumption seemed to be that large print was being read more often from preference than from necessity.

The overwhelming impression when working with large print was certainly that a very large proportion of retired people were drawn to the section and Table 7 shows that librarians were absolutely correct in their first conclusion, as expected; in fact the table of borrowers and browsers actually underestimates this bias because of the inclusion of several teenagers and young people whose apparently idle curiosity led them to browse and display a passing interest almost invariably without borrowing for themselves or for anyone else. It seemed right to include them in such a record because they did browse for a while and were at least aware of the existence of the material, but the average age of those who *borrowed* large print for someone was higher and the average age of the actual *readers* was higher still. (Incidentally it ought to be mentioned here that for observation purposes ages — by decade — could only be guessed and therefore were unlikely to be 100% accurate; they were at least the educated guesses of an experienced interviewer, however, tested from time to time when interviewing and proving to be remarkably accurate, with very occasionally a tendency to underestimate age in the well-preserved.)

TABLE 7

ESTIMATED AGES OF 602 LARGE PRINT BORROWERS AND BROWSERS OBSERVED AT THE SHELVES AND OF 200 ACTUAL READERS INTERVIEWED

10s		20s		30s		40s		50s		60s		70s		80s		90s		Library
M	F	M	F	M	F	M	F	M	F	M	F	M	F	M	F	M	F	
2	4	–	2	1	5	3	3	2	30	22	49	12	18	–	1	–	–	A
2	4	–	–	–	–	–	–	–	–	4	4	1	2	–	–	–	–	B
1	4	–	–	1	2	1	–	10	9	7	26	7	3	–	–	–	–	C
–	–	–	1	–	6	1	6	4	19	7	16	2	7	–	1	–	–	D
–	1	–	2	1	–	–	1	3	12	8	18	3	4	–	1	–	–	E
1	2	3	2	1	6	1	16	9	31	28	58	15	21	1	1	–	–	F
–	–	–	–	–	–	–	–	–	–	7	15	3	13	–	2	–	–	G
6	15	3	7	4	19	6	26	28	101	83	186	43	68	1	6	–	–	
21		10		23		32		129		269		111		7		–		602 borrowers and browsers observed
1		1		2		6		21		74		55		36		4		200 readers
22		11		25		38		150		343		166		43		4		802 in all

It will be seen that whereas Table 7 shows a total of 86 people in or under their 40s seen at the shelves (a percentage of 14½% of the 602) there were only ten people in or under their 40s among the actual readers interviewed (5% of the 200). This was not in any way because younger borrowers were less frequently approached for interviews, but because the majority of the younger borrowers interviewed were choosing for older readers and in those cases the actual *readers* then became the subjects of the interviews. If we take this point one stage further to include those in their 50s then Table 7 (which includes the browsers and those borrowing for other people) shows that there were 215 people in their 50s or under seen at the shelves (over 35½% of the 602) whereas the total of actual readers was only brought up from ten to 31 (15½% of the 200 interviewed). People of 60 and over formed just over 64% of the people seen at the shelves and 84½% of the actual readers.

It can thus be seen that not only the very young people were likely to be choosing books for older readers, but that a good proportion of those in their 50s who might have appeared to be choosing for themselves were in fact choosing for the elderly at home or elsewhere. 21½% of .the total seen at the shelves were in their 50s but on 10½% of the readers were in that age group. Even in the 60s, when it might reasonably be supposed that sight was failing to some extent in many cases and that the previous generation was less often alive and reading, the percentage seen at the shelves (44½%) exceeded the percentage of readers (37%) — though this degree of difference would be due partly to the number of young non-readers seen at the shelves. It was not until we reached the 70s that the balance swung in the opposite direction and there was a higher percentage of large print readers (27½%) than people seen at the shelves (18½%), and as one might expect, the percentage of people in their 90s choosing their own books was significantly lower, with 18% of the readers but only 1% of those seen at the shelves being in their 80s.

Educational and reading levels

In order to make the best provision for readers of all kinds it is obviously necessary to have some idea of their educational and reading levels, though several Chiefs referred the researcher to service points in order to assess these. Eighty-seven of the librarians in the West Midlands were able to offer an assessment in the case of their existing large print readers — three librarians classed most of them as 'illiterate', 34 considered that their large print readers (like their younger readers) had tastes and levels ranging right across the scale from illiterate to well-educated, 31 said that their reading tastes could best be described as 'light', eight answered 'average to well-educated' and 11 considered most of their large print readers to be well-educated.

The picture which emerged of large print readers as seen through their librarians' eyes was a united one of 100% elderly readers,

almost 100% indigenous, of both sexes but with almost 100% report-
ing a heavy bias towards the female; at that point the profession was
almost equally divided in opinion as to whether the readers were
mostly 'light' readers with a smattering of the illiterate, or readers
with levels ranging right across the board (not forgetting the group of
'old, educated females' referred to in the suburbs and some housebound services, occasionally with the epithets 'middle-class' or 'well-
heeled') and since the areas varied so significantly probably both
views were equally accurate.

During the course of the 200 interviews many readers were asked
about their school-leaving age when a rapport had been established
and a great many more volunteered the information in conversation
about reading tastes. It was possible to guess fairly safely at 'under
15' or '19 or over' by chance remarks or by the nature of employment in a few other cases, bearing in mind the norms of earlier years,
but in 15 of the 200 cases it was not possible to discover or estimate
this fact at all — either because the messenger did not know, the
nature of the employment was unknown or it was not diplomatic to
ask in view of the extreme proximity of other people. One hundred
and twenty-five of the 200 were known to have left school at 15
years of age or less, which was hardly surprising when one
remembered that in those days much earlier school-leaving was
common. Eight of the 125 specified ages between 11 (in three cases)
and 14 (in one case) and it was highly likely that others of the 125
left school at those ages but chose merely to answer 'under 15'. It
was also possible that more than the representative proportion of the
15 'unknowns' either left school at 15 or at one of these very early
ages. (This is of course one characteristic of large print readers which
is bound to change during coming decades.) Forty-two people were
known or were presumed to have left school at 16 years, two at 17
years, eight at 18 years and 8 at 19 years or over. Most of the 60
readers who had stayed on at school over the age of 15 years were
found in the two suburban libraries, A and D, and in the sheltered
housing G.

The interviewees were asked how they thought of themselves as
readers, within the scale ranging from 'intellectual' to 'mostly magazines and/or news' and it is interesting to note that a new point had
to be inserted into the scale for 'light *now*' because the number
spontaneously answering that way justified it — in other words a
significant number felt it worth mentioning that they were reading

lighter material at their present age than they had done when they were younger:

Intellectual — (1 female — varied from light to intellectual)	— 1
Serious — (1 male and 12 females)	— 13
Average/serious — (1 male and 3 females)	— 4
Average — (21 males and 49 females)	— 70
Light/average — (all 5 females)	— 5
Light *now* — (4 males and 15 females)	— 19
Light — (32 males and 50 females)	— 82
Mostly magazines/news — (1 male and 5 females)	— 6

Upon studying the list of reading matter of the respondents in the middle-to-lower brackets, it was difficult to detect any significant differences between the books being read by those who thought of themselves as 'average' in most cases and those who thought of themselves as 'light readers' — there was the same preponderance of mysteries, romances and general fiction, though here and there the very occasional biographies, travel and historical novels were included by *some* of the readers who thought of themselves as 'average' readers — and there was, of course, the drastic limitation of the material available. (It seemed to be rather like asking people in similar employment whether they thought of themselves as middle-class or working-class.)

Seventy-one of the readers were reading one or two large print books weekly and 63 of them were reading two to four books weekly. Twenty-three people read four or more each week, with the record-holder (like a high proportion of this group of avid readers) being female. Eighteen people estimated that they read one book each 10-14 days, eight read only one or two per month and the remaining 12 read less than one per month; the ratio of women to men in these lower groups was less than one to two and several of the women were limited by the frequency of housebound services and similar exchange frequencies. Not only did women readers outnumber the men by 70% to 30% but on the whole they also tended to read more books. Many of the readers of both sexes (but especially female) said that they would read more 'if they were available', for example, or 'if the stock was changed more frequently'.

The books borrowed by 113 of the 200 readers were also being read by other readers frequently and in some cases always. The additional readers were usually the husband or wife, or other residents in the same Home, but often they were sisters, daughters, other relatives, neighbours and friends. The majority of the large print readers were of course retired people on fixed incomes and since they were no longer working the topic of their past employment was less often introduced naturally into the conversation than it would have been had they still been employed. In spite of this and the fact that so many people were represented by messengers, it was still possible to discover the past employment of two-thirds of the respondents without giving offence and the 134 occupations could be divided into three 'higher' professional, 24 other professional, 37 clerical and minor administrative, 12 skilled and semi-skilled, 53 unskilled and five never employed.

Life styles

Of the 200 readers interviewed either personally or via their representatives, at least 53 were living alone (49 of them women) – and it must be remembered that as 35 of the 200 interviews were deliberately sought in residential establishments of one kind or another and not at random in the libraries, this really means 53 of 165, or that over 32% of the *random* sample were living alone; furthermore (on grounds that it might intimidate) the question was not always asked and the information was very often volunteered instead. It is therefore possible that a small proportion preferred to keep the fact to themselves and that the number might even have been a little higher than that shown below:

Age group	Male	Female
10s	—	—
20s	—	—
30s	—	—
40s	—	—
50s	—	1
60s	2	19
70s	1	14
80s	1	13
90s	—	2

Of the 162 interviewed in the six main libraries used 113 people were choosing their own books and 49 were having them chosen for them by other people; with the exception of the rural area (library E) where the percentage was much higher (45%), this overall 30% was shared fairly equally among all the libraries regardless of their location and the reasons were connected much more with the age, health attitudes and mobility of the old people concerned than with the degree of convenience of the library. Of the total sample of 200 interviewed 113 people (only 56½%) were actually travelling to a library and choosing their own books there (76 females and 37 males). Forty-nine people (24½%) were having them chosen in libraries by other people, three used a mobile library which stopped outside their home and 35 had books delivered either to their Home or home. (Incidentally the 37 men seen in libraries made up over 32½% of the total seen in libraries, whereas the total number of men in the sample *reading* large print was 30% and the number of men receiving them via services to Homes and housebound was only 17%).

All borrowers not served by the various delivery services were asked if and how they usually travelled to the library for their large print books and it emerged that by far the largest group lived within walking distance of the library used — 58 of them walked there; in all but nine of these cases the distance was considered to be of 'average' or greater convenience and in the other nine the walk seemed to be undertaken for reasons of exercise and/or economy. Twenty-four had their own transport (the largest proportion of these being members of the suburban community centre library), 23 used public transport (the largest proportion being members of the Black Country central library), eight got lifts in other people's cars and the remainder usually had a messenger.

With such a very high proportion of the respondents living on fixed incomes it was no surprise to discover that only three of the 200 had ever bought a large print book or had received one as a birthday present; one was a book called '*God calling*' and two were Agatha Christie novels. Even if the books were made available in the bookshops 185 of the 200 would not buy them. The most usual reason offered was 'I'm an old aged pensioner' or 'retired' (30) ' a widow' (4) — 'disabled' or 'on sick pay' (2) or simply 'I can't afford books *and* electricity!' Seven people stated that the books were 'no good when you've read them' or 'when you know who dunnit' and two said there was 'no point'. Another group would not buy them because they 'already had a houseful of books' (10) — 'had no space' or 'a small home' (15) or they were 'in a Home' (4). Nine people said that they 'didn't buy books of any kind' and ten said that there would be 'no point as they could read normal print'. Four people 'didn't get out to buy *any*thing' because they were housebound, two people commented on their failing sight and three people gave their great age as a reason, one of them saying that she was 96 and another that she was now giving away all her books to the people who were to have them after her. It was unfortunate that 126 of the 185 people who would be unlikely to buy large print books felt the need to give a reason, for the interviewer would not have embarrassed them unnecessarily by asking for one. The 15 (7½%) who said that they might buy the books if they were available in bookshops would be most likely to buy biographies (4) or religious books to re-read (3). Others nominated once each were thrillers, romances, 'Cooksons', good fiction, Westerns, non-fiction, gardening books, historical novels, cookery, dictionaries and encyclopaedias, Wisden, paperbacks, medical, French novels and books for technical 'A' levels.

Very few of the *older* people seen at the large print shelves were considered to be browsing; most were searching for something to take home and considering the ages of the majority of them the speed with which they tended to make their selection was astonishing. In Library A the average time spent at the shelves was 4.2 minutes; 16 people spent only 30 seconds there and ten of these had borrowed; at the other extreme an elderly lady spent 11 minutes making her choice and 15 people spent ten minutes. In Library B the average time was only 3.8 minutes, with three people taking ten minutes and two taking only 30 seconds. In Library C the average time (though not the mode) was considerably longer — 7.8 minutes, partly because a couple in their 60s stayed for an hour and three others stayed at the shelves for half-an-hour, 25 minutes and 20 minutes respectively. Only ten people stayed for around 30 seconds and half of these borrowed. In Library D the average time spent was 4.6 minutes, with no less than 20 members staying at the shelves for around 30 seconds only — 12 of them borrowed in this time, including two ladies in their 70s who each managed to find two books! The longest times spent were 45 minutes by one lady in her 50s and a quarter of an hour by two others. In Library E the average time was 5.7 minutes. Of eight women spending only 30 seconds at the shelves only three borrowed and the longest sojourns were 20 minutes (two people) and a quarter of an hour (four people). In Library F the average time spent at the shelves was only 3.5 minutes, with 31 people spending only around 30 seconds there. Out of these, only nine borrowed, because most of the remaining 22 were making rapid checks to see if anything new had come in. They were beaten to the desk by one woman who borrowed two romances in around

ten seconds and another who 'dallied' for 15 seconds over the
selection of one book. (So much for the leisurely rural way of life!)
Here three borrowers spent a quarter of an hour and 20 people spent
ten minutes or more choosing their books, the non-fiction readers
taking a conspicuously longer time than the others. Overall the
average time spent at the large print shelves was only *4.9 minutes* and
the mode (five minutes) was remarkably similar.

Reading tastes

Readers were asked how they chose their books and the following
methods (more than one per reader) were named:- browsing (97) —
using jacket colours as a guide (80 — though 104 said that they
found them helpful at different stages of the interviews) — authors
(61) — other readers' recommendations (25) — synopsis or blurb (19)
— staff guidance (16) — catalogue (10) — from booklists (9 — though
those in Homes and hospitals were not asked this question and they
would undoubtedly have increased the number had they been
consulted) — by messenger (6) — the library's own marking (4) —
titles (3) — returning to old favourites (2) — jackets (1) and tutor's
guidance (1).

We come now to the reading tastes of these existing borrowers and
in order to be able to give some positive, documented evidence to
librarians and publishers all 166 Chief Librarians in Britain were
asked in their questionnaires which large print books were the most
and least popular in their libraries; the 116 West Midlands library
workers at all levels were asked a similar question during their interviews; the 200 readers who were interviewed in six of the libraries
and various other establishments were asked what sort of book they
usually looked for, and the respondents in Survey C (both the elderly
and the visually handicapped groups) were also questioned about
their reading interests. Many respondents in all groups made joint
nominations and therefore there were many more replies than
respondents — See Tables 8, 9 and 10 overleaf.

Obviously no-one is going to be surprised at the tremendous popularity of the romances and there is no doubt that in spite of a bias
towards these books both in publication and purchase their readers
experienced extreme difficulty in finding something to read after one
or two years, depending on the number read weekly. The frequency
of ability to find a book as expressed by the 76 readers who were
looking firstly for romances averaged 2.5 — exactly halfway between

'average frequency' and 'rately', in spite of the fact that few of them had been reading large print for very long; romance readers also appeared to be the predominant group among those observed who made repeated visits to the shelves and went away empty-handed. Undoubtedly many more romances were needed and will continue to be needed.

TABLE 8

THE <u>MOST</u> POPULAR LARGE PRINT AMONG EXISTING USERS

216 questionnaire forms from 149 of 166 British libraries			Replies from 116 workers in 63 West Midlands libraries	200 replies from West Midlands large print readers in six varied and various other establishments	
First named and jointly first named	Second named	Third named	First named and jointly first named only	Looking for first choice	Acceptable alternative
Romances 180	Mysteries 75	Westerns 29	Romances 90	Romances 76	General fiction (incl. older) 50
General fiction 20	Westerns 23	Mysteries 25	General fiction 26	Mysteries 73	None/same again/or normal print 41
'Light Ulverscroft' 13	General fiction 18	General fiction 17	Mysteries 24	General fiction 43	Historical 32
Mysteries 10	Romances 14	Biographies 15	Westerns 12	Westerns 26	Biographies 31
Biographies 2	Biographies 7	Historical 14	Biographies 6	Biographies 16	Mysteries 31
Westerns 1	Family stories 6	Travel 4	Historical 5	Adventure 10	Romances 17
Historical 1	Historical 5	Romances 3	Adventure 5	Historical 9	Westerns 13
	Travel 2	Adventure 3	Family stories 1	N F 7	Travel 12
	Light N F 2	Light N F 2	Country/animal stories 1	Travel 5	Adventure 12
	'New Portway' 2	Family stories 2	'Ulverscroft' 1	Family stories 3	N F 11
	Adventure 1	Country life 1		Sport 1	War/sea/spy stories 8
	Country life 1	Older fiction 1		Classics 1	Country/animal stories 7
	'G K Hall/Prior' 1	Welsh books 1			Classics 2
	'Lythway' 1	'Lythway' 1			Religious 1
					Children's 1

TABLE 9

THE LEAST POPULAR LARGE PRINT AMONG EXISTING USERS

216 questionnaire forms from
149 British libraries

200 replies from West Midlands large
print readers in six varied libraries and
various other establishments to the
question 'are there some kinds you
would never take?

N F (except biography)	137	Westerns	87
Westerns	70	'Sloppy'/'slushy' romances	67
Classics	33	'Cruel'/'violent' mysteries	56
Quarto size, any type	30	Science fiction	32
Historical	17	N F (except biography)	30
Modern or heavy general fiction	12	Historical	16
'Magna Print'	5	'Modern'/'permissive'/'sexual'	11
Travel	4	American	4
Religious	4	Religious	3
American	4	Classics	3
'Watts'	4	'First person'/'old English style'	3
'G K Hall'	4	War/sea stories	3
Adventure	3	Fiction	2
Mysteries	2	'Heavy'	1
War/spy stories	2	Short stories	1
1920s reprints	1	None at all	1
Biographies	1		
Science fiction	1		
Children's	1		
'John Curley'	1		
'Lythway'	1		

TABLE 10

SHOWING THE REVEALING READING INTERESTS OF THE ENTIRE SAMPLE FOR
SURVEY C – THE ELDERLY AND VISUALLY HANDICAPPED COMMUNITIES NOT
CONTACTED IN LIBRARIES.
(NB Although this survey was mainly in respect of non-use of large
print some users did respond, particularly by questionnaire.) This
Table serves as a contrast and a complement to Tables 8 and 9.

Reading interests	Elderly in community (Incl. VH)	Elderly in OAP Homes (Incl. VH)	V H interviewed	V H question- naires	Totals
N F/general knowledge/ hobbies	9	4	20	82	115*
Mysteries	19	11	6	69	105
Romances	21	16	5	52	94
Biographies	9	4	4	44	61
Travel/ exploration ·	8	4	5	26	43
History/ historical	5	4	2	32	43
Adventure	4	5	5	15	29
Sagas/family	6	4	6	12	28
Religion	4	9	6	6	25
Animals/fish birds	1	1	3	12	17
War/spy	2	4	–	10	16
Science fiction	–	–	2	13	15
Sport/s	1	1	1	12	15
Classics	1	–	5	8	14
Westerns	5	2	–	7	14
Gardening	1	–	–	12	13
Poetry	2	3	3	5	13
Other languages/ novels	1	–	1	3	5
Other crafts	1	1	–	3	5
Cookery	–	–	–	4	4
Humour/ comedy	1	–	1	2	4
DIY	–	–	–	3	3
Sea stories	3	–	–	–	3
Fantasy	–	–	–	2	2

*Some of the NF subjects included in this category more than once each were politics,
medicine, yoga, sociology, science, music, economics, antiques, chemistry, child development, archaeology, technology, etymology, photography, philosophy, radio, natural history
and the supernatural – a far cry from budgies and window-boxes!

Note also that the mystery/thriller/detective category has actually outnumbered the
romances and that biographies, travel, history, adventure, family sagas, religion, animals,
war and spy stories, sport and even science fiction (usually so disliked by the elderly) were
all more popular than the ubiquitous Westerns.

It is necessary, nevertheless, to draw attention to the anomaly between the degree of popularity accorded to this category of books by librarians and the degree expressed by the 200 readers interviewed (Table 8). Almost as many readers were looking for mysteries, referred to as 'mysteries', 'detectives', 'thrillers' or 'crime' and even more were willing to take them as an alternative; many readers of both sexes commented on the bias of the existing books towards women writers or 'women's books'. As mysteries were the most popular category of books among the men and the second most popular among the women, much greater provision of these would have satisfied both sexes and seemed to be very necessary. The frequency of ability to find such a book as expressed by these 73 mystery readers averaged 2.6 — only fractionally higher than that of the previous group and still well below 'average frequency'.

General fiction — especially *light* general fiction — and biographies seemed to be more popular with the readers than the librarians recognized and this also applied to a lesser extent to travel, adventure and non-fiction books; several of the West Midlands librarians did make the point that non-fiction *would* be more popular if more were available. The readers of some of these latter groups naturally fared even worse in their quest for reading matter — their recorded frequencies of success in finding a book of the required kind averaged 1.6 in the case of travel (between 'rarely' and 'almost never'), 2.7 in the case of fiction and non-fiction adventure and as low as 1.4 in the case of general non-fiction. Except for classics — which, with only one recorded first-choice reader, ought in this particular case to be disregarded — no category of books achieved as high a rating as 'average frequency' for its readers' ability to find one, a fact which was all the more damning when one remembered the sense of gratitude felt by the age group as a whole and their generally uncomplaining habit. Table 10 gives a preliminary indication as to why some of the non-users *were* non-users!

From these Tables it can be seen that the readers seemed not to be as opposed to the *idea* of non-fiction reading as the librarians considered them to be; the latter were of course judging by their experience of the readers' use — or non-use — of the craft books and the very few other non-fiction books that were in existence. The readers were answering about their natural tastes and knew of no such limitations; on the other hand their lack of knowledge about the existence of most of the non-fiction books would in some cases be the reason why the category was not named here. Most of the 200 readers questioned about the large print they had seen (other than fiction) had either seen only biographies (69) or none at all (68) while a further 36 stated that either they were not interested in non-fiction or had not looked. Only 27 of the 200 knew of the existence of any travel books, 17 had seen religious books, nine had seen a book or books on gardening, nine had seen books on other crafts and very little else had been seen at all. Some of the libraries did have some of the few other non-fiction books available, however, regardless of the fact that their readers had not seen them; on their own admission many of the readers had a tendency to notice only what they were looking for.

The situation regarding Westerns was a difficult one. Obviously, as one librarian remarked 'Western reading in general is on the wane'(!) and there were large groups of people who would never read one even if it were the only alternative available; yet among the elderly male large print readers there still remained a nucleus of avid Western readers, at least at that time, and these well-established ratepayers found it difficult in most libraries to borrow a book they had not read. The average frequency of finding one was 2.5, exactly half-way between 'average frequency' and 'rarely'. (For detailed statistics about readers' ability to find suitable reading material in large print see Table 11.)

Considering that so little was available in large print science fiction was named surprisingly often by the readers; clearly there was a positive antipathy to this type of book among the elderly in general, whereas the antipathy demonstrated by the romance and mystery readers towards each others' type of books merely reminds us that 'one man's meat is another man's poison'. Some of the romance readers were of a nervous disposition or avoided the topic of death because of bereavement and almost the only men found anywhere who would ever read romances were a tiny minority in hospital and a few Asian males learning English.

Although the names of authors most popular or likely to be most popular with large print readers if available were not at any stage requested during the interviews with either librarians or readers it was inevitable that they would to some extent be volunteered. The list below is given in order of the number of mentions in each case and serves as a sort of light-hearted Pop Chart:

Named by librarians interviewed	Named by readers interviewed
1 *J Herriot*	1 *A Christie*

TABLE 11

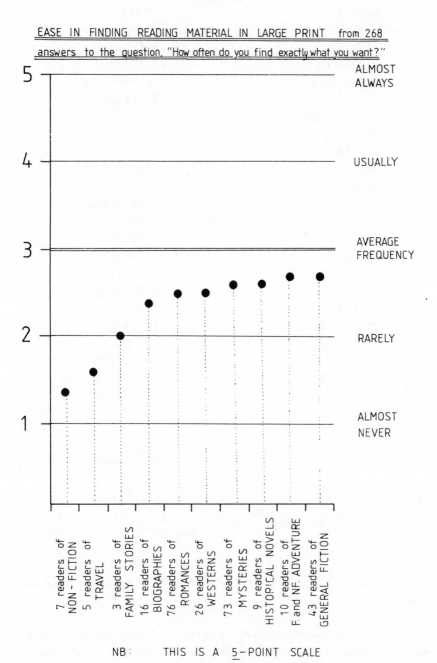

EASE IN FINDING READING MATERIAL IN LARGE PRINT from 268 answers to the question, "How often do you find exactly what you want?"

NB: THIS IS A 5-POINT SCALE

2   *C Cookson*
3   P Strong (verse)
4   E M Dell
5 = V Holt
     H Innes
     A S Swan
8 = B Cartland
     W H Davies
     M De la Roche
     M Powell
     D E Stevenson
     Mrs H Wood
14 = R M Ayres
     D Bagley
     M Dickens
     D Eden
     J Farnol
     N Lofts
     D Niven
     J Plaidy
     Miss Read
     M Stewart

and several authors
mentioned once each

2   *C Cookson*
3   *J Herriot*
4   *Miss Read*
5   *E Wallace*
6   B Cartland
7 = A Bridge
     J Galsworthy
9 = E M Dell
     V Holt
     N Lofts
     A Maclean
     D E Stevenson
     M Stewart
15 = M De la Roche
     N Shute
     P Wentworth
18 = F Barclay
     L L'Amour
     L Beckwith
20 = M Dickens
     D Du Maurier
     Mrs H Wood
24 = L Andrews
     F Archer (local)
     R M Ayres
     D Francis
     Z Grey
     H Innes
     F P Keyes
     J Plaidy
     R Sabatini

and several authors mentioned
four times or less

(Those italicized were named *very* many more times than their
closest 'rivals')

Considering the number of writers in the world the librarians were to
be congratulated, for the two lists bore a marked resemblance to
each other — and had the readers' list been continued further to

include the authors mentioned less frequently then even more of the names on the librarians' list would have appeared. The striking omission on the librarians' list was the name of Agatha Christie, whose outstanding popularity among existing large print readers — like that of Edgar Wallace — seemed to have been totally unnoticed or ignored; not only did she head the readers' list of favourites, but her named was mentioned almost twice as often as those of even Catherine Cookson and James Herriot and it might be worthwhile reminding readers at this stage that two of the only three large print books which had been purchased had been books by that same author. These lists possibly underlined a tendency shown earlier for librarians in general to recognize the great demand for romances but to underestimate the almost equal demand for mysteries and to a much lesser extent that for general fiction.

Table 12 shows the categories of books actually borrowed by the 602 readers and browsers observed, but it does *not* include those borrowed by the 200 readers interviewed. (The librarians concerned kindly agreed to keep records during the week following the research visit and these were later compared for consistency; allowing for additional issues to the 200 extra readers the sample was considered a reliable one, as five of the six libraries issued a sufficiently increased number of books the following week to allow for the 200 interviewed readers among them and one library issued a number only slightly higher. Some of the librarians expressed surprise that their large print issues were so high.)

In spite of the fact that the numbers in the categories borrowed did follow what has by this stage become accepted as the usual trend, it must be remembered that this table is only of superficial value as it merely shows what was *actually* borrowed and not what would have been borrowed had it been there. For example, it was most unusual to find more than a handful of books with blue jackets on the library shelves anywhere at any one time and some libraries often had none at all. Not only would romances have been borrowed even more often had they existed for selection, but it is probable that some *were* immediately borrowed from unobserved 'returned books trolleys' near library desks. Brown jackets were non-existent, while red and orange jackets, on the other hand, usually proliferated on the shelves. Some libraries had good non-fiction collections (bearing in mind the limited number published) and in other libraries non-fiction was almost non-existent on the shelves; in Library C an entire trolley filled with books in green and blue jackets was situated immediately

TABLE 12

BOOKS ACTUALLY BORROWED BY THE 602 READERS AND BROWSERS OBSERVED, BUT NOT INCLUDING THE 200 INTERVIEWED
(COLOURS REFER TO ULVERSCROFT CODED JACKETS)

Library	Red (general fiction)	Blue (romance)	Black (mystery)	Orange (Western)	Green (non-fiction)	Purple (historical)	Illustrated jackets (other publishers)	Totals
A	34	53	31	11	11	8	31	179
B	4	—	7	7	—	—	2	20
C	20	34*	9	6	4*	1	22	96
D	10	46	6	1	5	3	40	111
E	21	33	8	6	10	3	27	108
F	49	68	29	14	23	1	19	203
(Delivered) G	21	29	13	4	10	2	20	99
Totals	159	263	103	49	63	18	161	816

*In Library C an entire trolley filled with books in green and blue jackets was situated immediately behind the large print bookstack and some potential borrowers failed to notice them; it was also possible that some borrowings from this trolley were unseen and unrecorded.

behind the large print bookstack and not only did some potential borrowers fail to notice these but some actual borrowers were possibly unseen and unrecorded by the researcher. It is also necessary, when attempting to estimate the popularity of the 'other' publishers' books with illustrated jackets, to bear in mind that in some libraries it would have been greater had there been more, though to a certain extent this popularity was due to their recent appearance on the scene and the certainty that the books were newer and had not already been read. The table can therefore only be of real use when it is used in conjunction with the readers' detailed replies given during interviews with the other 200 borrowers.

Since comparatively little research work of this nature has been undertaken in residential Homes for the elderly, it might be worthwhile including brief details about the reading interests of the 67 OAP Home residents interviewed during Survey C before leaving the subject. Respondents were asked how they thought of themselves as readers — what their reading mostly consisted of — and certain categories were suggested to them as possible replies. Twenty people were not reading anything at all, though some mentioned reading done in the past and the remaining 47 people gave the following replies (more than one category per person in some cases):

29 — Magazines and news
25 — Light books
 9 — Average books
 4 — Serious books
 — — Professional books
 — — Intellectual books

Several people referred to the more serious nature of the reading done when they were younger, compared with the reading being done at that time. Where exact types were described spontaneously in more detail than the above categories the nominations were as follows:

16 — Romances
11 — Mysteries
 9 — Religion
 5 — Adventure
 4 — Biographies
 4 — Historical

4 — Family sagas
3 — Travel
3 — Poetry
2 — Westerns
2 — War stories
2 — Spy stories

and Crafts, Exploration, Politics, Hauntings, Medical books, Sport and Animals were named once each — a selection fairly similar to that of the large print readers interviewed at an earlier stage in the study.

Opinions, preferences and degrees of satisfaction

As mentioned previously, readers were asked how often they managed to find the type of book they were seeking (Table 11) and partly but not entirely as a cross-check much later in the interview they were asked to express their degree of satisfaction with the range available. Librarians were also asked to estimate their present readers' degree of satisfaction with the range and the replies to these questions are given in Table 13.

It can be seen that again the librarians presented a fairly realistic picture of their readers' opinions, the only difference being that a higher percentage of them gave 'average' as an answer, having slightly underestimated the degree of dissatisfaction expressed by the replies in category '1' and the degree of satisfaction expressed by those in categories '4' and '5'.

Most of the *librarians'* replies in the 'satisfied' category (9%) related to housebound services where they 'usually found them *some*thing' and to short-stay patients in hospitals; most of the *readers'* replies in the 'highly satisfied' and 'satisfied' categories were borrowers in the two libraries with the best collections and in the OAP Homes. One hundred and forty-five of the 200 readers had been reading large print for four years or less but 29 had been reading it for more than ten years — almost all of them female — and naturally this group was finding it very difficult to find anything new to read. Eight women and one man had been reading large print since it first became available in 1964.

These questions to this notoriously uncomplaining group of readers opened wide the floodgates and their unsolicited additional complaints about the range were far too numerous and monotonous to list effectively. In addition to many of the 'need more of this or

TABLE 13

DEGREE OF SATISFACTION WITH THE RANGE OF LARGE PRINT
MATERIAL AVAILABLE SHOWING 200 READERS' OPINIONS AND
100 LIBRARIANS' ESTIMATES OF THEIR READERS' OPINIONS.

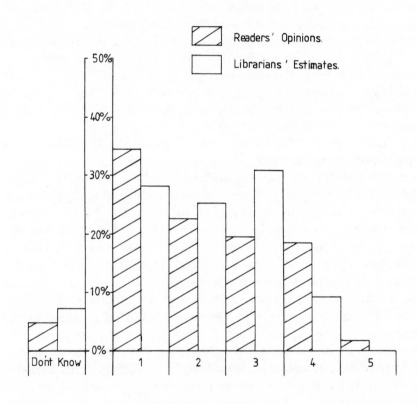

Readers' Opinions.

Librarians' Estimates.

1 = Highly dissatisfied
2 = Dissatisfied
3 = Average
4 = Satisfied
5 = Highly satisfied

that' types of complaint there were the readers who blamed themselves, like 'I'm reading too quickly, I expect — it's my fault'; the
readers who had already read so many of them in normal print in the
past; the readers who blamed recent local authority amalgamation
for what they saw as a poor deal; the many who 'mustn't complain,
but we do have difficulty finding anything'; the ones who 'often go
home without one', 'often read the same ones again twice', or consider 'it's a waste of time coming'; the readers who spoke for a group,
such as 'everyone's complaining bitterly'; the ones who considered
them 'a good *hors d'oeuvre*' or 'a good basic start, though they've
been here for years'; the addicts who bemoaned the fact that 'there
are always the same ones in', and those using more than one library.
Even the 'satisfied' readers gave cause for concern, with remarks such
as 'they'll see *me out,* probably' from a lady in her late 80s — 'it's
good, but I'm glad I'm not restricted to the range!' — 'it's a nice
collection — I don't often have to go without' — 'they're not bad
really as long as you can read normal print' and 'there are quite a
few yet — I suppose there will come a time . . . .'

A much smaller group complained about the triviality of the
range, with comments like 'The range is *rubbish,* when there are so
many wonderful biographies available' — 'It's very light reading,
unless they're all out?' — 'Some of them are insulting to one's intel-
ligence' — 'Most of my friends refuse them because they're so trivial'
and 'The range needs to be very much wider and more serious, the
same as on the other shelves'. Surprising as it might seem, this is only
a synopsis of the remarks made by these ageing Oliver Twists and it is
obvious that in most libraries the readers would read many more if
the publishers would produce them and the librarians would buy
them. For many years the problems of the partially sighted or the
otherwise visually handicapped did not receive the attention they
deserved because those of the blind seemed more urgent, and still
they were at a disadvantage regarding the reading material available
to them. What was required in theory was the same element of
choice available to other readers, yet in view of majority reading
trends it probably seemed extravagant to provide it.

Librarians *were* aware of this need for more titles and a wider
range and on the whole they were not complacent about the provision. However, it is true to say that if each central library and large
branch had stocked all or most of the titles published — even of
those published by Ulverscroft — then their present shelf collections
would have been considerably larger even than those seen and read

about which were considered to be good and to be reasonably satisfying their readers; but most librarians seemed not to take kindly to
pre-selection, being accustomed to selecting from an extensive range
the books which *they* believed to be best for their readers. Most were
already buying an extremely high proportion of everything produced
by Ulverscroft in spite of having unwanted reserves of large format
books on their hands, especially when compared with the proportion selected of other 'normal' print publishers' output. Many librarians felt that more titles ought to be available for them to choose
from without appreciating that the viability of each title depended
entirely upon *them* as almost the sole outlet — which of course,
explains the Foundation's limitation of the range to proven sellers.
However, many librarians at all levels expressed a wish for standards
of provision and guidance of this kind could well alleviate the
situation.

Though far from satisfied with the range, most of the readers were
extremely pleased with the books themselves, according to the librarians (See Table 14).

The readers' own degrees of satisfaction with different aspects of
the books were shown in Table 4(b). (See p.102). It can be seen from
Table 4(b) that a remarkably large number of readers were satisfied
and highly satisfied with the books — even 'delighted' would not be
too strong a word to use in many cases — and particularly with the
size of the print. Survey A showed that librarians considered the size
of print to be only fourth in importance of the factors which made
something easy to read but it was clearly the most important factor
in the present elderly readers' opinions — this was another of the
anomalies between the views of the two. This is probably explained
by the specialist bibliographical training of the professional group
who have been made aware of and critical about factors of book
production which are usually noticed much less by the readers, many
of whom had never before considered such things as clarity, layout
and paper and seemed very surprised to be questioned about them;
even when their attention was drawn to these factors some were
unable to give an assessment of them. (See the 'don't know' column
in Table 4b).

Answers to the question 'in your opinion what makes something
easy to read?' served as a cross-check and again a tremendous majority of the readers named the *print* (166 of 182 respondents) though
100 of them qualified the reply by adding 'the size' and 35 qualified it by adding 'the blackness' or 'darkness'. Thirty of the libra-

TABLE 14

READERS' SATISFACTION WITH
THE RANGE OF MATERIAL
COMPARED WITH THE BOOKS
THEMSELVES. - 100 Librarians' Estimates.

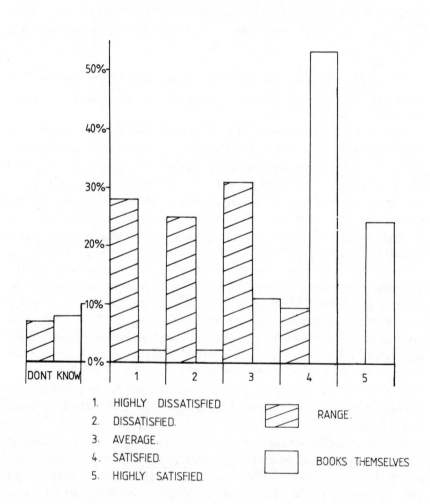

1. HIGHLY DISSATISFIED
2. DISSATISFIED.
3. AVERAGE.
4. SATISFIED.
5. HIGHLY SATISFIED.

RANGE.

BOOKS THEMSELVES

rians would have given answers about the degree of satisfaction in an even higher category than they did if it had not been for the weight of the books, which was still the most common cause for complaint by frail, elderly, arthritic or bed-ridden patients and another seven said that their readers would prefer illustrated jackets. Other librarians volunteered the information that most of the complimentary letters they received came from the elderly large print readers.

The readers themselves mentioned the weight of the books in many cases, though a good proportion of them appreciated some of the difficulties involved in further size reduction and many were satisfied with Ulverscroft's present format. Most were so pleased to have the books at all that they didn't like to complain about any aspects of them, but the size and weight factors (which caused so many borrowers to carry less books home than they would have liked to read and made the books so tiring to hold) were 'scored' less enthusiastically than the size of the print. Some of the most interesting readers' comments about size were 'they reduce my loan from three to one' — 'Watts' is much too large and I can't read G K Hall's in bed' and 'couldn't they have thinner bindings or paperbacks?' (According to one leading publisher these would need a run of 20,000 copies. If a softback were applied to existing paper —carefully researched and improved upon before use — a saving of only two ounces would result, which would not justify the consequent reduction in durability.)

The reader who seemed least impressed by the print had been a printer's assistant before retirement. Two readers praised G K Hall's print for being larger and darker, another would have liked print in general to be darker, one said that the print could be as large and dark as the publishers could afford to make it and one man whose eyes were worsening said that he would have to leave them, as he couldn't see them at all until his new spectacles arrived. These were the exceptions, however, and as can be seen by the figures in Table 4b the great majority of the readers were extremely pleased with the print, which was in their view the factor which made the books easy to read. Apart from two contradictory remarks — one about waste space leading to extra pages and another about more spaces being needed — the clarity and layout questions were answered without comment and the only remarks made about paper here were five regarding transparency — one relating to Portway specifically and one exonerating Ulverscroft.

The readers were asked which size of book they preferred, whether they preferred any other publishers' books to Ulverscroft's and whether they found distinctive covers helpful, immaterial or embarrassing. One hundred and fourteen of the 200 people questioned were unable to state a preference either for quarto or octavo size books, in most cases because they had never seen the large older format books but in a few cases because the unfortunate borrowers (using a large library's collection) had never seen the smaller new ones! Of the 86 who had seen or used both sizes 85 very definitely preferred the present octavo format for its convenience and the 'odd man out' was an elderly male resident in a Home who 'liked a nice big book'. The readers were delighted when the new format was introduced and it was referred to as 'the biggest step forward to date'. The 95 reasons given for preferring the smaller books were: 'could carry more home (with the shopping)' (31) — 'easier to handle' (26) — 'lighter to hold', 'very frail' or 'in wheelchair' (23) — 'easier to hold in bed' (10) — 'took up less space' or 'fit into shelves' (3) — 'could only use one hand' (1) and 'more like other books' (1).

Because 112 of the 200 readers had never seen any large print books published by any other firm than Ulverscroft only 88 were in a position to express any preferences. Sixty-eight of them (over 77%) preferred the Ulverscroft books (49 women and all 19 men) and 20 (nearly 23% — all women) preferred the other publishers' books.

Some of the 68 Ulverscroft fans (one of whom wouldn't accept that the others *were* 'proper large print books') enlarged upon their replies, giving such reasons as 'they're a reliable/wholesome/clean/ sound/safe/not too permissive series' (13) — 'better titles' (2) — 'you can't recognize the others' (2) — 'the others have very heavy, black print' (1) and 'I like the uniformity of lettering on the spines (1). Regarding the 13 comments about the 'respectability' of the Ulverscroft range it was also interesting to note that of the 49 readers who did not always read to the end of the books borrowed well over a third gave a similar reason — the accidental borrowing of 'violent', 'permissive', 'sexual' books or 'coarse language'. The other reasons were inability to get interested or to finish by the time due for exchange; failing concentration; books which turned out to be not type expected; difficulty in the case of new readers; eyes tiring and illness.

Comments from the 20 women who seemed to have transferred their allegiance to the newer publishers included 'I like the illustrated covers' (15) — 'they're newer!' (3) — 'they're more like other books'

(2) — 'I dislike the charitable blurb and the feeling of being treated as almost blind' (1) — 'G K Hall's are clearer print' (1) and 'there are misprints in the large Ulverscroft' (1).

According to at least one leading ophthalmologist (Brier, 1973) 80% to 90% of all partially sighted patients are either totally colour blind or have a strong deficiency in colour perception, and if this is true of most of the visually handicapped it calls into question *any* system of colour-coding book jackets; the small symbols carefully added to the spines of illustrated jackets by a few conscientious librarians had certainly passed unnoticed by all the readers interviewed. Some borrowers and readers had even failed to notice that Ulverscroft covers *were* particularly distinctive — they didn't know that there was any system of colour-coding in existence and many were in any case having books chosen for them by others. Nevertheless 182 borrowers who *were* aware of the distinctive covers were prepared to give an opinion on their usefulness and 104 of the 182 (over 57%) found the distinctive covers helpful (73 women and 31 men); 76 people (over 41½% — 52 women and 24 men) considered them immaterial and two elderly women considered them embarrassing. Incidentally, most of the 20 women who stated that they preferred the illustrated covers also said that they found the colour-coded Ulverscroft covers helpful, so one could only assume that perhaps a combination of the different jacket styles would be most popular of all (i.e. an illustrated jacket incorporating a coloured spine and/or a very wide, conspicuous band, or a colour-coded Ulverscroft-style jacket incorporating a large photograph or picture.) Small pictures, although providing a guide to the contents, would not make the books resemble others and small symbols would pass unnoticed — as had those used by some of the libraries.

On this point of embarrassment felt by large print readers, when 97 West Midlands librarians were asked if they had ever noticed it among their elderly or visually handicapped readers and browsers 80 of them (82½%) said that they had never been aware of its existence and some added remarks such as 'it is all in the minds of librarians' — 'librarians are more touchy than the public' — 'partial sight isn't a stigma like illiteracy' — 'they're accepted now they've been around for a few years and they're smaller' — 'they're all in the same age group' and 'the method of approach overcomes any initial tendency'. Seventeen of them replied in the affirmative (17½%) but almost all of this group qualified their answers by adding 'only very occasionally', 'only at first' or 'but not so much as when they were larger and more conspicuous'. When librarians were asked who these people were it emerged that most of them were the literacy students and new readers with a confidence problem, who were 'furtive and acutely embarrassed to use anything at all different and are even difficult to get into a library'. However, there was an additional but even smaller group mentioned and that consisted of a tiny minority of 'educated elderly ladies who were proud of their abilities and wouldn't give in', 'old men with magnifying glasses' and — extremely rarely — 'younger visually handicapped people'.

The 97 were also asked if they could think of any borrowers who could benefit who were prejudiced against large print and a great racking of brains followed before 43 decided that they had never known of anyone, two librarians were unable to answer and 52 could recall at least one borrower or occasion. The categories referred to by these librarians most often were 'normal' print readers refusing reservations in large print and new readers — who preferred illustrated jackets. The others were late middle-aged and recently pensioned females who enjoyed boasting a little about their faculties or who liked to dress and appear younger than they were; readers who feared abridgement; readers who considered the available titles too trivial; teenagers who either wouldn't admit to partial sight or considered them to be children's books; people who only read paperbacks; readers afraid to become addicted to a limited range and people who found the quarto books too heavy to carry.

Excepting, of course, such groups as the housebound and prisoners, who were not asked, few people really wanted to complain about convenience of access to their library or to the large print shelves when questioned; almost half of the 20 who rated it 'below average' were readers in the library which had a severe space problem and where the books were at floor level; the remainder found entrance steps a little difficult to climb (especially in winter) and main roads difficult to negotiate. In addition to this being a fairly stoical group, the readers in most of the libraries selected for readers' interviews were fortunate in the location of the large print collections, with nothing too high, the shelves too low in only one library and the books even spread for maximum convenience across the eye level shelves of a large non-fiction stack in the busy Cathedral city library. All the collections were situated on ground floors, some locations having been chosen for their prominence and others for their quietness; chairs were available nearby in all of them, with low tables also provided in some. Lighting was classified as between 'average' and 'very good' in all six libraries after working in each for a week, including the evening sessions; lettering on signs varied from excellent to non-existent but only two of the six libraries displayed notices referring to large print books. The shelf stocks of the books themselves ranged from about 150 volumes in a small library to about 530 in one of the large ones.

Perhaps surprisingly, none of these latter factors appeared to have much effect upon the degree of use or non-use of the respective libraries, though clearly the readers of large and/or revised collections were more satisfied than the readers of small and/or outdated ones, regardless of housekeeping methods. If this were considered to be worthy of further research then the various factors involved would need to be carefully isolated — a refinement that was impossible in such a widespread investigation as this one.

Success and failure at the shelves

In addition to the evidence of many interviews, the observation at the shelves provided further evidence that although books were chosen quickly, some borrowers were finding it extremely difficult and sometimes impossible to find a book of the required type which had not already been read. For each library the forms of the people considered to be seriously searching for a large print book to take home were identified and separated from those which referred to browsers passing time or displaying idle curiosity only and as shown in Table 15 quite a number of the searchers were obliged eventually to borrow normal-size print, to return later to the shelves, or to go home without a book.

Tables 12 and 15 demonstrate — among other things! — that readers having their books delivered or borrowing from the libraries where car parks and more cars were available tended to take more books per borrower than the people who had to carry them home; that the very good large print stock in the little-used library (B) was satisfying the few readers it had; that the numbers of large print loans in all the other libraries would be higher if bookstocks were adequate and in some cases considerably higher, and that a number of the libraries' younger normal-print readers (some of whom might come into contact with people in need of large print material) were becoming aware of its existence.

Of the 129 readers who were searching but who failed to borrow a large print book after one or more visits to the shelves, over half of

TABLE 15

SUCCESS AND FAILURE AT THE SHELVES

Library	Total observed at L P shelves (or in delivery service)	Total seriously search- ing	Total borrowed some L P at first attempt	Total who failed to borrow L P at all but then borrowed N P	Total who failed but returned for sec- ond and third attempt	Total who failed to borrow any book	Total no of L P books borrowed
A	154	137	97	28	2	10	179
B	17	12	12	–	–	–	20
C	71	58	46	8	1	3	96
D	70	59	51	6	–	2	111
*E	54	49	43	6	–	–	108*
F	196	179	97	55	18	9	203
G (Deliv- ered)	(40)	40	38	2	–	–	99
Totals	602	534	384†	105	21†	24	816 ◊

NB   ◊   This figure does not include books borrowed during these weeks by the 200 readers interviewed

     *   Library E opens for only 4 days weekly

     †   Many people who did borrow 1 or 2 books only were clearly searching for more and not *all* those who returned were successful

them were men – a significantly larger proportion than of the group as a whole and a further possible pointer to earlier suggestions that a) the shortage of 'mens' books' might possibly be as great as the shortage of romances or b) that there could have been a slightly higher proportion of the male than of the female readers able to read normal-size print and 'poaching'.

It should also be pointed out that a total of 12 of the readers overall who had been assessed as not seeming to be searching seriously with borrowing in mind did in fact borrow a book; presumably the intentions of some were wrongly interpreted but their forms were not altered because it was obvious that others without a real intention of borrowing became attracted by what they saw. This brings the actual total of large print borrowers from among those observed to 417 — the 384 who succeeded in borrowing large print at the first attempt, most of the 21 who returned and succeeded in borrowing something at the second or third attempt and the 12 who borrowed but had not been thought to be searching. NB The books borrowed by the 200 readers who were interviewed are not included in Tables 12 or 15 (which show the categories of books borrowed only by those *observed*).

An adequate stock seemed to be the most important contribution the librarian could make for this group of existing readers and even this was ineffective if either the need or the knowledge of its existence was lacking. Regarding the need, this was proved satisfactorily by the almost non-existent use made of a very good collection in Library B — a collection backed up by excellent signing, genuine staff concern, pleasant facilities for the elderly, an outreach programme and even well-displayed booklists. Further investigation revealed that decaying terraced housing in which many elderly indigenous people had recently lived had been razed or vacated and many had been re-housed in OAP Homes and housing some distance away; the younger Asian population had spread, taking over most of the few remaining shops and the local post office had closed. The library was in any case situated on a difficult main road and it also emerged that additional provision was being made in the new OAP Homes and in nearby centres, so that the elderly residents no longer needed to return to the distant library and carry their books so far.

Although Survey C was primarily undertaken to investigate *non-use* among the community, those who *were* regular readers and those who read large print 'sometimes' (144 readers) were also asked how many books they read per month and their degree of satisfaction with the range and with the books themselves, as a double-check.

The average number read per month was two for the elderly readers in the community, where the answer was usually only one or two, and four was the highest number. The average number worked out at 3½ for both the elderly readers in Homes and the visually handicapped readers of all ages interviewed; the highest numbers were six and eight respectively. The average number of books read per month among the postal correspondents was 6½; one (a man in his eighties) read up to 48 per month and the mode was four — the number read by 21 people. (Incidentially, 96 people who completed this section were averaging well over 600 books per month among them, with 18 people averaging double figures and six averaging in the twenties.) Sixty-three retired readers and 18 of the younger ones constituted the group that could be considered the more avid readers and this confirmed the findings of Survey B. The extremely large numbers were almost all read by solitary people on the housebound round, as mentioned previously.

For consistency, replies about satisfaction with the range and with the books themselves were categorised on the 1–5 scale used in the earlier surveys. This was a simple operation in the case of the interviews, but the appropriate place on the scale was sometimes difficult to estimate in the case of the postal respondents who could not be questioned further. For this reason the findings have been summarized informally and in each case they mirror very closely the findings of Reader Survey B:-

The average degree of satisfaction with the range worked out at 'under three' in OAP Homes, 'over three' among the elderly readers in the community, 'under two' among the visually handicapped interviewed and 'about two and a half' in the largest group, the postal questionnaires. Again this meant that overall the degree of satisfaction with the range was well below average (three) in spite of the old ladies who were 'just delighted with everything that's done for them these days'. The average degree of satisfaction with the books themselves worked out at about four — 'about four and a half' in OAP Homes, 'over three and a half' among the elderly readers in the community, 'over four' among the visually handicapped interviewed and 'over three and a half' in the postal questionnaires. This meant that overall the degree of satisfaction with the books themselves was in the satisfied category (four). It then began to seem obvious that the publishers had done *their* best (as far as it went) and that it now remained for the librarians to improve their stocks and at the same time increase the publishers' sales to a level which would encourage experimentation with the range.

Suggestions for improvement

These were the suggestions for improvement received as a result of an unguided and open-ended invitation — i.e. each reader's major criticism — but it must be remembered that some of the postal respondents probably replied specifically to express these criticisms.

1 More extensive range/variety of subjects	26
2 Need more large print books in library	21
3 Lighter weight/smaller size	16
4 More biographies	11
5=More non-fiction	8
More classics	8
7=Illustrated covers	5
More for young people	5
9=Universal colour-coding	4
More romances	4
Textbooks needed	4
12=More travel books	3
More poetry	3
More history	3
More well-written/semi-serious books	3
Shelved with kind/convenient height	3

Other suggestions were:- illustrated books, larger print, whiter paper, books on antiques (2 each) and more who-dun-its, less cowboys, more Ultratype, more on royalty, more wildlife, more war books, more information, more authors, more supernatural, crosswords, railway, technology and musical record charts (1 each). One reader suggested that book markers should be attached 'so that ignorant people don't turn corners down'; one commented about heavy type on thin paper in recent additions; one remarked that Magna-print looked dirty; one thought that the books should be disinfected after use and another regretted that the 'excellent Ulverscroft and Lythway titles were being swamped by American publications with distasteful subject matter and unintelligible language'. The last word was left with the complainant who objected that 'sighted borrowers take the who-dun-its' — and who might sometimes have been mistaken!

Other activity at the large print shelves

Who *were* the people at the large print shelves, apart from those who actually read large print? There was the tiny group of teenagers and other young people displaying what proved to be idle curiosity or interest in everything in the library; in some libraries there was a con-siderable group of would-be borrowers who were unable to find any-thing new, as has already been demonstrated (both of which groups left empty-handed) and there was the larger group of people of all ages who were taking books for elderly or housebound readers, many of them living alone.

The 30% of the borrowers taking books for other people underlined the old saying that 'blood is thicker than water' for 34 of the 49 were relatives, often husbands or wives — in fact every one of the 14 in the industrial area's central library (library C) was a relative. The remaining 15 'messengers' overall comprised six fellow-residents in OAP Homes, four friends, three literacy teachers and two neighbours. The good deeds ranged from daily visits in one case to only occasional visits in eight cases, with the majority borrowing weekly. Although the great majority of the readers who didn't choose their own books from the library were either elderly, handicapped, ill or housebound, six of those not in residential accommodation were stated to be 'busy' and five (including the three literacy students) refused to venture into a library.

When the 116 West Midlands librarians were asked about their large print readers and in particular about any *other* readers who had been observed in addition to the elderly and visually handicapped, the replies on the following list were given:

General public, general browsers, readers seeking/reserving specific titles and authors, people who liked to read in bed, Cookson-and-romance-seekers, the middle-aged for ease, messengers for old people and borrowers who rejected tiny print;

Literacy students, literacy teachers, dyslectics, new readers and teenage boys with low reading ages;

Librarians, library staff, volunteers and social workers; Immigrants learning English, male Sikhs, Asian ladies and Bengali ladies;

Mentally handicapped adults, and physically and mentally handicapped children;

Students, technical students requiring classics and children (some reading mysteries);

Hospital patients on drugs, post-operative patients, people without or awaiting spectacles, night nurses, depressed patients,

and Tramps (who apparently liked to make it very obvious that they really were reading and therefore entitled to be in the building.)

THE VISUAL
ABILITY
OF THE USERS

Ability to read normal print

One of the most important questions to be answered by the study was the degree of visual ability of the existing large print users. Were they mainly just elderly people borrowing the books out of preference, together with a few younger 'poachers', or did the group include a significant number of people with varying degrees of visual handicap?

After interviewing librarians and reading unsolicited comments on questionnaires, the conclusion was reached that most librarians considered the books to have become a series of leisure reading for elderly readers who found them 'easy on the eyes'; after interviewing a random sample of 200 readers in various borrowing situations it was apparent that *more than one in three of the readers were unable to read normal print.* This was by far the most important difference between the librarians' opinions of their readers and the replies given by the readers themselves and, in fact, one of the most significant findings of the study, one which alone justified the time and money spent in terms of its potential for attitude—changing in the profession.

After searching questions about the books and a few enquiries about the convenience of the libraries, all the 200 readers were asked the vital question 'can you read books in normal-size print?' Those who replied in the affirmative were asked a few further questions about their preferences and their reasons for reading large print and their interviews were then ended; those who replied in the negative were asked a series of graded questions relating to increasing degrees of visual handicap and these were discontinued as soon as it was apparent that they had become irrelevant.

Even among this generally uncomplaining age-group, it became apparent that one had to allow for the difference between those who tended to think of their glasses as 'half full' and those who thought of them as 'half empty'. Although it was probably that the 65 who said that they were unable to read books in normal-size print included a very small number of people with no specific eye complaint who could most likely manage to do so if it were important or essential, it was absolutely *certain* that the group of 135 who said that they were able to read books in normal-size print included a significant number with quite serious eye problems who did so with considerable difficulty, for example the man who was 'almost blind' and who wore two pairs of glasses in order to read occasional Westerns by his favourite author, J T Edson. It was, therefore, much more likely that the number quoted (65 of 200) unable to read normal-size print was an extremely conservative estimate rather than an exaggerated one — and had the wording of the question been extended to include the words 'without undue difficulty' then that number would have been extended from 65 to something between 95 and 109!

Librarians were not in any way to blame for underestimating the degrees of visual handicap experienced by their readers. Spectacles are very good these days and even the researcher with a special interest and time to concentrate on the group was unable to estimate from appearances, in most cases, what the answer to the question 'can you read normal print' would be. After observation at the shelves and prior to the experience of a few surprising interviews, their librarians' assessment had seemed fairly acceptable. Not only were many of the visual defects unnoticeable, but personal contact between staff and the group tended in any case to be minimal owing to their extreme independence and their desire never 'to be any trouble' by asking for things. Furthermore, there were the younger people at the shelves who often *appeared* to be borrowing for their own use and not actually needing large print, but were in fact borrowing for someone else — usually for an elderly, housebound person who would probably never be seen at the shelves borrowing and needing large print.

The eye conditions of the 200 readers interviewed

These 200 replies are shown below as raw data in lay terminology, just as it emerged in note form from the interview papers, partly owing to classification difficulties but primarily because of its more immediate impact on the layman than unknown specialist terms:

The 135 who said that they *could* read books in normal-size print:

91 unconditional answers

13 said they had great difficulty, very weak eyes or thick glasses

6 could only do so with a magnifier

1 had only one eye

1 blind in one eye after measles

4 had one extremely weak eye

1 had one very bad eye and other tear duct blocked

1 never used one eye – a 'lazy eye'

1 very cross-eyed

1 had been almost blind all life and wore very thick glasses

1 wore two pairs of spectacles, one pair on top of the other

1 said eyes had been affected by stroke

1 had sight affected by mastectomy and double thyroid operation

1 had glaucoma and had had iridectomy

1 had glaucoma – and had operation on one eye and other 'going' – bad sight for 25 yrs. Read by day only, with magnifier

1 had very painful eyes since an ear and nose operation

1 said that beginnings and ends of lines 'always rise and fall and go out of line'

1 broke hip and was left with clot behind one eye and sight affected by shock. Did not wear glasses, but could then only read larger-than-average 'normal' print with magnifier (93 years)

1 had very sore and inflamed eyes and wore dark glasses always – had measles as child – conjunctivitis often, plus thyroid condition. Used magnifier

3 had double cataracts developing – all used magnifiers and had difficulty

1 post cataract operation (double) and poor sight since young

1 had one cataract 'done' and one waiting – 'skipped' a lot when reading

1 had cataract on one eye – was blind for six months at 11 following sunstroke, then ulcers on eyes. Needed magnifier

The 65 who said that they could *not* read books in normal-size print:

14 unelaborated answers

1 had no eye condition (dyslectic)

2 had always been long (far) sighted

3 had always been severely myopic no particular condition – in 1 case extremely thick lenses and in 1 case heredity (everyone in family similar)

3   had only one eye, in 2 cases result of car accident

1   had only one eye — had cataract removed from that recently and had blood clot behind — was blind for several months

1   'might need an operation' — no particular complaint — just could not see very well

1   blind in one eye and cataract in other — also very cross-eyed

1   had no sight in one eye, very little in other and no peripheral vision — had to take drug to save residual vision and this made her ill — all very sudden

1   cornea 'gone' on one eye and too late for graft

1   lost sight in one eye two years after conjunctivitis led to other germs

1   ex-stroke patient, one side damaged

1   had glaucoma — also stroke which affected eyes five years ago

3   had sugar diabetes — 1 said that it had led to problems of the retina

1   got German measles after aged 60 years and eyes affected — had no tear ducts — had acupuncture of eyes

2   had multiple sclerosis which affected vision — 1 lost sight of one eye

2   had angina — one 'couldn't look in daylight' and one had also had cataract operation on one eye

1   eyes were affected by shock — car accident and wheel-chair bound

1   weak eyes since five years old — also wore collar and had arthritis

1   two corneal grafts — emergency operation took £660 life savings + £400 raised by children and grandchildren

2   wore extremely thick glasses

1   had double vision since 1921 — had cataracts developing

8   had cataracts on one eye — awaiting operation — one had been 'running badly' for several years

1   had cataract operation on one eye and was awaiting operation on other eye

1   had cataract operation on one eye — wore very thick spectacles — also had Parkinson's disease

1   had cataract operation on one eye and second operation pending, but back of eye diseased

1   had cataract operation on one eye and wore intraocular lens and very thick spectacle lenses

1   had cataract operation on one eye and had 'something' behind it — could hardly use that eye — 'laser beams useless'

4   had had double cataract operations and all wore very thick lenses

3   had cataracts on both eyes and were awaiting double operation — one told 'too old'

NB The list of *non*-visual complaints and handicaps listed was by no means comprehensive. The readers were not asked for these and did not always mention them; the researcher only included them here when it seemed that there was a possibility that the complaint or handicap might have some bearing on the visual handicap. (Visual handicap was often linked to or accompanied by other illnesses, complaints and diseases, but owing to time restrictions multi-handicap could not be specifically investigated in this study.)

The difficulty experienced in reliably identifying visual handicap by observation

To list the numbers of visually handicapped or 'hard-of-seeing' users estimated by the librarians would serve little purpose, for in spite of a consistent definition in each case it was clear that interpretations varied and the replies were in any case mere speculation. Most librarians gave replies in the '1-10', 'only a handful', 'less than 1%' or 'very few' category regarding the users in the libraries themselves and 25–40% regarding the users in Homes and housebound services ('but these have 7 to 14 books each' in some cases). Typical first reactions to the question were 'many with failing sight but only five to six with real visual difficulties', 'only about six with gadgets or very restricted vision' and 'lots wear spectacles but none worse!' The only conclusion which it is safe to draw from the librarians' replies to this question is that there *was* a definite tendency to underestimate the degrees of visual handicap encountered in the libraries and it was interesting to note that the librarian making what seemed to be the best provision was one of the few seeming *not* to underestimate the need, replying 'there are many with magnifying glasses'.

Table 16 shows that of the 602 people observed at the shelves — many of whom did not borrow at all, were borrowing for some other reason (were new readers etc.) or would be borrowing for someone older who was unable to travel to the library — only five were *visibly* visually handicapped, ·389 wore spectacles and 208 did not. The stereotype of a groping figure in dark glasses does a disservice to the visually handicapped and was *never* encountered at this stage of the study. These statistics of people seen at the shelves no doubt explain why so many librarians tended to underestimate the proportions of their actual large print readers with visual handicaps, and of course the group 'merely' wearing spectacles included many of these — the 389 or nearly 65% — compared with only five who were conspicuously visually handicapped and an unknown number for whom spectacles did not solve the problem.

TABLE 16

VISIBLE SIGNS OF VISUAL HANDICAP AMONG 602 BORROWERS AND BROWSERS OBSERVED AT THE LARGE PRINT SHELVES BUT NOT INTERVIEWED

Age / Sex	Visibly visually handicapped																Wearing spectacles																Not wearing spectacles															
	10s M	10s F	20s M	20s F	30s M	30s F	40s M	40s F	50s M	50s F	60s M	60s F	70s M	70s F	80s M	80s F	10s M	10s F	20s M	20s F	30s M	30s F	40s M	40s F	50s M	50s F	60s M	60s F	70s M	70s F	80s M	80s F	10s M	10s F	20s M	20s F	30s M	30s F	40s M	40s F	50s M	50s F	60s M	60s F	70s M	70s F	80s M	80s F
Library																																																
A	–	–	–	–	–	–	–	–	–	–	–	–	–	–	–	–	1	1	–	–	–	–	1	–	1	1	22	18	41	12	12	–	1	4	–	2	1	4	3	2	1	8	4	8	–	6	–	–
B	–	–	–	–	–	–	–	–	–	–	–	–	–	–	–	–	–	–	–	–	–	–	–	–	–	–	2	3	–	1	–	–	2	4	–	–	–	–	1	–	2	1	1	1	1	1	–	–
C	–	–	–	–	–	–	–	–	–	–	–	–	1	–	–	–	–	–	–	–	1	1	1	1	6	7	4	19	5	3	–	–	1	4	–	–	1	1	4	2	3	7	1	–	–	–	–	–
D	–	–	–	–	–	–	–	–	–	–	–	–	–	–	–	–	–	–	–	–	–	–	2	–	3	2	16	2	13	6	–	1	–	–	–	–	1	3	4	1	3	6	2	2	–	–	–
E	–	–	–	–	–	–	–	–	–	–	–	–	–	–	–	–	–	–	–	–	–	–	–	–	–	–	10	5	15	3	4	–	1	1	–	2	1	–	1	3	2	3	3	3	–	–	–
F	–	–	–	–	–	–	–	–	–	–	1	1	–	–	–	–	–	–	–	–	1	2	–	3	5	18	19	38	12	18	1	–	1	2	3	2	4	1	13	4	13	8	19	3	3	–	1
Delivered																																																
G	–	–	–	–	–	–	–	–	–	–	–	–	–	–	–	1	–	–	–	–	–	–	–	–	–	–	1	1	1	3	1	1	–	–	–	–	–	–	–	–	–	–	5	4	1	1	–	1
Totals	–	–	–	–	–	–	–	–	–	–	1	1	1	1	–	1	1	–	–	–	2	6	–	7	14	73	51	14	35	55	1	4	5	15	3	7	2	13	6	19	14	28	31	44	8	12	–	1

NB According to Going (1973) only 6% of the elderly have sight sufficiently good for them to read without spectacles and 13% of the spectacles worn are unsatisfactory

The method adopted to estimate whether the people *observed* were or were not likely to be able to read books in normal-size print was simply to note whether or not they demonstrated any interest whatsoever in these during the observed visit to the library. Again referring to the 602 people seen at the large print shelves (who were not always borrowing either for themselves or for anyone else and who would therefore include many more people showing such an interest than would a group exclusively composed of large print *readers*) the results are shown in Table 17.

TABLE 17

FROM WHICH IT WAS ASSUMED THAT ALMOST HALF OF THE LARGE PRINT BORROWERS AND BROWSERS OBSERVED (EVEN INCLUDING THE NON-READERS) WERE UNABLE TO READ NORMAL PRINT COMFORTABLY

602 people seen at the large print shelves

Library	*Yes* — shown interest in other material			*No* — no interest shown in normal-size print		
	M	F	Total	M	F	Total
A	23	42	65	19	70	89*
B	6	9	15	1	1	2†
C	17	25	42	10	19	29
D	9	27	36	6	28	34
E	5	24	29	10	15	25
F	35	73	108	24	64	88
Delivered G	2	10	12	8	20	28*
Totals	97 °	210 °	307	77 °	217 °	295

It is interesting to notice † how few of even the very small number of browsers in Library B (the library where the need was lacking) were interested exclusively in the large print material, * how many were interested *only* in large print in Suburban Library A, and how much greater the proportion of these there was in the delivery services to the exclusively over-60s in group G. ° Draws attention to the slightly higher proportion of men than of women who might possibly have been 'poaching'.

The group displaying an interest in material other than large print not surprisingly included most of the under-50s and six of the very young people included in that group were additionally interested in literacy material *only*. (It is also worthy of mention that three people who were noticed borrowing books in *normal*-size print were wearing very thick spectacle lenses and using magnifying glasses. Two of the three were in the library with the poorest large print stock.)

Preference for large print.

The overall proportion of people showing no interest whatsoever in normal-size print during their observed library visit was even higher than the one in three suggested as likely by the responses from interviewees; even allowing for the possibility that a few people briefly displayed such an interest in some corner unobserved by the researcher, the proportion would still be much higher than one in three in spite of the fact that this higher proportion included the non-borrowers and borrowers for others. In the researcher's opinion the group which made up the difference in proportion between the percentage of those interviewed who were *unable* to read books in normal-size print and the percentage of those observed who had no wish whatsoever to do so should be catered for *in addition* to the former group, since there is no crime in elderly ratepayers preferring to avoid discomfort and to read something which is usually described as 'easy on the eyes'. Reference to the list earlier in this chapter reminds us that a number of the 135 people who were able to read books in normal-size print suffered from a variety of eye complaints, discomfort and difficulty (quite apart from others who made no mention of these factors but mostly read large print 'because it was easier') and this was presumably the category of reader which swelled the 'not-interested-in-normal-print group' from a third to almost a half.

The 135 interviewed readers who were able to read books in normal-size print were asked which books had been borrowed more often and which were preferred. Forty-three of them borrowed less large print, eight estimated that they borrowed an equal amount of each and 84 borrowed more large print — seven of these adding that lately they had not borrowed the others at all. When it came to preference, the situation was even more loaded in favour of large print (which was to be expected since they were contacted at the large print shelves) with only seven saying that they preferred reading normal-size print, three liking them equally and 125 saying that they preferred reading large print. As some worded it, they 'had to be desperate to read normal print' and the main reason why most of them ever did so was 'in order to get enough to read'. Several indicated that they would not read the others at all if there were more large print books, though some added that they did not like carrying them home.

The main reasons for reading large print volunteered spontaneously here in the readers' own words were: 'easier or restful to read or on the eyes' (58) — 'less eye strain' (25) — 'read in bed' (13) — 'eyes ageing' (9) — 'attractive titles or reliable standard' (9) — 'don't need to wear spectacles' (7) — 'sight deteriorating or operation pending' (7) — 'quicker to get through' (6) — 'eyes tired at night or after work or after knitting' (5) — 'better in bad or electric or night light' (5) — 'don't need such a bright light on in bed' (4) — 'can't always read the normal print or eyes fade' (4) — 'don't like or need a magnifier' (4) — 'can read for longer' (3) and 'eyes do not get so heavy or hot' (3). Other spontaneous reasons volunteered were that new readers felt encouraged by progress, readers liked to knit and read together, eyes were very sore or painful, small print blurred or gave the readers headaches, large print was blacker, spouses liked to share the same books and one reader mentioned blindness in one eye.

It had been intended to ask the 135 readers who were able to read normal-size print for their reasons for reading large print, but as so many of them had already volunteered one reason and the researcher had no wish to appear stupid the typewritten list of suggested reasons was read out later and checked over with them 'to find out *every* reason that applied' in each case; Table 18 shows the interesting and fairly consistent results.

It cannot rightly be assumed from *o* that 52 people were so-called 'poachers' because almost all of them coupled this reply with at least one other — such as 'more restful' — but in view of the prevailing opinion that the majority of those who were 'poachers' were middle-aged women seeking romances, it is interesting to note here (and in the totals marked *o* similarly in Table 17) that a higher proportion of the men might possibly have come into this category. Clearly the main reason for reading large print out of preference was that it was 'easier on the eyes' and this was shown consistently by both methods of responding; it was interesting to note x the sizeable group which read large print in order to avoid wearing spectacles or using a magnifier, ◊ the predominance of females in the groups relating to eye complaints and † the number of women who read in bed, possibly related to the number who lived alone.

TABLE 18

EVERY APPLICABLE REPLY (FROM A LIST OF PREPARED SUGGESTIONS) TO THE QUESTION 'WHY DO YOU READ LARGE PRINT BOOKS?' ASKED OF 135 READERS ABLE TO READ BOOKS IN NORMAL PRINT

		Male	*Female*	*Total*
1	No copy in normal print	20	32	52º
2	New reader	2	3	5
3	Read more quickly	4	11	15
4	More restful	37	76	113*
5	Poor lighting	6	14	20
6	Read in bed	9	48†	57
7	Elderly	15	31	46
8	Eye operation pending	1	6	7◊
9	Post-operative	—	5	5◊
10	Eye complaint	—	1	1◊
11	Others: Don't need spectacles/magnifier	8	11	19x
	Eyes hurt/sore/painful/headaches	1	5	6◊
	One eye/one eye weak etc.	3	2	5
	Awaiting new/first spectacles	3	2	5
	Reliable writers/good titles	—	4	4
	Handy/read by others in family	3	1	4
	Always had poor sight	2	1	3
	Various (similar to spontaneous replies)	2	10	12

º   Most of these apparent 'poachers' coupled this reply with at least one other
*   Clearly the main reason for preferring large print, among those with a choice
◊   Note the predominance of females in these groups relating to eye complaints
x   Note the fairly sizeable group which preferred large print to the use of simple aids.

When asked whether they had ever checked the ordinary shelves for clear or larger-than-average print, surprisingly only 42 of these 135 readers 'able to read normal print' had done so. However, one must remember that this would not always have been possible as many of the 93 who had never done so were either housebound or did not visit the library personally.

The use of spectacles and other aids

One hundred and nineteen of the 135 interviewees who could read normal print wore spectacles when they did so, in some cases other people's spectacles and in one case two pairs together. The 16 who did not wear spectacles included most of the younger new readers, two ladies in their 80s and one of 96 who all considered it 'too late to bother', one reader who had sat on hers and a reader who said that there weren't any spectacles which would help. Table 16 (p.198) shows the number of the 602 people observed who wore spectacles while browsing or selecting large print books in public; spectacle wearing among the 500 members of the general public interviewed is discussed later in this chapter, and among the elderly and visually handicapped respondents it is discussed in the chapter on non-use.

We come now to the subject of the extent of visual handicap experienced by the 65 readers who answered that they were *not* able to read books in normal-size print. These readers were asked a graded series of further questions which were discontinued when it became apparent that they were irrelevant; a few of those who *could* manage to read normal print (with great difficulty) were also included and therefore the number replying to each question varied and will be stated separately. Only 15 of 69 readers worried in case reading harmed their vision and only 22 of them became *less* interested in reading when their vision deteriorated; in fact most said that they had more time to read since retiring and now that they were less busy or unable to sew or knit.

Of 76 readers questioned, 37 wore reading glasses, 18 wore special glasses (mostly cataract spectacles), 15 wore bi-focals, two wore tinted glasses and four wore none at all. These four comprised one dyslectic with no eye problems, one lady in her 50s who 'soon would' and two ladies who considered themselves 'too old to bother'. Forty-one people named additional aids: one a bookstand, one an intraocular lens, and in the remaining 39 cases magnifying glasses. No reader using a binocular, Optacon, microfilm reader or low vision aid other than magnifying glasses was encountered among the 200 readers interviewed. The 39 magnifying glasses consisted of 26 merely defined as 'popular' glasses, seven special aspheric magnifiers, three stand magnifiers, one 'coil', one rolling rod and one supplied free of charge with a directory. Two readers used a stand aspheric magnifier together with a 'popular' hand magnifier and also wore spectacles with thick lenses.

Even if they really wanted or *needed* to read something in normal-size print for its content, only 45 could ever manage to do so and most of these managed with 'extreme difficulty or urgency', 'very close to the eyes', 'in daylight only', 'with magnifiers' and 'in short sentences or spells'. The material mentioned as meriting this effort included football coupons, letters, tax returns, legal matters, forms, addresses, news and travel brochures. The 24 who could never manage to do so comprised ten cataract sufferers, three people with one eye/blind, two diabetics, two angina sufferers, two elderly women who had always had weak eyes, an ex-stroke patient, a victim of multiple sclerosis, a reader with two corneal grafts, one with no tear ducts and one with permanent conjunctivitis.

Eighty-one people were asked whether they always read large print books clearly. Forty-seven replied in the affirmative, some adding 'so far' or 'with aids'; one said 'except fancy print that's too black' and two people remarked that the blurb in Ulverscroft books made them feel guilty about taking them/at all/from the nearly-blind. A further eight people answered a much more doubtful or hesitant 'yes', some of these elaborating by adding 'usually, but not always' and the 26 who replied definitely in the negative were questioned further on this point. Twenty-one of the 26 who did not always read large print clearly were female and only five were male. Four women and one man (five in all) said that it blurred, four women experienced a running together of the print, five people mentioned faintness of print (two men and three women) and three people mentioned dazzle. Other things experienced were lines jumping, double vision, inability to focus, ghosting and fog, eyes being 'pulled', headaches and eyes aching and letters going upside down 'like them Indian letters'. The 26 held the print at a variety of distances from the eyes when reading, ranging from 'very close' and 'about six inches' to 'on a table', with the mode being 'about a foot away' or 'about average'; two people tried all sorts of distances and positions in an endeavour to achieve satisfactory results.

Only the lady wearing dark glasses made an adverse comment about the library lighting, saying not surprisingly that she found it too bright; the remaining 13 who actually used the library building considered the lighting at least adequate. At home 12 of the 26 relied on a ceiling light, ten used a good reading lamp, two read by the window, one used an orange light bulb in a standard lamp and one respondent was unable to answer on the reader's behalf.

Eighteen of the 26 had had their eyes tested and/or their spectacles changed within the previous two years, which seemed at first to compare well with the findings of other surveys, but it must be remembered that these 26 people were not selected at random from the public at large, nor were they merely the elderly or even the large print readers – these were the 26 readers from seven service points who were the most likely group (or among the most likely group) to be receiving specialist eye treatment. One of the most surprising things learned from this study by the researcher was that if a delayed return were made to any or all of these libraries in search of these 26 very visually handicapped readers, 20 of more or them would not be distinguishable to either the library staff or to a researcher who had previously interviewed them, a fact which serves to underline the point made earlier about librarians understandably underestimating the degree of use made of their large print books by readers with visual handicap.

Registration

None of the 69 people asked knew their own visual acuity and only 12 of these 69 people most likely to be registered had ever even heard of the Partially-Sighted Register kept by their local authority; one person for whom it had been considered too late for a corneal graft was actually *on* the register. One wondered how many of the general public – or even of the large print readers – knew of the existence of the register if so many of *this* particular group were unaware of its existence? The 11 people who *were* aware of the existence of the register comprised a doctor's receptionist awaiting a cataract operation, two people severely myopic all their lives, two multiple sclerosis sufferers, two diabetics (one of them a Sister-Tutor), two ex-stroke patients (one of them with glaucoma and registered disabled) and two people blind in one eye and with additional problems.

The 57 who were definitely unaware of the Register or whose representatives felt certain that they too were unaware included many with serious eye complaints, a highly educated ex-private nurse going blind and reading Moon and one woman who had actually been blind for a two year period and had not even been told by anyone that she had been entitled to a blind pension. On the other hand, there were the two possibilities that some of the 57 might have been registered by professional people without their knowledge and that a few of the very old people might have been informed earlier and have since forgotten. Many of these people added the information that they were aware of registration of the blind and a few of them mentioned the Disabled Register. This was clearly an area which — while being outside the scope of this study — needed investigation on a much wider scale than was possible here if the Partially-Sighted Register was to achieve its potential value.

During the course of Survey D, the Link-men Survey, an attempt was made to sound out opinion about the estimated extent of this shortfall in the Partially Sighted Register with interesting results but not with any measurable success. Most of the people in the miscellaneous Group 1 had no idea how many of their partially sighted contacts were registered, though a few could quote *some* specific cases of the definitely registered, the definitely unregistered and the registered blind with sufficient residual vision to read large print. The estimates ranged from 50 — 100%; one replied 'very few, in my opinion, although most will eventually be registered as blind' but most of Group 2 (the social workers and health visitors, etc) did consider that over 80% of *their* specific contacts were registered.

The medical experts in Group 3 were the *least* united of all the groups in their estimates. These ranged from replies like 'none', 'only 2 or 3', 'very few', '½%', 'hardly any', '5%' and '10%' through some '20%', '30%', '48%', '50%' and '60%' replies to '75%', '80%', '90%' and '100%', 'almost all', 'all' (underlined), 'all at the eye clinic', 'all with irremediable defects', and 'all who might benefit by talking books'. Of course, each of the six main groups embraced differing sub-groups, roles and types of contact and in the case of Group 3 it was mostly the ophthalmologists who estimated that the higher proportion of their partially-sighted contacts were registered and mainly the opticians who estimated the lower proportions; the estimates from low vision aid centres averaged 48%. (Incidentally the majority of those who replied to the question and for whom it was relevant said that they did 'discuss registration with patients or encourage them to register', though three discussed but did not encourage it and five replied in the negative; five of 11 ophthalmologists had done unsolicited registration with colleagues in the welfare services or with Medical Officers, five had not done so and one did not understand the question.) The great majority of the social workers and all 20 health visitors did encourage registration, though a few social workers expressed reservations and three did not do so 'because their clients would be financially better off on the Blind Register'.

Because questions about hospital libraries were substituted on the third pages of forms for hospital workers, respondents in Group 4 were not asked additional questions about their partially sighted contacts. The members of Group 5 (workers with the blind and partially sighted in schools, colleges and voluntary agencies) considered that most of *their* partially sighted contacts were registered, though in most cases they were not registered as partially sighted but as blind; the language and literacy workers in Group 6 had very few partially sighted contacts and little knowledge about their registration details.

This was obviously an extremely complicated subject to tackle in so short a time, though the answers did successfully indicate the extent of the confusion which existed about registration and statistics based upon the Register. Failure in identification of the 'registerable' partially sighted and of the 'unregisterable' visually impaired had undoubtedly led to an under-provision of large print books and of library services for the visually handicapped in many areas, particularly by those librarians heavily dependent upon printed statistics. Given a more effective method of identification there would have been a more conspicuous need (and perhaps even pressure) for expansion, though without any obvious benefits at the present time there can be little incentive for the less severely visually handicapped adults to register under the existing system, even if eligible.

Visual ability of 500 interviewed members of the public for comparison

All respondents were shown a sample of (10-12 point) normal print which was changed for an identical specimen as often as it became worn or soiled and they were asked 'can you read this print comfortably, with reading glasses if normally worn?' Their abilities were then classified into five main categories:

1 Easily without glasses (or contact lenses)
2 Easily with glasses (or contact lenses)
3 'Could, but no glasses'
4 With difficulty
5 Not possible

In Table 19 it proved necessary to sub-divide columns 4 and 5 in order to show respondents with visual problems (at a)* separately from those with literacy, language or mental problems (at b). By studying this Table it can be seen that exactly 6% of the people encountered in the street had such *visual* difficulty in reading normal print (with reading glasses if normally worn) that they would be unlikely to do so and that almost 6% found it impossible to do so — in other words 6% of the sample were seen to be 'visually handicapped' by the definition used throughout this study (though it must be remembered if applying the figures more generally that this sample of people 'out and about' in working hours included approximately double the proportion of elderly people actually alive in our society at present) and exactly 6% came into the category of people *also* needing large print provision, making a total of 12% in all — though of course not all of these would be readers.

It was suspected that some of the respondents who said that they 'could but had no reading glasses with them' would also be unable to read normal print for either visual or literacy reasons, however, and where visual problems were suspected the reply was marked with a query and noted. The sex and age groups of the people shown in Table 19 to be unlikely (4a) or unable (5a) to read normal print for visual reasons and the areas in which they were interviewed are shown in Table 20. Looking at the total sample interviewed, classified by age groups, one can see that of those in their 60s 12% found normal print difficult to read and a further 14% found it impossible, and that of those in their 70s 20% found it difficult and a further 23% found it impossible.

In addition to these *definite* responses there were the 72 people who were unable to prove or to disprove their ability because their reading glasses were at home and whose visual ability seemed in some way suspect in 14 cases (11 of them female). These consisted of one female in her 80s, two females and a male in their 70s, three females in their 60s, two females and a male in their 50s, one female in her 40s, a female and a male in their 30s and a female in her 20s. These have *not* been shown in tabulated form or included in the above

TABLE 19

VISUAL ABILITY OF 500 MEMBERS OF THE GENERAL PUBLIC

Area where interviewed	1	2	3	4a*	4b	5a*	5b	Totals
Suburban	21	37	16	2	—	4	—	80
Assorted shopping	38	40	24	9	1	9	1	122
'Academic'	68	42	8	5	1	1	—	125
City inner zone	31	28	16	9	3	10	7	104
Rural	31	19	8	5	—	5	1	69
Total	189	166	72	30	5	29	9	500
Percentages	38%	33%	14%	6%*	1%	6%*	2%	100%

Key

Column 1 — Read normal print easily without glasses (or contact lenses)
      2 — Read normal print easily with glasses (or contact lenses)
      3 — 'Could, but no glasses'
      4 — a) Read normal print with difficulty — visual problems*
           b) Read normal print with difficulty — literacy, language or mental problems
      5 — a) Not possible — visual problems*
           b) Not possible — literacy, language or mental problems

figures because in these cases visual disability could be strongly suspected but could not be proved. It seemed probable that *some* of these 72 people would come into our 'visually handicapped' category or find the normal print specimen difficult to read, however, and if the researcher's estimates of 14 were accurate this would bring the joint total up from 59 (12%) to 73 (15%) of the entire sample of 500.

This means that *between 12% and 15%* of the adults out walking in these areas would be unlikely or unable to read normal print for visual reasons, in addition to the 3% (14) unable or unlikely to do so for reasons of literacy, language or mental problems (4b and 5b in

TABLE 20

SHOWING THE SEX AND AGE GROUPS OF THE 59 MEMBERS OF THE GENERAL PUBLIC
UNLIKELY OR UNABLE TO READ NORMAL PRINT FOR VISUAL REASONS (OF 500 INTERVIEWED)

Area where interviewed	Unlikely – 4a								Unable – 5a								Totals
	10s	20s	30s	40s	50s	60s	70s	80s	10s	20s	30s	40s	50s	60s	70s	80s	
Suburban	–	–	–	–	–	–	F F	–	–	–	–	F	–	F	F F	–	6 Females / — Males
Assorted shopping	·	–	F	F	–	F F F F M	F	–	–	–	F M	–	–	F F F M M	F F	–	14 Females / 4 Males
'Academic'	–	M M	–	M	M	M	–	–	–	M	–	–	–	–	–	–	– Females / 6 Males
City inner zone	–	–	–	M	F M	F M	F F F	F	–	F	–	–	F	F F F F	F F F M	–	15 Females / 4 Males
Rural	–	–	F	–	M	–	F M M	–	–	–	–	–	F M	M	F M	–	4 Females / 6 Males
Total	–	2	2	3	4	9	9	1	–	2	2	1	3	11	10	–	F 39 / M 20
Percentages of the totals		30% of the 30 at 4a				30% of the 30 at 4a				38% of the 29 at 5a				35% of the 29 at 5a			66% of all 59 at a / 34% of all 59 at a

Table 19) bringing the total to between 15% and 18% in all. There was no reason to suppose that this selection of outdoor areas would vary greatly from any other, though obviously the proportion interviewed in 'academic' and city inner zone areas was significant, as were the facts that few working people were interviewed and that 25% of the respondents were in or past their 60s.

These interviewees were entirely selected at random; the brief encounters took place outdoors in such places as street corners, shopping centres, post offices, 'bus stations, outside colleges and academic centres and in all sorts of places where people could be found quickly and in large numbers. As explained in the earlier chapter on methodology, five very varying areas were pre-selected in order to produce a cross-section of respondents in as effortless a manner as possible in the time available. Again registered blind people were encountered who did not use white canes, dark glasses — or even in some cases, glasses — and again by no means all of the respondents who proved to be severely visually handicapped were *visibly* visually handicapped. In addition to serving as a further reminder to librarians and other laymen working with the group of the difficulty in identifying all cases, this also suggests that probably the proportion of the 72 'without glasses' who would find normal print difficult or impossible to read was slighly higher than the 14 mainly estimated from appearance.

ATTITUDES AND AWARENESS

In libraries

The West Midlands Branch of the Library Association in its Report on Library Services to Hospitals and Handicapped People in 1970 recommended among other things that cooperation between the libraries and the voluntary bodies involved in hospital library service should be encouraged, that Chief Librarians be asked to survey access facilities for the physically handicapped as a matter of urgency and that new developments be publicized in order to keep the needs of hospital libraries and the handicapped in mind.

In some cases the libraries visited were situated on ground floor level only and in others the buildings, reference or lending departments were entered by an assortment of steps, stairs, lifts and escalators. In many of those with steps and stairs there were either separate entrances for the elderly and the disabled, ramps for wheelchairs, or special facilities at the touch of a bell, but there were still some (mostly ancient) premises without such ease of access and in one library where special toilets for the disabled had been provided these were situated at the top of a flight of stairs and kept permanently locked. The locations of the large print books were mostly but not always appropriate according to the librarians' own reasons for choosing those locations, but this subject has already been discussed in the chapter on large print stocks.

The workers in 34 libraries were asked if there were any concessions made for retired people, such as the waiving of fines or reservation fees or the issue of extra tickets. In this respect the results were very encouraging, with only three authorities making no concessions whatsoever and even in one of these the staff claimed to be perturbed about the large print users and the partially-sighted. Thirteen of the libraries charged no fines and either waived or halved reservation fees to OAPs at the time, 11 of them charged no fines (though there was a pending change of policy on one of them), two charged no reservation fees for large print, in four the staff usually exercised discretionary powers and in the remaining library one extra month was allowed before fines became due. A notice referring to the introduction of such a concession for the partially sighted in one library was seen in the local press.

Under the Public Libraries and Museums Act 1964 a local authority is specifically authorized to 'use its premises or allow them to be used for the holding of meetings. . . and other events of an educational or cultural nature', therefore in 23 of 27 establishments inspected it was relevant to ask if there was a spare room available for public meetings, etc. 11 of the 23 had no spare room and 12 did have a room available for such meetings. Five of the 12 had never to their knowledge used the room for any of the groups enquired about; the remaining seven used the room for adult literacy classes and five of these also used it for either Age Concern or other OAP groups and/or pre-retirement classes. Six of the seven took the opportunity provided by these meetings on their premises to provide library publicity (mostly by means of Ulverscroft lists, though in one case large print did not feature in the publicity) and in the library which specialized in providing pre-retirement information and courses, a very senior librarian took an active part in the classes. None of the libraries had housed any meetings of blind or partially sighted societies (and incidentally, no bulk provision of large print books to any of these was traced.)

We come now to awareness and attitudes in libraries, specifically related to the visually handicapped. Seniors in 31 libraries were asked if they had consciously made concessions to the visually handicapped in their choice of either lighting or lettering on signs and posters and the replies fell into three categories:- 'Yes', 'No but . . .' and 'No'. Ten libraries came into the 'Yes' category. Excellent lighting and/ or signs were provided and genuine concern expressed by the librarians. (The ten did, however, include some who had been concerned about the health and safety of all the users and not only the visually handicapped.) The 'No but. . .' category consisted of nine libraries difficult to distinguish from the previous group, where although the librarians said that they had not consciously considered the visually handicapped, the overall standard was good and was thought by them to be good. The remaining 12 librarians merely answered an unqualified 'No'.

Of 47 librarians in 31 libraries, 13 librarians in only seven libraries thought that they had seen copies of the Library Association's leaflet 'Reading for the Visually Handicapped' and in four of these seven libraries there was at least one copy in someone's possession at the time. It was not displayed for the use of the public in any of them, though one authority had supplied one copy to each branch. The remaining 34 librarians in 24 libraries had never seen or heard of the leaflet and several expressed interest. None of the 47 librarians had read Alison Shaw's *'Print for Partial Sight'* and most had never heard of it, but two now intended to buy a copy. One four of the 47 had ever approached a publisher regarding the size or quality of print. Polite and evasive replies had been the only result and two had retaliated by cancelling orders and using financial loss as a weapon.

The senior staff in 30 libraries were asked if they had ever had a visually handicapped member of staff or committee and also whether or not any staff member had ever attended any conference on visual handicap or been a member of a relevant organization or committee. Twenty-two of the 30 libraries had never had a visually handicapped staff or committee member and eight librarians replied in the affirmative; none of the latter felt that there had been any effect on the service however, usually 'because the person concerned had not really been in a position to affect it'.

The seniors in 26 of the 30 libraries knew of no-one who had ever attended any conference, or been a member of an organization or committee, connected with visual handicap. Four of them most certainly did: it emerged here that two of the Chief librarians came into this category and both attempted to provide a channel of communication by circulating their committees and staffs. One of the four was a senior committee member who had had no effect on the service whatsoever and one was an area and hospital librarian who subsequently started using talking books and providing poetry therapy.

It might be interesting — if perhaps a little irrelevant — to know that of 47 librarians asked, 36 of them, including everyone under the estimated age of 40, referred to large print among themselves as exactly that — 'large print', whereas four older ones still called them 'the Ulverscroft' and seven others used both names and in some cases 'tried *not* to say 'Ulverscroft''.

Finally, 50 librarians were asked if they thought it might be a good idea for the publication of all large print to be a non-profit making service, and if so, by whom it should be undertaken. The majority (35) approved of the idea, some hoping that prices would thereby be cut or remain stable and one feeling that it would result in a better range. There were such additional comments as 'an excellent idea', 'laudable', 'it shouldn't be Mr Thorpe's job to cater for the whole of society' and 'it should be a social service and not a profit-making venture'.

A fascinating list of potential providers was produced, with the Social Services heading the list (10) though seven of these felt that the Social Services should be given a Government subsidy and two wanted librarians to be involved as advisers. The Library Association was the next most popular candidate (9) and four of these respondents also considered that Government aid should be forthcoming. Seven people opted for the Ulverscroft Press expanded with help from the Central Government or Social Services; six nominated the National Library for the Blind (with no help at all!) and three people thought that there should be a Central Government Unit, Board or Foundation and that the books should be made available 'in the same way as aids to dyslexia, literacy, sight or hearing'. Two people considered that the D E S should be responsible and as a few people suggested an alternative possible provider there were also the following ideas each with one 'vote' — the Arts Council, the National Health Service, the British Council, a large charitable trust and Portway Reprints.

Six people were undecided. One of these said 'yes, if it resulted in a wider range; no, if it led to deterioration like other nationalized things' and one pointed out that if you removed choice you removed competition — before finally deciding that perhaps it could be tried on a small scale to see if the range were improved. Nine people disapproved of the idea, saying such things as 'it would be a better service if it paid commercially', 'I'm glad the commercial publishers joined in and increased the range', 'you'd get more of the sort of institutionalized books like Ulverscroft' and 'it should be profitable if it were better distributed and librarians recognized the need that does exist'. One of the nine did concede that a non-profit making service might be necessary 'if prices got out of hand'.

For the purposes of the study it is interesting to note the underlying desire expressed even here for an increased range and the fact that (in spite of unused large format stock) *not one of the 116 people interviewed suggested in any way or at any stage of their interviews that the need had already been met,* and this unanimity in the profession was surely highly significant!

About libraries and reading

Groups 1, 2 and 5 in the Link-men Survey were asked to estimate how many of their visually handicapped contacts read large print books, but the majority did not know.

The Books on Wheels ladies in Group 1a were an obvious exception because by the nature of their service this applied to most of their partially sighted clients and also their elderly clients with failing vision. Two did answer '25%' in respect of the partially sighted and three answered '20%', '50%' and 'about half' in respect of people with failing sight and difficulty in reading normal print, but another answered '80%' and *everyone* else in the group answered 'all'. The average percentage of large print readers among the considerable numbers of OAP Homes residents estimated to have failing vision worked out at 34%, (1b) but this was based only on 14 of the 19 respondents' hazarded guesses, among additional remarks ranging from 'not a lot read at all', and 'they get lazy when they get to eighty' to 'a large number would if sufficient were available'.

Many of the social workers and health visitors in Groups 2a and 2b were also exceptions who knew about the reading habits of their contacts and who often quoted actual numbers from their casebooks, from which the following percentages were worked out — 32% of the social workers' partially sighted contacts and 36% of the health visitors' partially sighted contacts were *known* to read large print books. (The district nurses were omitted here only because the sample was too small.)

In Group 5, the workers with the blind and partially sighted in schools, colleges and voluntary agencies, the estimates about large print reading were as far-ranging as the medical Group 3 estimates about registration had been, from 'none at all', 'very few' and 'very, very few' through '20%', '25%', and '30%' to '80%' and 'all to some degree'. The general opinion of this group seemed on the whole to lean towards a lower percentage of readers, however, and there were such additional remarks as the following — 'there's so little suitable', 'most don't like it', 'the partially sighted are often less active than the blind', 'they don't read much for leisure', 'reading's not easy for them and talking books are so effortless' and 'children can adapt with aids to remarkably small print and adults tend not to read for pleasure'.

Sixty-seven residents in OAP Homes were asked about family attitudes to reading when they were young. It was discovered that 29 people had been discouraged when young, usually because 'there was too much to do' or 'too many of us to look after'. Ten of this group (34%) were now readers in spite of this early attitude in the family and 19 were non-readers. Fifteen people said that they had been 'allowed' to read when young and these were now divided almost equally into seven readers (47%) and eight non-readers at the time of their interviews. Twenty-three people had been *encouraged* to read and of this group 19 were reading still (83%) and only four were non-readers; all four had severe visual problems. These results will obviously be of interest to librarians but 67 people formed too small a sample upon which to base any positive conclusions; however similar results were also found among the 133 elderly people living in the community and these are all discussed together at length in the chapter on non-use and non-users of large print.

No matter how librarians might regard the fact, reading books and using libraries were not synonymous nor were reading books and reading. Twenty of the 67 residents never read anything at all by then — including newspapers — but 46 of them never used a library — even including small branches and loan collections in Homes. In the absence of further information, one could only assume that reading material was obtained from most of the sources mentioned — paperbacks, gifts, 'swops', own books (especially the Bible) and of course the newspapers and ubiquitous women's weekly magazines. Of the 21 people who did at that time use libraries, branches or bulk loans, ten used them regularly and eleven used them sometimes. Of the 46 who never used libraries of any kind then, 30 had never done so at any time in their lives and 16 had used them previously. The reasons given for ceasing to use libraries by these 16 ex-borrowers in Homes were: visual problems (6) — moved away from familiar library (4) — gave up when busy (3) — not available in Home (3) — Homebound or too far to walk (3) — concentration failure (2) — and own books (1). (More than one reason per person.)

The 500 members of the general public interviewed briefly were also asked about their libraries, in order to put statistics of use by the elderly and the visually handicapped groups into perspective. In case some respondents were tempted to answer incorrectly for reasons such as prestige or the wish to please, they were not asked directly whether or not they used their public libraries but were asked if they knew the address. This was recorded, where known, but it led to the much more significant 'incidental' conversation as to whether or not the library was used and *this* was the answer which was really sought and was later classified.

Thirty-three was considered to be the generally accepted percentage of 'active' library users in the community but according to their replies this sample seemed to be atypical in this respect, with 242 of the 500 contacts (48%) claiming to use their public libraries at least 'sometimes'. This variation of 15% could probably be accounted for by four factors, however — a) 125 people or 25% of the total sample were interviewed in 'academic' areas and 74% of these were library users; b) five of the 27 users in the city inner zone used only a community library open for one half-day weekly in a local chapel and would probably not have used the library building; c) many people, especially those in the rural areas, said that they used their libraries 'only very occasionally' or 'only now and then' and these were classified as users rather than as non-users for our purpose (though probably they would not have been considered 'active' by the researchers who produced the 33% estimates) and d) the researcher was not library-based and had no means of checking replies other than by addresses. Regardless of the apparent overall variation of 15%, taking all these factors into consideration, therefore, it seemed likely that these figures would be likely to conform to rather than to contradict the generally-accepted and more carefully researched earlier estimates of library use or to suggest any increase. (Table 21 shows the replies in detail.)

It must surely surprise librarians to learn that so many non-users did not even know the whereabouts of the nearest public library or branch library to their home, because accurate addresses were not insisted upon if the respondent described its location, appeared to know where it was situated or claimed to use an alternative branch or central library. In only one group — the rural respondents — were the non-users who did *not* know its whereabouts outnumbered by the non-users who *did* know and many of the rural respondents had 'scored' in this respect by replying that a van or mobile library which had been seen in the village was their nearest library!

Presumably most of those who did not know the whereabouts of the library were just not interested in reading, unless they stated otherwise, like most of the people who did not volunteer any other reason for not using a library. Applied to 149 people who came into these two categories together with 13 respondents who *said* that they were not interested in reading, this would make a total of 162 or over 32%. The other reasons volunteered in 109 cases for non-use

TABLE 21

500 MEMBERS OF THE GENERAL PUBLIC WHO WERE QUESTIONED ABOUT THEIR LIBRARIES:

Area where interviewed	Library users (to some extent)	Non-users who knew address or location	Non-users who did not know address or location	Totals
Suburban	44	12	24	80
Assorted shopping	47	30	45	122
'Academic'	93	9	23†	125
City inner zone	27 °	17	60*	104
Rural	31	26	12	69
Total	242 (48%)	94 (19%)	164 (33%)	500

† Most of these used an 'alternative' library, e.g. college or special
* Note the proportion of non-users in the City inner zone who did not know the whereabouts of their nearest library in spite of generous provision in Homes, schools, church halls and community centres etc. and an old, well-established central library situated on the main road
° 5 of the 27 used only a community library open for one half day weekly

were: that they were too busy (31 — with 11 of them in the inner zone — had visual problems (16) — had just moved into area (14) — used an alternative library — college, university, work, private, voluntary (14) — could not get there, or there was not one 'in the area' (11) — collected or bought their own books (8) — were illiterate or barely literate (6 — 4 of them in the inner zone) — worked away from home (3 — all in rural areas) — books obtained by another member of family (2) — had 'left school now' (2) — had a daughter who worked in a library (1) or that the books were too filthy and scribbled in (1).

In connection with visual handicap

When the 26 visually handicapped residents in OAP Homes were asked if anyone had encouraged them to use their vision for ink-print, many more of them replied in the negative than of the respondents of the younger visually handicapped groups, reflecting older ideas such as 'we ought to save it' and 'I ought to rest them'; 20 replied 'no', five replied 'yes' and one could not remember earlier advice. Several replied 'they didn't need to encourage me', one adding 'when I bought *private* spectacles'. Four people had someone to read to them, one had talking books in a previous Home but by then her hearing was impaired, and 21 had neither; most of those who did not have either facility either stated or gave the impression that they did not wish for them and that the need had been met. Only five of these 'visually handicapped' residents ever heard the BBC Radio 4 programme 'In Touch' on Sundays; the usual reasons given for not listening were unawareness, 'no radio', 'clashes with our tea-time' and lack of interest, but it was very probable that a number did not think of themselves as visually handicapped and therefore did not connect such a programme with their own situation.

In view of the changed attitudes towards the use of residual vision today, all groups of link-men were asked whether or not they encouraged clients to make use of their remaining sight, because old attitudes towards 'sight-saving' would clearly have a bearing on the mention or recommendation of large print books. The overwhelming majority did, in fact, encourage its use — 274 (or 84%) of the 328 who were presumably not offended by the question — though a few did qualify their replies with 'sometimes', 'with reservations' or 'depends on the amount of time available'. A further 18 were undecided about the appropriate reply or said that the question did not apply to their work and only 36 (less than 11% of those who answered) replied in the negative. The majority of these were in the miscellaneous category or were language and literacy workers but there were isolated examples in all categories except 2 and 3 usually the reply given was 'it's not our function', 'it's outside my role' or 'I wouldn't interfere'. The largest single group was found among the workers in OAP Homes where six of 19 people replied in the negative; one who did answer 'yes' added that 'a lot of the older ones think they should rest them, though, and they won't have it', which confirmed the findings among the residents themselves.

Many of the interviews with the general public at the Question four stage would surely not have been out of place in Esther Rantzen's 'That's Life' programme on television. The 500 respondents were asked 'when I mention low vision aids, what, or which ones, come to mind?' and after a suitable interval the words 'meaning optical aids to reading' were added if necessary. The result was often amusing, with very many replies of which the following were only a small selection — 'no, I'm a bit of a backward one; I only work for the council' — 'you don't know my mind! Absolutely nothing!' — 'sorry, not in my line' — 'would you mind repeating the question?' — 'you really want to know? nothing at all!' — 'no, I can't think of it; it's *gone!*' — 'oh, I couldn't help you there duck!' — 'sorry — how do you mean?' (several) — 'I don't know much about this National Health Service' — 'come again?' — 'well it depends what you mean' — 'you've got me there!' — 'no, love, I can't help you there' — 'lower what?' — 'meaning exactly?' — I haven't a clue' — 'nothing, love — I'm not a clever one' — 'bifocals for one eye' and 'you can or you can't, can't you?' There were also many straightforward expressions of ignorance or puzzlement such as 'it's terrible in my position — I'm a social worker with elderly people but I don't understand. I've heard the phrase' — 'I haven't come across that phrase' — 'you'll need to define that for me' — 'what exactly do you mean?' — 'you don't mean *visual* aids?' — 'I honestly don't know anything like that — I'd help you if I could' and 'sorry, I've never thought about that sort of thing' — again only a very small selection.

Nineteen of the 500 people named four or more aids without the question being explained and a twentieth person did so afterwards. These were all younger people with the exception of one lady in her 70s and they included three known users, one large print reader, a geriatric nurse and an eye nurse, a lecturer and an Oxford student. Only 35 people (including two known users) named three aids, surely a very moderate achievement when spectacles and magnifying glasses were usually two of the three aids named?

One hundred and thirty-nine people named magnifiers and spectacles (with which contact lenses were grouped for classification purposes) and 234 people could think only of spectacles or none at all. Fifty-one people named magnifying glasses only, often using the terms 'spy-glasses' and 'them Sherlock Holmes things' or miming the use of hand-held magnifiers to bring the name to mind. Twenty-one other people each gave either only one or two replies but these were in different categories from those above, such as anglepoise lamps, lighting, large print, braille, CCTV, tape recorders, binoculars, telescopes, the TV literacy programme 'On the move', and 'square pegs screwed into the pupils' (which apparently had applied to the hospital neighbour of one man interviewed.)

The respondents themselves were aware that they knew very little about such things unless they were personally involved and a certain amount of resentment was expressed that not enough was done to publicize the availability of all kinds of aid, particularly those available on the National Health Service. 'Things don't get advertized' — 'it's like everything else! only a few people *know* about them' — 'there's a few goodies like that and the old people 'outside' never get to hear about them' — 'glasses, large print, good lighting; I only have one eye myself and *I* didn't know you could get anything else' — 'I'm going to ask my doctor. I'd love to be able to read the paper' and 'they never tell us'.

The total aids mentioned by the 500 people (other than the ubiquitous replies 'spectacles' and 'magnifying glasses', are listed here: — Contact lenses (107) — bi-focals (29) — large print (19) — supplementary lenses or 'special thick lenses to fit on' (18) — binoculars (14) — monocles/monoculars (13) — braille (12) — good light/ing (10) — CCTV (10) — telescopes (9) — tapes/tape-recorders (7) — cataract spectacles (6) — microscope (6) — anglepoise lamps (5) — filmstrips (5) — slides (5) — 'glasses that go dark in the light' (3) — Moon (3) — telescopic spectacles (3) — TV (3) — projectors (3) — maps (3) — models (3) — blackboard (3) — tri-focals (2) — opera glasses (2) — charts (2) — films (2) — flannelgraphs (2) — teaching aids (2) — sheets of plastic (2) — visual aids (2) — 'special stands you put the book under' (2) — torch magnifiers (2) — cassettes (2) — and then (1 each) enlargers, recumbent spectacles, sunglasses, epidiascopes, pictures, diagrams, lorgnettes, pegboard, telephone, typewriters, talking books, guide dogs, young children's special books, audio-visual aids, 'blow-ups on TV', 'the optical' (!), a good optician, 'On the move', 'a square peg screwed into a man's pupils' and the Optacon (described only).

Most of the 12 people who included braille among the 'low vision aids' which came to mind and others who mentioned braille without including it in their final replies wrongly assumed that *all* blind people could read and write braille. Those with whom a conversation ensued knew that braille consisted of different arrangements of embossed dots but they did not realize that an average novel transcribed into braille took up ten to 12 large volumes, nor that a person's age and health could affect the sense of touch. The 15 young to middle-aged respondents who included good lighting or anglepoise lamps among their replies appeared to be better informed about the importance of lighting than their elderly counterparts, though 15 among 500 people was nevertheless a disappointing proportion when researchers such as Cullinan (1978 and 1979) have proved that changing attitudes to artificial lighting in the home could be very important, especially for the elderly. Almost all of the 107 respondents who mentioned contact lenses were below the age of forty and (as might be expected) almost all of those who named educational visual aids were interviewed in 'academic' areas.

PUBLICITY
METHODS

Past methods and present readers

How did the present readers find out about the existence of large print books, if they did not notice the collection for themselves when browsing in the library?

Forty-eight West Midlands librarians were asked if they ever encouraged anyone *other* than the elderly and the visually handicapped to look at them and it emerged that the majority of these (31) offered large print to the general public occasionally, to help with waiting lists or when readers were seeking a specific title not on the ordinary shelves. Five librarians had offered them to adult literacy students and new readers, four had recommended them to workers with mentally handicapped adults, three had offered them to children and each of the following had been offered large print books by one (different) librarian — playgroup mothers who did not read, people temporarily affected by medicine, library students, Asian teenagers, (elderly) new borrowers, people who had already found them restful for evening reading and one librarian's wife when she was awaiting new spectacles, though, rather interestingly, she was later discouraged when she became 'hooked' in case the range became too limiting too soon! Mention should perhaps also be made here on the significant number of *library* workers at all levels reading large print. Eleven of the people asked had never offered them to anyone other than the elderly and the visually handicapped and one of these added 'we've provided them and that's that!'

Coming next to the *main* group of large print readers, the elderly and/or visually handicapped, how did librarians consider that *they* found out about large print?

The replies given on the national questionnaire forms to the question 'which is your most effective method of communicating with users and potential users of large print?' were as follows:-

103 — Personal contact by staff
 63 — Providing/displaying large print lists and catalogues

51 — Displaying the actual books in the library
44 — Via housebound reader service and visits
42 — Posters and notices
39 — Books in OAP Homes, hostels, day centres, lunch clubs, or
     by liaison with wardens
34 — Prominent siting of the books
33 — Word of mouth, or personal recommendation by other
     readers/relatives/neighbours
32 — Via Social Services Department, social workers, domiciliary
     service, Housing Department, district nurses or health
     visitors
29 — Talks to groups, clubs, societies, Age Concern, senior citi-
     zens, retirement groups or Home Helps, training
     programmes
14 — In hospitals
13 — Mobile and travelling libraries
13 — Via WRVS, Red Cross and other volunteers visiting the
     elderly
12 — Civic newspapers, library guides, reports, newsletters, printed
     and local radio book reviews
12 — Distributing leaflets
 7 — Effective, clearly-guided shelving
 6 — Having an adequate supply
 5 — Via local blind associations, visually handicapped associations
     and handicapped clubs
 5 — Health centres, doctors' surgeries and opticians
 4 — Readers' advisory desks

If indeed all this activity *was* going on nationwide then the list was
truly impressive. However, from talking to West Midlands librarians
— who must surely be similar in many respects to their counterparts elsewhere — the researcher gained the distinct impression that
in many cases most of these activities were undertaken only on very
rare occasions if at all, but naturally and honestly recalled when such
questions were asked. Also, when the list was scrutinized some of the
methods did appear to be rather passive; for example one hoped that
'displaying the actual books in the library' referred to some sort of
a display stand or exhibition and not just the fact that the books
were there on the shelves. 'Prominent siting of the books', while
obviously considered to be desirable, required little positive effort as
did 'effective, clearly-guided shelving' and 'having an adequate

supply'. 'Providing/displaying large print lists and catalogues' needed to be better done than it was in the West Midlands on the whole if it were to be effective, for here in 25 public libraries whose stock and facilities were examined only nine had any lists on display at all.

Forty-five people from 29 different libraries were asked if any member of staff had ever publicized large print in any of the following ways:- by giving a talk on local radio or TV, in a local newspaper or magazine, in a library report or handout, by giving a talk or lecture to a local group – or via the Social Services or voluntary associations.

Fifteen people from 11 libraries did not know of anyone who had ever done any of these things; one of these added 'We should! The partially-sighted and people like that very rarely come in – they probably don't even know we've got them!' The remaining 30 people from 18 establishments all knew of someone from their authority who had publicized large print in at least one of the ways mentioned and the totals for each method were as follows:

By giving a talk or lecture to a local group – all 30 people from all these 18 libraries (though in most cases large print was only mentioned in a talk about facilities in general.) As might be expected, it seemed that the most effective were those talks given to pre-retirement courses and the elderly, especially where either *books* were available or lists of names and requests were taken at the end of the talk.

Via the Social Services or voluntary associations – 21 people from 12 libraries. In some cases this was informally done via individual social workers; in one case it was considered superfluous as the Social Services already knew and had offered to rebind the large print stock; in one case the surplus large print stock had been donated to the Social Services Department and one case should probably be discounted altogether in view of the added remark that 'one assumes they already *have* this sort of knowledge' (together with inside information that liaison was bad in this area following social workers' pressure for closure of some of the libraries as a means of saving money!)

In a library report or handout – 12 people from five libraries (though again large print was merely mentioned in passing and in fact proved not to be included at all when two recent library reports were traced.) Undoubtedly, the most effective mentions in this category were made in a free civic newspaper, which brought an influx of new large print readers. In a local newspaper or magazine – nine people from four libraries remembered this being done but none were aware of the effects and finally, on local radio or TV — only one library had tried this and it was not possible to measure its effectiveness.

It seemed that on the whole, therefore, the two methods *known* to be the most effective in bringing in new large print borrowers were the talks to groups of elderly people and the article in a free civic newspaper, though of course some of the other methods were likely to have had good but immeasurable results.

Forty-four people in 30 libraries were asked whether or not they had ever featured large print books in displays or exhibitions:

Twenty-seven people from 20 libraries had never done so and the remaining 17 people from 10 libraries (only one-third of the libraries) had done so at different times. Four of these libraries had displayed large print books in their usual library displays, three of them *featuring* large print for a short period and one including it in a general display. In one library the books were all borrowed, in one the librarian said that she thought it had resulted in new readers, in one 'some people had been very surprised to find that it existed' and in one the effect was unknown. Two libraries had displayed the books in their window cases, one embarking on an all-large print display in all its full-time branches and one 'just adding the odd book' to a normal print display. Neither was sure whether or not there had been any increased issues or new readers. Two libraries had featured large print in their library display three years previously at a large public show, but rather disappointingly neither of them felt that it had had any effect whatsoever. One library placed large print books in troughs on the counter to attract attention and this simple method resulted in them 'really being noticed and borrowed'; the remaining library displayed them for a week in a local 'Aids for Disabled' exhibition which 'probably bucked up the issues because some of them had never seen large print before'.

Increasing sales

West Midlands librarians were then asked if they could suggest ways of increasing the sales and therefore the range of large print books. There were 61 different suggestions for changes in the large print books themselves:

Eleven reversed the factors in the question and suggested (perhaps unrealistically) that an increase in the range would increase the sales;

nine librarians — none of whom knew of their existence — considered that the introduction of paperbacks would increase sales; seven thought that the 'other' publishers must reduce the prices they charged for the books; six felt that the production of more romances would lead to higher purchase; six suggested less distinctive or 'institutionalized' jackets; four considered that weight reduction would be the main factor; four thought that publishers should concentrate on books popular several years ago for the elderly, whereas one thought that popular titles should be produced more quickly; two suggested pictures; two suggested abridged editions and there was one person in favour of each of the following ideas: the inclusion of 'comforting' books, the selection of titles together with librarians dealing with the public rather than with the Library Association, short stories, more light classics, coverage of popular subjects in non-fiction, booklets like those produced by Reader's Digest for new readers, non-fiction not 'specially produced for large print, that commercial publishers should 'copy Thorpe's print and spacing' and that there could be a continuation print in photographically enlarged print at the end of any run in normal print.

There were 55 separate spontaneous mentions of the need to increase or improve publicity in some way: nine librarians considered that countrywide work like these personal interviews and the survey, together with the production of some standards or 'more similar cooperation from the Library Association' (as one worded it) would publicize large print to librarians, 'increasing interest, making people look at their stock and talk about them and thus increase the sales'; two others also pointed out again here that standards of provision were needed for librarians. Eight people felt that we should make the general public aware, since (as one of them remarked) 'a lot of the potential market for large print don't even know it exists;' five thought that both publishers and the Library Association should publicize large print more to librarians — and to the *right* librarians, not always the chief. For similar reasons another four considered that the 'other' publishers should publish and circulate lists like Ulverscroft instead of sending books on approval which weren't always seen by everyone interested. Three suggested publicity via local radio and there were three suggestions about aiming publicity at each of the following groups: OAP Homes, hospitals, opticians and librarians in training. Two suggested aiming publicity at the Rotary Club and two at voluntary societies and one suggested each of the following: publicizing the availability of large print books for purchase as gifts, circulating people with reading difficulties, the surprise tactic of integrating *spare* large print among normal print, book-marks, advertising in women's magazines, that a large advertising campaign was needed, that there should be more posters and that the Ulverscroft posters should be more striking.

Finally there were ten suggestions regarding the marketing of the books: four people thought they should be available in bookshops, feeling that people who did not actually need them would not choose them on grounds of price; three felt that colleges should begin to stock them; two that they should be on sale in specialized shops for the handicapped and one that an increase in library book-funds was the answer. Not all the above ideas were practicable but the raising of the question alone stirred up an interest locally and some of them might well be worthy of pursuit.

Reaching potential readers

Every one of the 116 librarian interviewees in the West Midlands was asked for ideas on ways of communicating with *potential* users in the community as a parting question and the replies received are shown here:

40 – OAP clubs and social centres

39 – Liaison with Welfare and Social Services Departments

28 – Word of mouth or leaflets via relatives, friends and neighbours

28 – Radio, including popular serials

24 – OAP Homes, hostels, almshouses and wardens

22 – Talks to OAP gatherings

22 – Libraries or publicity in community centres

18 – Leaflets through doors or in books issued

18 – Church clubs, halls, magazines, Mothers' Union, clergy

18 – Meals on Wheels

16 – OAP lunch clubs

15 – Age Concern, Help the Aged and other OAP associations

14 – WRVS

14 – Opticians' waiting rooms

14 – ITV, including popular serials

13 – Notices in family doctors' waiting rooms

13 – Posters in post offices near pension desk

13 — Voluntary societies and volunteers working specifically
      with the elderly
11 — Social workers
11 — 'Yours' and other local OAP magazines
11 — WIs, Townswomen's Guilds, etc
10 — DHSS stickers or leaflets in pension books
 9 — More or better publicity in libraries
 7 — Clinics, health centres and Area Health Departments
 7 — Home helps
 7 — Get teachers to ask children to publicize or distribute
 6 — Displays, exhibitions, collections, demonstrations
 6 — Press advertisements in large print
 6 — Notices in corner shops
 6 — Welfare librarians going out into the community
 5 — Pre-retirement courses
 5 — Posters in pubs
 5 — Book-marks
 4 — Partially-sighted and blind organizations
 3 — District nurses
 3 — Concentrated drive, campaign or Large Print Week
 3 — Notices in supermarkets
 2 — Chiropodists' waiting rooms
 2 — Health visitors
 2 — Via the housebound service
 2 — Accident and emergency clinics
 2 — Diabetic and thyroid clinics
 2 — Coffee mornings
 2 — Rotary clubs
 1 — Bingo clubs
 1 — OAP days in hairdressers'
 1 — Hospitals
 1 — Rent collectors
 1 — Probation officers
 1 — Posters on hoardings
 1 — Posters in underpasses
 1 — Stickers and balloons at carnivals
 1 — Another poster poem advertising large print

From the above it can be seen that there was no shortage of ideas
or enthusiasm in the West Midlands; one can only assume that if
these were harnessed to the cause and if both the money and staff

time were available a worthwhile publicity campaign could be
launched.

Slogans

Before finally leaving the subject of publicity from the librarians'
viewpoint, for a little light relief let us consider some of the slogans
kindly suggested by West Midlands librarians — in some cases after
driving round the area deep in thought!

Bed-time reading
Big is beautiful
Books for bedtime
Books for reading in bed
Books for tired eyes
Easy on the eyes
Easy reading
Evening reading
Eyes getting tired? Why not try a clearer print?
Is yours the large type?
It's clear to see why I'm in large print!
Large is lovely
Let us open your eyes
Let's face it — I'm your type!
Look, see and read
Read with ease
Right reading for sight left
Sight-savers (though this is not approved by experts in the field).

The readers' angle

From the earlier Survey A it had become apparent that in spite of an
imaginative variety of publicity methods being used or suggested, few
people came into libraries specifically to borrow large print books
having heard about them from outside sources or through the
libraries' extra-mural publicity methods, so how *did* the borrowers
find out about them? The majority of the West Midlands librarians
who were asked this question believed that most people came across
the shelves and saw the books there for themselves, being already
library users (42) and the second largest group believed that they
found out from friends and by word of mouth (29) most of these
also being existing borrowers. 'Staff contact' was the reply given by

16 librarians, usually meaning contact within the library with existing borrowers and nine thought that a good proportion found out
during their introduction to the library on joining, or during their
interviews when requesting housebound services. 'OAP Homes
services and wardens' and 'using the community centres and other
centres where the books are located' were each suggested by four
perceptive librarians and the remaining suggestions were talks,
literacy tutors, WRVS, by accident, notices, hospital services,
doctors, Social Services and prison! As one interviewee remarked
'most of them don't! Confidence regarding access to libraries hasn't
yet been fully developed' and another pointed out the anomaly
where 'library users come across the books by accident but the
housebound are *invited* to use them'.

Again the 200 borrowers' factual version tallied fairly closely with
the suppositions of the librarians. In the case of 90 of them — 45%
and by far the largest group — either they or their messengers had
merely found the shelves while using the library; 27 were told about
them or shown them by other readers and another 26 had seen the
books in OAP Homes; 14 had first been guided to them by members
of the library staff; eight had first seen them at an OAP centre; in a
further seven cases either the reader or a relative/friend worked or
had worked in a library; five had been introduced to them via the
housebound service; three had first seen them on travelling libraries
in another area; another three had been introduced to them by their
literacy tutors and three couldn't remember. Two people had seen
them when in hospital, in two cases they had been seen or borrowed
when a parent had read the books in earlier years and two people
had been told about them by people at work (one being a visually-
handicapped reader). The remaining five readers had been introduced
to the books by a doctor, a district nurse, the matron of a nursing
home, a neighbour who delivered one with flowers when the reader
broke her leg and — in one case — by seeing them advertized in the
library! Having taken a great deal of trouble to interview readers in as
wide a variety of library and other borrowing situations as possible,
there is no reason to suppose that the sample varied greatly from that
of any other group of large print readers elsewhere (except where
unusual circumstances or methods prevail) and therefore it seemed
reasonable to assume that the largest number of that minority group
of users who were not already library members (the group which particularly interests us here) found out about the existence of large
print books by seeing them in OAP Homes and centres (34 in all,

17%). In addition to suggesting that the books themselves were their own best advertisement, this must surely be one reason why the younger non-library members seemed not to be joining libraries to read large print — and it seems logical, therefore, to suggest making bulk loans or finding ways of flooding colleges, centres and club premises where groups of younger visually handicapped people can be found with attractive selections of the smaller-format books by *all* publishers. This, of course, pre-supposes that the present financial crisis is at an end, that more titles are available and that librarians are better-informed about their availability and have standards which guide them regarding adequate provision in libraries of different sizes and in varying locations.

Early in the interviews, in order to provide information which would enable us to reach their peers, readers were asked for their own ideas about the kinds of publicity which would be most likely to reach *them* regularly and as guidance the following suggestions were offered to them: BBC radio, independent local radio, commercial TV, local press, via optician or Social Services, talks in clubs, lists in the library, or any other ways they could think of. The fact that 93 of them opted for lists in the library rather defeated the object of the question, though the *way* in which it was often suggested — as a 'jolly good, novel idea' — and the frequency with which it turned up did reinforce the previous findings about lists not usually being seen and also suggests that book lists would be appreciated by more readers than librarians realized. The fact that this question immediately followed that on booklists must be taken into consideration here, however, as some of the respondents might still have been thinking along those lines — and at this point it must also be pointed out that 22 respondents were not at all interested in publicity or lists, giving such replies as 'I don't need it — or them' and 'we want books on the shelves, not lists!'

Apart from the 93 who opted for booklists in the library, the most popular suggestion was for lists in OAP Homes (28 — an answer reinforcing both of the last two points made) — talks in clubs (23 — reinforcing the opinions of the librarians, as discovered during the first survey) — the local press (16) — BBC radio (15) — via opticians (9) — letters or leaflets through the letterbox (7) — commercial television (6) and then a string of ideas identifcal to those listed by librarians and mainly featuring various OAP and church clubs, groups, magazines and organizations.

Awareness among the general public

In a sample of which 15% to 18% would be unlikely to read books in normal-size print for one reason or another and of which 48% claimed to use their libraries at least 'sometimes', how many had seen any large print books? Respondents were shown a specimen of Ulverscroft print and asked 'which books have you ever seen with print this size?' and pre-coded columns had been prepared for classified replies such as 'three or more publishers', 'two publishers', 'Ulverscroft only', 'irrelevant examples' and 'none at all'. The researcher quickly discovered that the general public paid little attention to publishers' names, however – the people who actually named one publisher were rare indeed and respondents who *had* seen large print books had to be questioned further in order to discover from their descriptions exactly which books they were likely to have seen.

Only two of the 500 had seen books by 'three or more publishers', though *none* of these were named – one respondent was interviewed in a rural area and one in an 'academic' area. Four of the 500 people had seen books by 'two publishers'; one was interviewed in a suburban area and three in 'academic' areas; Ulverscroft was actually named three times, Watts was named once and described once and the British and Foreign Bible Society was named once. Of the 140 people who had seen only Ulverscroft large print books, 19 actually named them (correctly or approximately) and 121 described them variously as 'a set in identical covers', 'those that all look alike', 'I've seen a special bookcase for old people', 'I've seen some without pictures on the cover', 'they're terribly heavy to carry', 'the ones with the backs all similar', 'they all look alike and they're all kept together', 'they're all alike, but they're rather heavy though' and 'I've seen the old people's books – is that what you mean?' (Inevitably some remarked 'They need more of them, tell them', 'there aren't very many', 'I've actually read some, but I like travel and adventure and non-fiction' or 'I've seen them in the library, but there aren't enough to make it worthwhile'.) In addition six people named other publishers – in one case Watts and in the remaining five cases the British and Foreign Bible Society. This meant that, in all, 152 of the 500 members of the general public – 242 of them library users – had at least *seen* large print books; even if they had never opened one, 30% of the potential users and the friends, relatives and neighbours who were expected to pass on information to them did know of their existence and of places where they could be found. This 'knowing 30%' comprised 39% of the people interviewed in suburban areas, 25% of those in assorted shopping areas, 39% of those interviewed in 'academic' areas, 21% of those in the city inner zone and 28% of those interviewed in rural areas.

Probably in this particular survey the 70% who did *not* know of the books were more significant than the 30% who did know. Of these (348 people in all) 243 respondents had never seen *any* books in print similar in size to that of the Ulverscroft sample and 105 gave irrelevant examples such as children's/school/picture books (88) — paperbacks/on bookstalls (12) and adult literacy material (5). Even *more* significantly the 348 people included 54 or 70% of the 77 respondents in their 60s, 27 or 61% of the 44 respondents in their 70s, four or 67% of the six respondents in their 80s, 44 or 75% of the 59 respondents who found it difficult or impossible to read the 'normal' print for visual reasons and 12 or 86% of the 14 who found it difficult or impossible because of literacy, language or mental problems. Disregarding the fact that there was some overlap between these age categories and visual or reading ability categories, this meant that overall over 70% of the people in the groups now known to form the majority of potential users had never seen large print books!

Many of these people would have liked to see them, however, for there were very many remarks such as 'nothing like that. I wish I had!' — 'I'd still be using the library if I had' — 'none at all. I wish there were' — 'my grandmother would have been pleased with those when she had cataracts and glaucoma' — 'I could read *that* print without an aid' — 'I wish there *were* some with decent print like that' — 'none; I wish they *would* print them a bit bigger' — 'none at all! I think *I* could read that' — 'none; I wish I had, because my father's registered blind but he can just see a little bit' — 'none. I've got cataracts coming and I would do with that myself' — and 'none! You've done me a good turn; I know several people I'll pass the word on to'.

'Word of mouth'

All 67 elderly respondents in Homes were asked if they had ever read, seen or heard of large print books. Nineteen had read or still did read them; 16 had seen them but for various reasons did not read them; only two had heard of them and 30 claimed that they had neither read, seen nor heard of them.

The 30 who claimed never to have been aware of their existence

TABLE 22

'WORD OF MOUTH' AS A PUBLICITY METHOD

ANSWERS GIVEN WHEN *ALL* THE ELDERLY AND VISUALLY HANDICAPPED RESPONDENTS IN SURVEY C WHO HAD READ, SEEN OR HEARD OF THE BOOKS WERE ASKED 'HAVE YOU EVER TOLD ANYONE ELSE WHO MIGHT NEED THEM ABOUT LARGE PRINT BOOKS?'

Group questioned	None at all	Friends	Relatives	Neighbours	Other library borrowers	People in B of PS group	VH clients	'Linkman' or agency!	No. who had done so	Total no. of responses
Elderly in community (incl. V H)	55	11	1	7	3	1	—	—	15	70
Elderly in OAP Homes (incl. V H)	34	3	1	—	1	—	—	1	3	37
V H interviewed (incl. elderly)	25	4	5	2	2	4	4	—	16	41
VH questionnaires (incl. elderly)	66	76	29	21	19	2	2	3	166†	232*
Totals	180	94	36	30	25	7	6	4°	200	380

* The motivated respondents

† Several circled the word 'other' without definition; others gave no details whatsoever, which made the claim suspect in some cases. Replies from those interviewed were obviously more reliable here and these presented a very different picture — i.e. 114 who had *not* told anyone else at all and only 34 who had done so

° These were a clergyman, a braille teacher, a visiting welfare worker and an official of a society and in each case this was done so that they would be able to 'spread the word' to others

(NB One person replied here 'I wouldn't dare! The range is no good — there's no choice')

were shown samples of normal print and samples of Ulverscroft large print. Twenty-one of the 30 (70%) found the large print easier and less tiring to read than the normal print (including three who were

unable to read the normal print at all and five who found it very difficult) and nine of these 21 people were then fairly likely to read
large print books if available in the Homes; the other 12 were considered unlikely to do so, mainly due to a lack of interest in reading.
Eight of the 30 found no improvement, either because they were
able to read normal print, unable to read large print or illiterate, and
one respondent preferred the 'normal' print.

Thirty-four of the 37 who did know of their existence had never
told anyone else about them, which is very significant for librarians
when many rely on 'word of mouth' as an important publicity
method. The remaining three, between them, had told friends (3) —
relatives (1) — other Home residents (1) — other library borrowers
(1) and a visiting welfare worker 'so that she could tell others' (1).
Incidentally, one lady who had not thought to inform anyone else
about their availability added that most of the blind people with
whom she associated used them already, 'especially the older people'.

All the elderly and visually handicapped respondents in Survey C
who had read, seen or heard of the books were asked if they had ever
told anyone about them, and (as might have been expected) the
actual readers were the most likely group to have done so. Table 22
shows the amount of publicity being obtained 'by word of mouth',
and in the chapter on the non-use of large print books it will be seen
that 132 of the potential users had never read, seen nor heard of
them.

THE LINK-MEN

Implications of the response rate

Since so many librarians regarded word of mouth as an important
publicity method when making provision for the elderly and the
visually handicapped it was important to discover how well-informed
the link-men themselves were about large print books and as
mentioned earlier this was one of the main aims of Survey D.

The response rates themselves provided useful information. It was
probable that in some cases they were low because the group was an
exceptionally busy one; because the survey coincided with hospital
and social worker strikes and other industrial action — or because the
most appropriate approach had not always been selected. In other
cases, however, individuals approached entirely failed to see its
relevance to themselves in spite of explanation and this in itself was
very revealing, for it was considered extremely unlikely that such
people would pass on information about large print to potential
readers. In the case of one entire group repeated efforts had to be
made in order to obtain 25 replies (in spite of assurances that returns
from non-users would be as useful as returns from users) and this
clearly indicated that few of those initially approached felt that
large print books had any connection with their language or literacy
work. The feeling was obviously shared by the workers and volunteers in the miscellaneous category, except for WRVS Books on
Wheels ladies — those groups whose links with elderly and/or visually
handicapped people were undeniable but whose links with either
books, large print books or libraries were possibly doubtful; it was
almost certain that many of these people demonstrated this either
by not replying at all or by filling in their forms hastily or incom-
pletely. On the whole, however, it was likely that — together with
lack of interest — ignorance of the topics under investigation was the
most common reason for failure to reply; the 'testing' of knowledge
was impossible to disguise completely and any insecure people would
intensely dislike making a return which revealed their ignorance.
Overall there were about 850 non-returns and even if as a very conservative estimate less than half of these were caused by ignorance of

the questions under discussion this would apply to 35% of the so-called 'link-men' approached.

Awareness of the range of material available

What of the 346 people (29% of those contacted) who did complete and return their forms — how much did they know about large print books? Certainly most of these had seen them, which must prove gratifying to librarians. Excluding the Books on Wheels ladies and the hospital librarians/assistants who actually *worked* with books, 250 of 272 (92%) had seen them, which, in addition to being gratifying reinforced the theory that those 'in the know' were more likely to reply than those who had never seen the books. (Incidentally three WRVS ladies and one hospital librarian had never seen large print books, which was surprising, though possibly the former were work-ing in an administrative capacity and the latter with hospital staff only.) Every single respondent in categories 1c, d and e; 2; 5a, b, d and e; and 6b had seen large print books and the only categories in which those who had seen them were outnumbered by those who had not were 1f and g (the Home helps and Meals on Wheels ladies). The people concerned were not library users and most of them were people who were interviewed, which was highly significant.

This definitely suggested that if a larger sample had been inter-viewed at random in place of the written responses of knowledgeable or motivated respondents, more people would have been found in the 'unseen' category. Perhaps the most surprising discovery made at this stage was that four of the 31 opticians who answered the question and three of 19 workers (mostly interviewed) in OAP Homes and centres had never seen large print books, though three of the former group did 'sometimes' use their libraries.

The majority had seen only Ulverscroft books though some ticked the 'other' column without being able to specify other publishers by name. Some did not even know of the Ulverscroft series by name and no doubt its presence on the form reminded many others who might otherwise not have remembered it. The answers to the question 'which publishers' large print books have you seen?' were as shown in Table 23.

There were many references to large print books other than Ulver-scroft which could not be named, but librarians probably realize that 'other' people pay less attention to publication particulars; neverthe-less even among the people who *were* willing to reply to a question-

TABLE 23

THE LINK-MEN'S ANSWERS TO THE QUESTION 'WHICH PUBLISHERS' LARGE PRINT BOOKS HAVE YOU SEEN?'

Publishers named	Misc.	Social workers, health visitors and district nurses	Doctors, ophthalmologists and opticians	Hospital librarians and other workers and volunteers	Special schools, colleges and voluntary associations for the VH	Literacy and language workers	Totals
	1	2	3	4	5	6	
Ulverscroft	71	52	34	40	33	22	252*
Magnaprint	11	5	1	9	6	3	35◊
Lythway	12	1	1	10	4	3	31
Chivers	5	2	1	7	6	2	23
New Portway	6	—	1	6	1	—	14
Watts	3	2	—	6	1	1	13
Curley	5	—	—	6	—	—	11
G K Hall	3	—	—	6	—	—	9
B and F B Society	2	1	—	1	2	—	6
Prior	2	—	—	1	2	—	5
N L B	—	3	—	—	—	—	3
Totals	120†	66	38	92°	55	31	370
No. of respondents in each group	103	65	59	53	41	25	346

* *It must be borne in mind here that the name 'Ulverscroft' appeared on the form*

† *Most of the 'other' publishers mentioned by this group were named by the WRVS Books on Wheels ladies. Twelve of the group had never seen any large print books*

° *It can be seen from these figures how many more publishers' books were known to hospital workers (not only the librarians) than to the other groups*

◊ *It is interesting that Magna came to mind more often than all the other*
publishers not named on the form and that although comments were not
specifically invited there was no evidence among the link-men of the criti-
cisms expressed by librarians

NB Firecrest and Robert Hale were mentioned twice each and the following
were each mentioned once: Cassell, Hulton, Harrap, Unwin, Viking, Keith
Jennison, William Clowes, Grolier, the Xavier Society, Magnet, Benn, JCA,
Gideons International and the Scripture Gift Mission, while others referred to
children's books, to literacy material or to American books.

naire about large print books there were 26 replies from respondents
who had never seen one, in addition to those from very many more
who could not name any publishers. Furthermore, since the vast majority had seen only the Ulverscroft series it was also possible that
some of them had seen only the earlier large format books, in which
case these would be thinking of large print and presenting it to their
contacts in those terms, if at all.

The medical group (3) in particular had obviously had little time
for library browsing, the comparative irrelevance of the books for the
language and literacy group (6) was again indicated, and considering
how important are the links between client and social worker, health
visitor or district nurse, the figures in column 2 were somewhat
depressing. It was interesting to note, however, that social workers
were the only group to mention the NLB's large print at this stage,
presumably because of braille borrowing and because dealings with
that library were often left entirely to Social Services Departments
these days. Considering that these 346 replies were all that emanated
from 1,200 supposed 'link-men' the situation could not be regarded
with complacency and it was hoped that publication of Table 23
might assist publishers and librarians when they were determining
how best to publicize the material.

Thirty-seven respondents in the Link-men Survey (11%) had read
both the Library Association's 'Reading for the Visually Handicapped'and Alison Shaw's 'Print for Partial Sight', not unexpectedly
19 of these were in the hospitals and seven were in each of Groups
3 and 5, including four of the five researchers. A further 34 respondents (10%) had read only 'Reading for the Visually Handicapped' (making 21% in all) and three others had read only 'Print for
Partial Sight'. The language and literacy workers were again understandably the least aware group with none of them having read
either, but this also applied to 87 of 97 respondents in Group 1,

52 of 65 workers in Group 2, and 45 of 56 respondents to the question in Group 3.

Effective publicity sources

We now knew how many of the respondents had seen large print books and although many were vague about details the majority had at least *seen* them. Was it the librarians' publicity methods which reached the 320 and if not, how *did* the books first come to their attention?

Two hundred and three entries were made under the heading 'via public library', which was a creditable 63% of the 320 who had seen large print books, 59% of the total 346 respondents, or 17% of the 'link-men' originally contacted. The publishers were responsible for the awareness of the next largest group and although the fact was rarely stated at this point this usually meant Ulverscroft; 75 entries were made under the heading 'via publishers', which was 23% of the 320, 22% of the total 346, or 6% of the original 1,200. Hospital libraries came third with 36 (11%, 10% and 3%) and Social Services Departments fourth with 20 (6%, 6% and 2% respectively.) The various 'other' replies were as follows: seen clients/patients/friends/ contacts reading them (17) — professional press/church newspaper/ New Beacon/reviews (10) — via a club/society for the blind/partially sighted (7) — in an OAP Home/centre (7) — forgotten (5) — on hospital wards/ brought by visitor (4) — on the radio (3) — at meetings/ conferences/training courses (3) — in a school/college library (3) — via the Library Association (2) — from a bookshop/list in shop (2) and (once each) an Education Department, an eye clinic, a literacy scheme, a book exhibition, from own enquiries and in discussion with a Chief Librarian. In a survey of link-men, meaning people who informed or who could inform potential large print book users of their existence, it was interesting to note that in so many cases the information was passed in the unexpected direction — i.e. that 17 of the 'link-men' found out themselves about the existence of the books by seeing visually handicapped people reading them!

The groups which had been *entirely* dependent on public libraries for any initial contact made with large print books were the workers in OAP Homes and centres, the Citizens' Advice Bureaux, the officials and organizers of Talking Newspapers and the language workers with immigrants, but unfortunately not all of these people used their libraries. In addition other groups which had been heavily dependent on their public libraries were the Meals on Wheels ladies, the home helps and the health visitors, though again these were not always library users. As might be expected, 15 of the hospital librarians and workers, four general practitioners and three of seven clergymen first saw the books in hospital libraries and ten of the social workers made their first contact with them via Social Services Departments.

The extent of contact with the visually handicapped

If in some cases the distribution of publicity material must be strictly limited by the time and money available, then it seemed useful to identify the areas where it could be most effective and in addition to earlier questions about the willingness to display posters and/or distribute lists most respondents were asked to estimate the *number* of their contacts who were partially sighted and also (in appropriate cases) the number with failing sight who found difficulty in reading normal print.

The 23 volunteers and workers in Group 1a who gave their replies in numbers averaged about five partially sighted contacts each and about 15 each with failing vision and difficulty in reading normal print. Sixteen workers in the Homes (1b) averaged five partially sighted contacts and 27 contacts with failing vision, some of them adding in the second case such remarks as 'all', 'most', 'almost 100% even if they don't admit it', and 'all those over 70'. Thirty-one social workers in Group 2a (many of whom worked specifically with the visually handicapped) averaged 46 partially sighted contacts each and 15 of the health visitors (2b) averaged 17. Ten of the general practitioners (3a) averaged 34 partially sighted contacts and 99 with failing vision; eight people in the ophthalmologists' group (3b) averaged 348 and 1,218 contacts and 17 opticians averaged 121 partially sighted contacts. (Low vision aid specialists were excluded here because their highly significant estimates of 5,000 − 10,000 would have distorted the others' figures.) Eight of the workers in Group 5a averaged 46 partially sighted contacts, 13 workers in 5b and 5c (considered together for this purpose) averaged 105 and four officials of the Partially Sighted Society (5e) averaged 59.

Most of the remaining groups were excluded here because too large a proportion of their replies were given in percentages or in verbal terms which were not quantifiable; some failed to answer the question, others were unable to make an estimate and the hospital workers were not asked. It must be stressed that these figures from comparatively small samples were intended as guidelines only; they could not in any case be shown as tabulated statistics because in many cases they were based only on estimates from very varied sub-groups.

A great deal depended in any case on where the line was drawn between a person registered blind but with residual vision, a registered and an unregistered partially sighted person, and a person with failing sight; it was too much to hope that all respondents — or even all groups of respondents — could have been consistent in this. Respondents in all groups experienced some confusion between the partially sighted and those with failing vision — many quoted only those registered as partially sighted and some lay workers' figures were not included above because exactly the same number appeared in each of the two columns. Since some librarians and others think and plan only in terms of the *registered* partially sighted it might be advisable to point out to them again at this stage that this number is very much smaller than the *'registerable'* partially sighted and that in any case — to quote one ophthalmic optician — 'for every partially sighted person there are about twenty with *poor sight'*.

Low vision aids

So many definitions of low vision aids have been encountered during the course of the study that ophthalmologists and opticians were asked 'how would you define a low vision aid?' and 44 respondents gave 44 different replies, which could, however, be divided into broad categories. Probably the least complicated replies were those in such general terms as 'other than an ordinary spectacle lens', 'an optical appliance to improve the vision they have', 'one having a magnifying function', 'an aid to poor vision', 'in my case a hand or stand magnifier' and 'it is a *low vision aid'*! There were many more specific replies probably likely to prove fairly incomprehensible to most laymen, such as 'any reading addition above 4.00 D', 'anything to improve reading better than N12', 'any addition over 4.00 dioptres' and 'any lens over and above a reading addition of X6' — one respondent replied 'as a misnomer! An aid for *low vision acuity* is one to assist visual performance in addition to the spectacle or contact lens correction which is best but which is inadequate'. From the researcher's own point of view probably the clearest definitions were those like 'any appliance which can be utilized to augment residual vision', 'any device used to improve vision when conventional spectacle correction is inadequate for a patient's needs', 'any piece of equipment that would improve acuity when glasses cannot help', 'an optical aid for near vision giving better reading vision than conventional reading spectacles' and 'any device which enables a partially sighted person to regain some useful vision'. (One respondent added 'they are often ugly, uncomfortable and unacceptable to the patients who often do not use those supplied to them', a remark which confirmed some of the replies given by non-readers in the Community Survey.)

General practitioners were asked whether or not there was a Low Vision Aid Clinic in their area and only 60% replied in the affirmative; it is worth mentioning, however, that some of the respondents who answered in the negative were practising in the same areas as others who replied in the affirmative, which suggested that even where it did exist the service was not always well-known even in health circles. One doctor wrote, 'there's an optician supposed to supply LVAs but our services are almost nil — detailed advice is *not* given at the Eye Hospital of this area'. When all the Group 2 workers from different parts of the country were asked the same question the results were 32 affirmative replies, 14 negative replies, and 17 respondents who did not know.

A great variety of advice was likely to have been given 'to clients who could benefit from low vision aids' by the workers in Group 2, many of whom were specialist social workers for the visually handicapped. Ten would have been referring them to a Low Vision Aid Clinic and a further six would have been referring them to their general practitioner who could do so. Eight would either have referred them to an Eye Hospital or a hospital with an Eye Clinic or told them to enquire at an Eye Hospital; six would have referred them to an ophthalmologist, six would have referred them to the Social Services Department and a further four to a social worker for the blind; two would have referred them to blind clubs or agencies and one would have referred them to an optician for a magnifier. Five would have advised them individually as follows: follow-up advice on the use of the aid and lighting, etc. (2) — the availability of a white stick and 'phone dial (1) — the need to keep the correct distance between the book and the aid, together with good lighting and the use of the right aid for the purpose (1) and 'avoid over-strain'! (1). The remainder either gave vague replies or otherwise indicated that they would not give advice, one adding that 'they're too old to adapt to them'.

The doctors responding referred very few patients annually for low vision aid prescriptions — ten was the highest number mentioned and most of those who did know of a clinic in their area referred only from two to six patients per annum; the opthalmologists, who were asked the question in reverse, averaged about 74 patients per annum referred *to* them for low vision aid prescriptions. Replies to the question 'in what proportion of cases do you complete the section of Form BD8 which asks whether a low vision aid would be helpful?' were insufficient for any conclusions to be drawn from them, though it was worthwhile recording that nevertheless they ranged from 'nil' to '100%'!

The respondents in Groups 1 and 6 did not usually know whether or not their contacts used low vision aids (other than spectacles) though 19 workers in OAP Homes did know of eight people who did so and respondents in most of the other categories each mentioned several users of magnifying glasses. Group 5 workers were asked whether or not their organizations had ever provided any low vision aids and 17 people replied in the affirmative, though in some cases the aids were only loaned and in one case they were provided only very occasionally or in cases of extreme difficulty when not available via the National Health Service.

The publishers (probably meaning mainly Ulverscroft by booklists and Chivers by advertisements) had been first to draw the attention of 23% of the *cognoscenti* to the existence of large print books and it seemed that their not inconsiderable efforts had been directed mainly towards the WRVS, the social workers, the ophthalmologists, the opticians, the hospitals, the whole of Group 5 (the special schools, colleges and voluntary associations with the exception of Talking Newspapers) and the literacy workers. More workers in some categories had first heard of the books from the publishers than had done so via their public libraries — these were the RNIB and the other societies and agencies, the special schools and colleges and the researchers. The opticians were almost equally divided, with 12 under 'public libraries' and 13 under 'publishers'; of the four who had not seen the books at all, one never used his public library and the other three used it only 'sometimes'. Possibly this suggested that the 12 whose attention had been first drawn to the books 'via their public libraries' had seen the books there in their private capacity as borrowers rather than having had any publicity material directed specifically towards them by librarians *because* they were opticians —

and of course at this stage of the enquiry this could have applied in the case of all the other workers who ticked 'via public library'.

Having discovered how many of our link-men had any information to pass on and how they *first* found out about large print books, the researcher therefore went on to investigate the specific distribution of publicity material on a regular basis to the link-men. In answer to the question 'have you ever received any publicity about large print books?' the answers and sources were as shown in Table 24, from which it can be seen that just over half of them were never contacted. Only 27 (16%) of the 171 uncontacted respondents were even aware that free lists were available from libraries and publishers; in no less than 10 sub-groups there was not one single person aware of the fact; only the 16 uncontacted social workers achieved semi-awareness as a group, with eight of them knowing and eight not knowing.

When the link-men's *first* contact with large print and their contacts as ordinary borrowers are excluded, we get a much more realistic picture about the amount of publicity material being actually distributed. It is now clear that the publishers — in addition to making the very first introduction to large print in 23% of the cases — were probably responsible overall for the distribution of one-and-a half-times as much effective publicity material as the public libraries, which is surely a situation unique to large print? Among certain very significant groups in the field of visual handicap the publishers were responsible for more than double — and in some cases three to six times — the amount of the material circulated by libraries, as can be seen from the Table.

Table 24 also shows that about half of these link-men interested enough to return questionnaires had not received any publicity material from any source whatsoever and that 72 (or 44%) of those who did so, received it very infrequently — in some cases only once, or only when specifically requested. Interviews and conversations with members of Group 5 had indicated that the group had less-than-average contact with public libraries because braille books and talking books were obtained from different sources, because normal print was usually difficult or impossible to read, because voluntary societies made so much provision for the visually handicapped and because of low expectations about the suitability of the service in their particular circumstances. Librarians attempting to provide any kind of library service for the visually handicapped would surely be well advised to make contact with these people in Group 5 and the

TABLE 24

THE LINK-MEN'S ANSWER TO THE QUESTION 'HAVE YOU EVER RECEIVED ANY PUBLICITY ABOUT LARGE PRINT BOOKS?' TOGETHER WITH SOURCES:

Groups	No	Yes	Public Library	Hospital Library	Social Services	Publishers	Other	Several times per annum	Once or twice per annum	Less than once per annum	Only on odd occasions
1 Miscellaneous	55	*43	33	4	3	14	6	15	14	1	11
2 Social workers, health visitors and district nurses	39	†26	3	2	13	◊11	10	5	4	1	16
3 Doctors, opthalmologists and opticians	38	°20	5	1	—	◊15	8	3	—	1	16
4 Hospital librarians, other workers and volunteers	16	37	12	7	1	26	1	11	20	—	4
5 Special schools, colleges and voluntary associations for the V H	9	32	4	—	2	◊25	6	10	3	—	18
6 Literacy and language workers	14	11	5	—	—	5	3	2	4	—	4
Totals	171	169	62	14	19	96	34	46	45	3	69

N B The number of replies did not balance with the number of respondents in each group because some people had received publicity material from more than one source and others failed to complete some sections of the questionnaire

* Thirty-four of the 43 were WRVS Books on Wheels volunteers, in regular touch with the libraries whose books they distributed; when these were discounted, only 9 of the remaining groups in Group 1 had received any publicity material, including only one of 19 OAP Homes and centres, one of the seven clergymen, two of nine Citizens' Advice Bureaux, one of the seven Meals on Wheels ladies and one of four home helps

† Twenty-three of the 26 were social workers; only one of six district nurses
  and two of 20 health visitors had received any publicity material at all

º Fourteen of the 20 were opticians and six were ophthalmologists; not one
  of the 13 GPs had received any publicity material whatsoever.

◊ Note the amount of publicity material directed by the publishers to these
  important groups

  The 34 'other sources were as follows: The Library Association (5) — RNIB
  and other societies for the blind (4) WRVS headquarters (4) — conferences/
  meetings/courses (3) — Partially Sighted Society (2) — professional press (2)
  — newspaper advertisements (2) — forgotten (2) and (mentioned once each)
  The DHSS, The Disabled Living Foundation, an Education Department,
  a college library, a literacy scheme, the Health Education Department of an
  AHA, a book exhibition, LVA patients, a mail order for the partially-sighted
  and an optician who worked on Ulverscroft's print

circulation of large print information might provide a suitable introduction in many cases; the researcher was unable to trace any bulk
provision including large print to any blind welfare organizations
in the West Midlands, though a collection had been *offered* to one
college for the blind. Closer liaison with at least the health visitors
and workers in OAP Homes and centres would also be an advisable
adjunct, even if it proved necessary to arrange this formally via heads
of their appropriate departments.

Publicity from link-man to client

The WRVS Books on Wheels ladies, the special schools, colleges and
societies and the hospital workers seemed to be the most likely
groups to pass on the information to their clients but no group
seemed especially *un*likely to do so. The number of visually handicapped people estimated as having been informed by these recipients
of publicity during the previous year totalled around 20,000 and
ranged from 'only 1 or 2' at one end of the scale to '5,000', a precise
'2,466' and '2,000 plus, via staff', with the average for actual
numbers quoted working out at almost 170 per respondent to the
question.

The majority of those who had passed on information of some
kind had done so to both sexes though in very many cases the
recipients were all or mostly female and in only one case were they
mostly told people of over retiring age; 34 respondents said that
though in some cases they were of all ages and in a few cases they
were younger people. (Seventy-three respondents said that they had

mostly told people of over retiring age; 34 respondents had said that they were either *all* ages or 25 years to 80 years; ten respondents had mostly informed middle-aged people and five told mostly young people between the ages of 12 years and 19 years.) A fascinating variety of people had been informed for a variety of reasons — geriatric patients, old ladies, the elderly, elderly frail, elderly library users, elderly visually handicapped, elderly with failing vision, elderly with senile eye conditions, elderly with limited concentration, old ladies with long-term fractures, the old and diabetic, the physically and mentally frail, the intelligent, the elderly housebound, housebound disabled, hospital patients, stroke patients, all patients, older patients with retained intellect, past readers, long-stay patients, psychiatric patients, introverts, patients with poor vision due to illness, patients on drugs affecting visual acuity, everyone with impaired reading vision, people without spectacles, people recovering from eye operations, Eye Hospital patients, hospital patients with eye defects, the registered blind, the registered partially sighted, the newly registered, the unregistered with poor sight, the registered blind who could read with aids or difficulty, the visually handicapped, those unable to read normal print, people unfamiliar with print, people with glaucoma, people with cataracts, people with central macular degeneration, people with poor visual acuity, people whose residual vision needed encouragement, people with *retinitis pigmentosa,* people with multiple sclerosis, LVA patients, people who will be partially sighted, parents for children, hospital staff, practitioners, ophthalmic trainees, social workers, nursing staff, WRVS volunteers, students, the general public, school children, young adults undergoing remedial education, adults with literacy problems, cases of poor literacy, new readers, people who found small print hard, near-independent readers, slow readers, students of low academic level, those whose language was not English, black people, literacy tutors, volunteers, the occasional young, all ages and a cross-section — which ought to hearten any large print publisher who perseveres to the end of the list!

Untapped publicity potential

Of the 171 respondents who had never received any publicity material 138 or 81% would welcome it, only 30 would not do so and three failed to reply to the question. (The five in OAP Homes who replied in the negative made such remarks as 'it would be up to the

chief' or 'it wouldn't be my decision'; the two Meals on Wheels
ladies said 'we're in and out in five minutes' and the two home helps
said, 'I can't see that I'd use it' or words to that effect.) No group
was particularly prominent among the 30 respondents who would
not welcome publicity material though in general it was noticed that
most of these responses seemed to be from among the better-
informed individuals — the group of 27 uncontacted people who
already knew that free lists were available and the overall group of
160 who were aware that large print classics were available from the
NLB.

The 171 people who had never received any publicity material
would be likely to display or distribute anything received in future
in a similar manner to the other group; again it would be to both
sexes but to many more females than males, again it would be to all
age groups but mainly to the elderly, and most of the potential recipients and their reasons for need were so remarkably similar as to
obviate the need for repetition. In addition, however, the following
were also mentioned: arthritics, the newly retired, Asian ladies
learning English, all the community centres in the area, the mentally
backward, patients suffering from nervous disease, people attending
eye clinics, people of moderate income who did not possess reading
lamps, doctors using the hospital, OAP club attenders, people with
wrong spectacle lenses, patients lacking stimulation, all diabetics, bed
and chair bound people, spastics and people who had lost concentration ability.

Ninety-one of the 171 uncontacted people (53%) would be willing
to display a poster about large print and 104 (61%) would be willing
to distribute lists to their contacts. Many of these respondents indicated that they would be willing and able to publicize it by both
methods and only 27 (16%) were unwilling or unable to do either. In
approaching these groups with such publicity methods in mind it
seemed that common sense would usually be a safe indicator of
success — the very few people who replied in the negative were
mostly workers in a junior capacity in OAP Homes who needed to
seek the approval of their seniors, hard-pressed Meals on Wheels
ladies who must of necessity and for obvious reasons keep their visits
short (and who should only be asked to pass on names), hospital
librarians whose libraries had no section for patients and (in the case
of posters) various workers who had no permanent premises visited
by their clients.

It was extremely significant that so many people particularly in Groups 2 and 3 had never received any publicity material and that — though these might be considered by many as overworked professional people, too busy to involve themselves in such matters — a large proportion of them indicieted that they would be willing to display posters and/or to distribute lists. For example, not one of the 13 GPs had received publicity material from any source whatsoever, yet 11 of them would be willing to display a poster and eight would even be prepared to distribute lists; only one of the 13 replied in the negative. Of 15 previously uncontacted opticians 14 would welcome publicity, 12 would display a poster and 12 would distribute lists. The display of six posters and the distribution of lists by four ophthalmologists could have been achieved by making such a request to nine who had never been contacted; ten posters and 12 list distributions would have resulted from an approach to 16 uncontacted social workers; 14 posters and 12 list distributions could have been achieved by an approach to 18 uncontacted health visitors (of a total of 20!) and eight posters and 12 list distributions from an approach to 18 uncontacted workers in OAP Homes and centres. The situation would probably have been different in the case of the non-respondents, however, and this sobering thought must be borne in mind.

All 346 respondents were asked whether or not they would be willing to draw attention to a specimen large print volume if one could be provided for them and again the resulting replies were most encouraging. Two hundred and fifty-two respondents (73%) stated that they would be willing to do so, only 72 (21%) would be unwilling or unable to do so, nine were either uncertain or felt that the question was not applicable in their circumstances and 13 failed to complete this section of the questionnaire. Again Groups 2 and 3 both responded very favourably, with 50 of the 61 respondents to the question in Group 2 and 50 of the 56 in Group 3 being willing and able to do so (82% and 89% respectively.) Several of the 252 respondents who replied in the affirmative added that they already did display the books, however, and several of the 72 who replied in the negative added that they would be unable rather than unwilling to do so. From this entire section it was clear that there were large pools of untapped resources and goodwill available to the publicity-minded, but that being a link-man involved a two-way exchange of information.

NON-USE AND NON-USERS

The isolation factor

Why did some people read and other people not read? What made a reader? It was considered necessary to isolate some of the factors thought to be connected with this very basic but complex question first before attempting to discover the main reasons why some of the *visually handicapped* were non-readers, or non-readers of large print books.

When all 515 elderly and visually handicapped respondents in Survey C were classified either as readers or as non-readers it was necessary to make a subjective judgement from the information on the entire form and therefore this could not possibly be 100% accurate. It certainly did not indicate the type or the amount of reading being done, since some readers 'sometimes have spasms of reading' and others read 'as many as I can get hold of'. The term 'readers' included braille and Moon readers and also people reading only newspapers and magazines, though not those undertaking obligatory school-work only. The term was used in its widest sense and certainly did *not* mean only readers of books — it could more clearly be defined as *'readers by inclination'*.

Since age, sex and life-style were likely to be influential factors when considering reading or non-reading habits (not necessarily connected at this stage to the reading or non-reading of large print books) the two groups were therefore analysed initially by these characteristics, as shown in the sample analysis. It must be remembered, however, that while many — such as all questionnaires except those from schools — *were* random results in respect of life-style others were the direct consequence of the methods used, e.g. interviewing in residential or in one-sex or one-age group establishments. These figures can not be seen, therefore, to bear a specific relationship to the composition of society or the group as a whole.

In all, 191 respondents lived alone and it seemed reasonable to suppose that solitude might encourage reading — that a higher proportion of these would be readers than of the respondents living with others. Table 25 shows the group under consideration, with the 262 postal questionnaires excluded from the lower part b) because of the motivation factor previously mentioned — 222 of these were classified as readers (c. 84.7%) and this barely varied between those living alone and those living with others. Those interviewed personally and shown in the lower part of the table were selected at random and were therefore more reliable in this particular respect.

Later in their interviews OAP *Home* residents had mostly given as a reason for not using a reading machine 'lack of interest in reading' whereas OAPs in the community had mostly expressed a fear of gadgets or mechanical things, which seemed to point to the isolation factor, yet the final result was both inconclusive and disappointing — probably because of the inclusion of other variables and the inability to isolate the factor of living alone. If the sample had not included other factors such as visual handicap and studying then the findings for the sample of the elderly would have been even more unexpected — 66.6% of the elderly living with others being readers and only 54.8% of those living alone. Were the answers of Home residents affected by the proximity of others? Was reading material — magazines, newspapers, paperbacks, bulk loans, etc. — more readily accessible in residential Homes? Would the results have been different for *book* reading alone? Certainly those who lived alone and *were* readers did read many more books than those who lived with others and were readers, which is mentioned elsewhere in the report and already known by librarians in charge of housebound services. This part of the study did not help to reveal the elusive factor and had to be regarded as a failed experiment.

Another attempt was made to study this isolation factor when everyone was asked, 'Are you in touch with any friends or relatives nearby?' Clearly, however, as this was of less significance to people living communally than to those living alone and 'nearby' meant different things to different age groups, this was destined to be a second abortive attempt, as is shown by the figures in Table 26.

Of the 262 motivated respondents who replied by post 200 stated that they were in touch with friends and/or relatives nearby and 62 stated that they were not. 167 (approximately 83.5%) of the group 'in touch' and 55 (approximately 88.7%) of the more isolated group were readers, mainly underlining the proportion of readers that *was* motivated to reply and, though being a step in the right direction, proving very little else.

TABLE 25(a)

THE ISOLATION FACTOR – READING AMONG THE ELDERLY AND VISUALLLY
HANDICAPPED GROUPS CONTACTED IN SURVEY C

AT a) SHOWING THE PROPORTION OF THE 515 WHO LIVED ALONE, INCLUDING
THE MOTIVATED POSTAL RESPONDENTS

Groups	Living with others		Living alone		Totals
	M	F	M	F	
Elderly in community (incl. V H)	11	18	16	88	133
Elderly in OAP Homes (incl. V H)	13	54	–	–	67
V H interviewed (incl. elderly)	23	23	5	2	53
V H questionnaires (incl. elderly)	83	99	15	65	262
Totals	130	194	36	155	515

TABLE 25(b)

AND AT b) SHOWING ONLY THE 253 RESPONDENTS INTERVIEWED PERSONALLY
AND THEREFORE CONSIDERED A MORE RELIABLE SAMPLE WHERE READING
AND NON-READING HABITS WERE CONCERNED:

Groups	Living with others		Living alone		Totals
	Readers	Non-readers	Readers	Non-readers	
Elderly in community (incl. V H)	17	12	57	47	133
Elderly in OAP Homes (incl. V H)	47	20	–	–	67
V H interviewed (incl. elderly)	14	32*	3	4	53
Totals	78	64	60	51	253
Percentages	54.9%	45.1%	54.1%	45.9%	100%

*Note the 32 visually handicapped people interviewed, mostly resident in
schools, colleges and a Home, who differed from the other groups

TABLE 26

A SECOND ABORTIVE ATTEMPT AT STUDYING THE EFFECT OF ISOLATION UPON
READING HABITS, WHEN THE 'RELIABLE' RESPONDENTS WERE ASKED 'ARE
YOU IN TOUCH WITH ANY FRIENDS OR RELATIVES NEARBY?'

Groups	Yes in touch		No, not in touch		Totals
	Readers	Non-readers	Readers	Non-readers	
Elderly in community (incl. V H)	43	37	31	22	133
Elderly in OAP Homes (incl. V H)	25	7	22	13	67
V H interviewed (incl. elderly)	10	23	7	13	53
Totals	78	67	60	48	253
Percentages	53.8%	46.2%	55.6%	44.4%	100%

Before finally dismissing Tables 25 and 26, however, one of the
most interesting facts to be reinforced by these figures was the
number of older people who did live alone and/or had no contact
with friends or relatives, in spite of the fact that 67 of the elderly
plus many of the visually handicapped were interviewed in residential situations. When asked whether or not the respondents attended
any meetings or gatherings with other people in a similar position,
the replies in Table 27 were forthcoming and it is hoped that the list
might prove useful to librarians and others attempting to contact
visually handicapped people, though many obviously lead very quiet
or private lives. There were more females than males among the latter
and more readers than non-readers, but not more than was proportionate.

Leisure activities

When asked about their main hobbies and leisure activities, a much
greater difference in replies was conspicuous between age groups
than between the visually handicapped and those able to read normal
print.

As might be expected, the very elderly in residential care named
the lowest number of leisure activities, in spite of probing by the
interviewer — 20 of them had either none at all or only radio and/or

TABLE 27

THE MEETINGS AND GATHERINGS ATTENDED BY THE ELDERLY AND VISUALLY
HANDICAPPED RESPONDENTS

Meetings/gatherings attended	Elderly in community (incl. VH)	Elderly in OAP Homes (incl. VH)	VH interviewed (incl. elderly)	VH question-naires (incl. elderly)	Total
60+ clubs, day centres, lunch clubs	110*	5	2	11	128
Blind/P S clubs, classes, societies, braille groups, rehabilitation	13	3	19	64	99
Church/clubs, choirs, Salvation Army, Mothers' Union, Sunday school, Bible groups, Scouts, Guides	38	15	7	6	66
Hobbies clubs, drama, music, sport, debating, talks, theatre, CSP, athletics, allotment, local history, political, radio, dancing, numismatics	4	1	24	10	39
Social/welfare clubs, Social Services, community centres, private firms	2	1	8	20	31
Bingo, whist drives, bridge clubs, chess	12	7	6	3	28
Classes-art, cookery, woodwork, typing, career, crafts, WEA	5	2	8	5	20
Group outings, concerts, parties	—	13	4	—	17
Handicapped/disabled/ PHAB, hospital/clinic group, Hard of Hearing Club.	4	—	—	11	15

Meetings/gatherings attended	Elderly in community (incl. VH)	Elderly in OAP Homes (incl. VH)	VH interviewed (incl. elderly)	VH questionnaires (incl. elderly)	Total
Other Townswomen's Guilds, committees, Womens' Institute, Rotary, charitable, Housewives National Register etc	—	1	6	5	12
Pubs	—	5	1	—	6
None at all	14*	35	28	152	229

*It must be remembered that most of this group was <u>contacted</u> in day centres and lunch clubs and that many listed more than one type of gathering. (Several of the younger visually-handicapped respondents remarked that there were no clubs or groups suitable for young people)

television and 37 had less than three. ('I'm 90 now and waiting for my harp! Surely I'm entitled to do nothing at all now, after a lifetime of hard work?') The remaining 30 named three or more activities but they usually included radio and television as two of them.

The elderly living in the community (also interviewed and probed) named a greater variety of leisure activities than those in Homes: 70 named three or more, usually including radio and television and 63 named less than three — of whom 29 had either none at all or only radio and television.

Very many more interests were named by the younger visually handicapped respondents, even those who replied by post and who presumably listed less than they would have done if interviewed. Their interests were as many and as varied as those of their fully-sighted peers, including such activities as train-spotting, ornithology, archery, numismatics, skateboarding and mountaineering, for example, and this is a fact to be borne in mind when making library provision for them. The 37 people of under 60 years who were interviewed named almost 100 *different* hobbies.

Age was clearly more significant than visual ability in this respect, however. The older visually handicapped respondents replied in much the same way as the older non-visually handicapped respondents and many of the very old did nothing at all. Four visually

handicapped old ladies who were interviewed in a residential Home
for the blind had no hobbies or interests at all and also disliked
radio and television, saying 'I just sit here and try not to hear it',
'I've never been used to it' and 'I've worked hard all my life and I've
always wanted to be a lady of leisure.'

TABLE 28

LIST OF HOBBIES AND LEISURE ACTIVITIES OF ALL THE ELDERLY AND
VISUALLY HANDICAPPED GROUPS (SURVEY C) IN ORDER BY THE NUMBER OF
TIMES MENTIONED

Elderly in the community (incl. VH) 133		Elderly in OAP Homes (incl. VH) 67		VH interviewed (incl. elderly) 53		VH question-naires (incl. elderly) 262	
Reading	72	Television	41	Radio	25	Reading	117
Television	68	Reading	35	Reading	22	Music	42
Radio	60	Radio	30	Television	20	Gardening	41
Knitting	24	Knitting	21	Music	20	Radio	40
Clubs/centres	21	Church	7	Records	11	Television	35
Gardening	19	Walking	7	Knitting	9	Knitting	28
Sewing	14	Sewing	7	Sport	9	Walking/rambling	23
Housework	10	Helping in Home	7	Talking books	9	Swimming	23
Bingo	9			Visiting	8	Watching sport	19
Walking	8	Drinking	5	Football	7		
Crafts	8	Crocheting	5	Walking	6	Records	16
Visiting	8	Bingo	4	Learning Moon/braille	6	Football	15
Crocheting	6	Talking	4			Cookery	12
Travelling	6	Crosswords	4	Charity work	5	Dancing	11
Cookery	6	Garden	4	Swimming	5	Sewing	11
Cards	6	Embroidery	3	Church	5	Correspon-dence	10
Music	5	Horse-racing	3	Travelling	4		
Animals/birds	5	Music	3	Typing	4	Travelling	10
Outings	5	Window-shopping	3	Blind and P S clubs	4	Charity work	9
Horse-racing	5	Art	2	Crocheting	3	Cycling	9
Church	5	Mending	2	Cricket	3	Horses/riding	8
Crosswords	4	Dominoes	2	Snooker	3	Athletics	8

Elderly in the Community (incl. VH) 133		Elderly in OAP Homes (incl. VH) 67		VH interview (incl. elderly) 53		VH question-naires (incl. elderly) 262	
Entertaining	4	Cards	2	Sewing	3	Visiting	8
Dancing	4	Draughts	2	Chess	3	Crafts	8
Talking	4	Crafts	2	Bridge	3	Tape recording	8
Watching sport	3	and		Crafts	3	Cricket	7
Charity work	3	Chess, Talks,		Politics	3	Painting	7
Riding in car	2	Correspondence, Hymn singing,		Cookery	3	Blind and P S clubs	7
Playing musical instrument	2	Politics, Visiting,		Model-making	3	Drama	6
Dominoes	2	Watching sports, Concerts,		Meals out	3	Talking books	6
Toy making	2	Cookery,		Amateur radio	3	Embroidery	5
Basketry	2	Travelling, Riding on buses,		Playing musical instrument	3	Cards	5
and		Weaving,		Running	2	Crocheting	4
Talks, Religion, Correspondence,		Blind classes, Charity work.		Fishing	2	Playing musi-cal instrument	4
Typing, Camping,				Cycling	2	History	4
Mending, Bowls,				Poetry	2	Committees	4
Baby-sitting, Records,				Gardening	2	DIY	4
Macrame, Bridge,				Athletics	2	Theatre	4
Concerts, DIY, Sailing,				Dancing	2	Dog breeding/ training	4
Mothers' Union, Keep Fit, Cycling				DIY	2	Cinema	3
Flower Shows,				Drama	2	Art	3
Parties, Drinking, Sunday school				Debating	2	Crosswords	3
teaching, blind classes, talking				Committees	2	Languages	3
books, occult				Animals	2	Antiques/ china	3
				Religion	2	Archery	3
				Work (social)	2	Housework	3
				Public speaking	2	Canework	3
				Wood-carving	2	Poetry	3
				Outings	2	Model railways	3
				Etymology	2	Drawing	3
				and		Night classes	3
				Tape recording, Electronics,			

Elderly in the Community (incl. VH) 133	Elderly in OAP Homes (incl. VH) 67	VH interview (incl. elderly) 53	VH question- naires (incl. elderly) 262	
		Quizzes, Languages, Theatre, Tlks, Train- spotting, Bowls, Breeding birds, Philately, Num- ismatics, Bingo, Cards, Whist drives, Dominoes, Collecting (Beer- mats), Nigh classes, Yoga, Housework, Canoeing, Camp- ing, Squash, Bad- minton, Volley- ball, Riding, Gymnastics, Golf, Trampolin- ing, Nature study, Skating, Rowing, Engineering, Basketry, Family life, Leatherwork, Sunday school teaching, Dress- making, Play- group organizing	Youth clubs	3
			Social clubs	3
			Philately	3
			Bingo	2
			Discos	2
			60+ clubs	2
			Politics	2
			Sociology	2
			Current affairs	2
			Photography	2
			Talking	2
			Typing	2
			Collecting (postcards)	2
			Model-making	2
			Driving	2
			Table tennis	2
			Tennis	2
			Fishing	2
			Camping	2
			Sailing	2
			Choir singing	2
			House plants	2
			Wrestling	2
			Running	2
			Wild life	2
			and	
			Wine-making, First Aid, Economics, Consumer affairs, Mountaineering, Basketball, Judo, Boating,	

Elderly in the Community (incl. VH) 133	Elderly in OAP Homes (incl. VH) 67	VH interviewed (incl. elderly) 53	VH question- naires (incl. elderly) 262
			Tapestry, Orni- thology, Toy making, Green- house culture, Bowls, Skate- boarding, Badminton, Weight-lifting, Gymnastics, Snooker, Breed- ing budgies, Rock climbing, Toy cars, Row- ing, Speedway, Canoeing, Weav- ing, Bus-rides, Opera, Needle- work, Pottery, Philosophy, Motor repairs, Science, Electri- city, Yoga, Archaeology, Bridge, Jig- saws, Church, Real ale, Kite flying, Domi- noes, Womens' Institute, Folk dancing, Inven- ting, Chemistry Whist drives, Working with children, Reviewing books, Engineering, Vintage cars, Helping on farm, Girls!

The question had been asked in order to ascertain whether or not a high degree of activity and a large number of competing interests could be shown to reduce the likelihood of reading, but this did not prove to be the mystery ingredient. Instead of any indication that busy people tended to have *less* time or inclination for reading, the results were mixed and inconclusive; in fact what was clearly revealed was a sizeable group of (usually elderly) people who had a great deal of time, who had very little to do and who *still* did not read.

Having extracted details of these hobbies and interests from all respondents, further use is made of the information by listing it in Table 28 as a guide for publishers, librarians and others interested in their welfare. This table listing the leisure activities of a comparatively small proportion of the visually handicapped gives some indication of the non-fiction range required even if readers were to be able to read only about their *hobbies!*

Education and employment

At the end of most interviews people were asked their school-leaving age and the nature of their employment (or past employment) if the information had not emerged spontaneously during the course of the interview and if it was unlikely to cause embarrassment or give offence; in some cases the former was estimated from other answers. As these questions might have proved a deterrent in print they were omitted from the questionnaire forms, therefore Table 29 shows only the results among the three groups interviewed.

TABLE 29(a)

EDUCATION OF ELDERLY AND VISUALLY HANDICAPPED RESPONDENTS

Left (or would leave) full-time education at the age of:

Groups	15 or under	16	17	18	19 or over	Unknown	Total
Elderly in community (incl. VH)	77	10	3	3	3	33	131*
Elderly in OAP Homes (incl. VH)	51	6	2	2	1	5	67
VH interviewed (incl. elderly)	13	15†	3†	11†	7†	4	53
Totals	141	31	8	16	11	44	251*

* 2 people did not ever attend school

† Some of the people who had stayed (or were staying) on at school after sixteen did so to receive special ordinary level education rather than higher education

TABLE 29(b)

PAST OR PRESENT EMPLOYMENT

Groups	Higher profes-sional	Lower profes-sional	Clerical admini-strative	Skilled/ semi-skilled	Unskilled/ manual	Unknown	Never employ-ed
Elderly in community (incl. VH)	—	13	17	15	47	38	3
Elderly in OAP Homes (incl. VH)	—	3	6	5	32	16	5
VH inter-viewed (incl. elderly)	—	11	7	2	5	5	23*
Totals	—	27	30	22	84	59	31*

* including 20 interviewed at school or college

Education and social class are usually considered to be important factors where reading habits are concerned. Table 29 shows that few of the respondents went on to higher education and that the majority (over 68% of those classified) were known or estimated to have left school at fifteen years or under, as might be expected since the majority were elderly people. It is probable that the actual number and percentage was even higher, as professional status was more often achieved by part-time study in the past. None of the 'higher professions' were represented and unskilled manual workers were in the majority in both elderly groups and in the total sample — only the visually handicapped group interviewed had more people doing 'lower professional' work than manual work, many of them being social workers.

If the supposition that education and social class are influential factors were to be reinforced, then the sample would have included more non-readers than readers and this was not the case; furthermore many of the early school-leavers were readers and many of the students failed to regard reading as a pleasure. It is obvious that an inconclusive result from such a small sample could not negate widely held theories about education and social class, however, so we had to continue looking for the other factors which caused our group to differ.

Attitudes to reading

If having higher education, living in isolation and having few conflicting leisure interests could not be proved to produce a higher-than-average proportion of readers — using the term again in its widest sense — then what else should be tested? An attempt was made to classify readers and non-readers by family attitudes to reading and this finally resulted in a breakthrough. Respondents were asked 'how was reading regarded in your family when you were young? Would you say that it was discouraged, allowed or encouraged?' Table 30 shows the gratifying results, which clearly underlined one of the important effects of a good start in life — lasting in most cases right through the retirement years, as was noted earlier among the residents in OAP Homes.

When interviewing, it was noticeable that more of the younger respondents than of the very old ones were encouraged to read, but this age bias was slightly less marked among the visually handicapped. Almost all of the old people who had been discouraged from reading when they were young mentioned large families, especially females, who had been expected to help in the home and were thought to be wasting time if they were seen reading. 'These things [reading, etc.] run in families and we were too poor for time-wasting', 'I was always brought up to sew in my spare time' and 'there were too many of us for that!' Until a rapport had been established some of them were ashamed to admit that they *had* been discouraged and therefore it is likely that some of the postal respondents who had been discouraged would mark their forms 'allowed'†. Even without allowing for this supposed swing, however, the results were still very much more positive than those discussed earlier and since so many visually handicapped people are elderly no doubt one of the reasons why some of them do not read has been revealed.

Non-reading specifically among the visually handicapped

Among the visually handicapped respondents by questionnaire the 21 non-readers encouraged to read and the nine non-readers allowed to read included 19 elderly people and five in their teens. Vision was the stated reason in 18 cases, lack of interest in seven cases (five in

TABLE 30

THE EFFECTS UPON READING HABITS OF FAMILY ATTITUDES TO READING —
515 REPLIES TO THE QUESTION 'HOW WAS READING REGARDED IN YOUR
FAMILY WHEN YOU WERE YOUNG? WOULD YOU SAY IT WAS DISCOURAGED,
ALLOWED OR ENCOURAGED?'

Groups	Discouraged		Allowed		Encouraged		Total
	Present readers	Non-readers	Present readers	Non-readers	Present readers	Non-readers	
Elderly in community (incl. VH)	21	35	20	18	33	6*	133
Elderly in OAP Homes (incl. VH)	10	19	7	8	19	4*	67
VH interviews (incl. elderly)	5	8	6	9	15	10	53
VH questionnaires (incl. elderly)	5	10	71†	9	146	21	262
Totals	41	72	104	44	213	41	515
Percentages	36%	64%	70%	30%	84%	16%	100%

NB Replies by questionnaire have been included here because the fact that so
many were readers is irrelevant when we were trying to discover why people
read or did not read.

* All four of these elderly people in the Homes and three of the elderly people
living in the community were severely visually handicapped; two were registered
blind

their teens and two over 80 years) and three were deterred by slow
reading ability.

This led on to these obvious but previously unmentioned deterrents to reading (in its widest sense) among those who were visually
handicapped — the nature and extent of the visual handicap itself,
sometimes further complicated by physical handicap. The following
replies were revealing examples which merited inclusion because they
were typical of many more: 'Reading is too uncomfortable for me. I

can read with very powerful magnification, but I'm too slow to keep up an interest in the story' — 'it's too laborious and my eye gets tired quite quickly' — 'I can only manage in spells' — 'I can read, but I don't. I'm learning braille but I don't read in it — you forget what a word was by the time you reach the end of it!' — 'everything blurs as it magnifies' — 'I don't read anything that I don't *have* to read — it's too much of a performance and I always get a headache anyway' — 'I didn't get to pleasure-reading speed with braille and just professional stuff with an LVA' — 'reading is strictly for business purposes now — there's no pleasure in it!' — 'I can only read a page or two and then I feel a bit sick and don't persevere — its such an effort' — 'reading's no pleasure any more — it's sheet hard work' — 'enlargement of words has gone beyond the optimum' — 'reading's too slow to be pleasant. That's why I like poetry; that's *better* for being read slowly' — I can read braille but I'm not too good so I can't be bothered' — 'I hate wearing telescopic spectacles' — 'I only read absolutely necessary information matter' — 'my fingers are less sensitive since I started having strokes' — 'it's hard work, so I only read mail and notices' — 'I only learned to read at fourteen so I'm very slow' — 'my sense of touch isn't what it used to be, so I can read very little braille now' and 'I used to read a great deal but I never learned braille I only went blind five years ago' (80 year-old).

Clearly, then, such factors as difficulty, inconvenience, discomfort, slowness of speed and lack of pleasure were all important reasons why many visually handicapped people read neither print, braille nor Moon as a leisure activity. An extension in greater depth of this part of the study on reading by a researcher with optical training, qualifications and experience would be enlightening; someone coming into regular professional contact with the visually handicapped would also be ideally situated for the collection of a much larger sample in less time without inconvenience to the interviewees and would be qualified to assess both the disability and performance.

The non-use of libraries

Early in the survey it became very apparent that the terms 'readers' (even 'book readers') and 'library users' were not synonymous and that there were many more people classified as 'readers' or 'readers by inclination' than were library users. Since one of the main subjects of the study was large print books which were only widely available in public libraries, it was considered advisable to follow the

investigation of reasons for non-reading with an investigation of the
use and reasons for the non-use of public libraries.

Respondents were asked 'do you use your public library?' and the
replies were categorized as regularly, sometimes or never. Even *this*
straightforward question was complicated by the fact that negative
replies were often given by housebound users unable to get to the
actual building and also by users of community libraries in such
places as church halls and of bulk loans in Homes, clubs and centres;
many of these simply did not realize that these *were* parts of the
library service, which is surely an indication that a little self-adver-
tising would be justified in these areas? It was possible to correct
these replies in the case of the interviewees from the remainder of
the information given (and this was often but not always possible in
the case of the postal respondents) but in all the circumstances it
is safer to regard the statistics for the postal group as approximate
(See Table 31).

The proportion of library users among these potential large print
readers was very much lower than the 48% suggested by the survey
with the general public in the same areas (Table 21) though it is
interesting to note that ·when the motivated postal respondents were
included experimentally, the proportion then became remarkably
similar. Table 31 highlights one very obvious reason why *some* of the
179 (71%) or 262 potential readers did not read large print books,
though it is not possible to estimate from these figures alone how
many were non-users of libraries because of a lack of interest in reading books and how many were non-users for other reasons, e.g. inaccessibility, dissatisfaction or the expectation that print reading
would be impossible — some had said that they would have used them
had tapes and records been available. A few visually handicapped
people did not know where their libraries were or 'where to get the
large print books from' and one replied, 'I get them in shops because
I don't know where the library is'. Student non-users replied, 'I
don't find it interesting', 'they have not got the sort of books I like'
and 'they do not cover the years 10-20 with large print'.

Of the 253 users, 150 had books out at the time (mainly those
who considered themselves regular users and whose information
seemed more positive and reliable) and 103 did not. Of the 262 non-
users, 122 had never used a public library at any time (79 of the
elderly and 43 of the visually handicapped of all ages, including a significant proportion of the older ones). The 140 non-users who *had*
used a public library in the past were asked why they did not

TABLE 31

TWO HUNDRED AND FIFTY-THREE RELIABLE ANSWERS TO THE QUESTION 'DO YOU USE YOUR PUBLIC LIBRARY?' BY ELDERLY AND VISUALLY HANDI–CAPPED INTERVIEWEES ONLY

Groups	Regularly	Sometimes	Never		Totals
Elderly in community (incl. VH)	17	19	97†	(73%)	133
Elderly in OAP Homes (incl. VH)	10	11	46	(69%)	67
VH interviewed (incl. elderly)	10	7	36	(68%)	53
Questionnaires* (incl. elderly)	97	82	83	(32%)◊	262
Totals incl.*	134	119	262	(51%)	515
Reliable totals	37 (14½%)	37 (14½%)	179	(71%)	253

29%

◊ The postal respondents would not be expected to include as high a percentage as non-library users as the random groups

† The elderly in the community were at a disadvantage when compared with the elderly in residential Homes which mostly had bulk loans available on the premises, but this was balanced to a certain extent by the fact that those in the community were on average slightly younger and more active

continue to do so and they gave the reasons listed in Table 32. Some interviewees were obviously saddened that they could no longer use their libraries; as one of them remarked 'it used to be one of the pleasures of my life, choosing my own books'.

Travel and accessibility

Respondents in Survey C were asked the distance from home to their nearest library, whether or not a convenient 'bus service existed, how they travelled there (or would have to travel there) and whether there were any difficult main roads to cross. Table 33 shows the results for those who replied to these questions and here in general 'user' was taken to mean 'user of the actual library building' (more in line with respondents' own replies); users and non-users of bulk loans to Homes and users of housebound services were included in Category A in Table 33a and in Category B in Table 33b, however.

TABLE 32

REASONS GIVEN BY THE 140 EX-LIBRARY USERS FOR NO LONGER USING A LIBRARY (OFTEN MORE THAN ONE REASON PER PERSON)

Reasons	Elderly in community (incl. VH)	Elderly in OAP Homes (incl. VH)	VH inter- viewed (incl. VH)	VH question- naires (incl. VH)	Totals
Visual problems	7	6	15	31	59
Housebound/disabled/ can't get to library/ Not available in Home or centre	35*	6	2	11	54
To slow/lost interest in reading/ gave up when busy	3	3	1	12	19
Moved away from familiar library	6	4	5	3	18
Old/unsatisfactory branch/books	4	—	—	7	11
Own books/braille library/postal book club	—	1	1	7	9
Various other reasons†	2	3	2	5	12
Totals	57	23	26	76	182

* The proportion here should surely be a cause for concern and could be borne in mind when planning/financing/publicizing housebound services and bulk loans to Homes, clubs and centres for the elderly and disabled. Incidentally, one handicapped old lady who no longer used the library because she was unable to get there was recommended to the librarian by her home help for the housebound service 'but it was no good' she said, — 'they said I needed to go in personally to request the housebound service and I can't get there!'

† The various other reasons given were concentration failure, poor reading ability, apprehension about going into a library building, the lack of records or tapes, library hours too short owing to working hours, only reading when alone, and only using the library in the past to read newspapers.

NB It is interesting to note that so few people gave dissatisfaction with their library or with the books as a reason for not using the library, yet at other stages of the form or interview, several people differentiated between the range of large print books in existence and the range stocked in their libraries and there were other forms with remarks such as 'the large print books in my branch are only changed once a year' — 'the lady should help find the books' — 'I'd like more large print to be kept at the library' — 'I can't read any longer and my library doesn't get cassettes, which is a great pity' — I can read all those I'm interested in in about three to four months' — 'according to booklists many [large print books] are available but they never seem to be in the library' — 'the library I used to use had records and tapes but this one only has books' and 'the top tier of six and the floor level are not suitable places to keep books for partially sighted people'

TABLE 33(a)

REPLIES BY THE ELDERLY AND VISUALLY HANDICAPPED GROUPS TO THE QUESTIONS 'HOW FAR AWAY IS YOUR NEAREST LIBRARY?'

Groups	Users			Non-Users				Totals
	A Under ½ mile	B ½ — 1 mile	C Over 1 mile	A Under ½ mile	B ½ — 1 mile	C Over 1 mile	D Un-known	
Elderly in community (incl. VH)	13	4	11	22	16	52*	15	133
Elderly in OAP Homes (incl. VH)	20°	—	1	35†	—	7	4	67
VH inter-viewed (incl. elderly)	6	1	10	11	5	10	10$^\diamond$	53
VH Question-naires (incl. elderly)	87°	49	42	18	35	25	2	258
Totals	126	54	64	86	56	94	31	511

* Many of these referred to the distance as an impossible one for them to travel

◇ The 10 included one whose home library had 'been knocked down'

o Note the tendency in these groups for increased use as distance decreased

† Indicative of the state of mind of the residents in this advanced age group

TABLE 33(b)

AND 'IS THERE A CONVENIENT 'BUS SERVICE?'

Groups	Users			Non-Users				Totals
	A Yes	B No need	C No	A Yes	B No need	C No	D Unknown	
Elderly in community (incl. VH)	12	7	9	16	15	55*	19	133
Elderly in Homes (incl. VH)	1	20	—	—	35†	7	4	67
VH interviewed (incl. elderly)	12	3	2	10	7	13	6◊	53
VH questionnaires (incl. elderly)	103	20	55	46	—	31	3	258
Totals	128	50	66	72	57	106	32	511

*   The elderly non-users unable to get to the library

◊   Including the one whose home library had 'been knocked down'

†   The same 35 very old residents

The questions about access, distance, convenience and travel to libraries (valid among the majority of Large Print User Study respondents) were asked during early interviews in the Homes but later discontinued, which coincided with the preliminary advice of the authority's Research and Development Officer. The questions were found to be inappropriate in these Homes, where so many Zimmers, sticks and wheelchairs were in use, where so many people were both elderly *and* visually handicapped by our definition, where so few of the residents got out into the community on a regular basis for any reason whatsoever and where so few of the interviewees used library building or knew of 'bus routes. It was finally accepted by the researcher that it was rarely possible and/or likely for the aged and infirm residents who had qualified for care in this Local Authority's Homes to visit libraries far afield and that this was a safe assumption to make.

The result seemed at first to be fairly inconclusive except for the postal questionnaires (and except, of course, for the residents in Homes) but as specific interviewing locations did not complicate the issue in the case of the postal responses these were probably the most reliable responses in this particular case. It was also very probable that fewer of the population lived nearer than '½ to one mile' away from a library than lived further away, therefore the numbers in column A for both users and non-users were likely to be a higher proportion of the population as a whole than were those in columns B and C. All things being equal, taking this factor into consideration one would expect less respondents in the two columns A than in the other columns.

Several elderly users said that they would use the library *more* if it were nearer and many elderly non-users living in the community* referred to the distance as an impossible one for them to travel; fortunately this *was* confirmed by the figures. Postal respondents and the elderly in Homes (each in the user category)○ also demonstrated this same understandable tendency, i.e. that the nearer the library was to their homes the more likely it was to be used (particularly by the elderly rather than the younger visually handicapped).

The 35 non-users in residential care† where bulk loans were available were mostly indicative of the state of mind of the residents in this advanced age group. Nevertheless, it was clear that some stalwarts of all ages would travel a great distance to get to a library if they were able to do so, while others failed to use one in the next road; it must be remembered, however, that half a mile was probably as prohibitive to many elderly and handicapped people as fifty-miles would have been to the younger and more able-bodied.

From Table 33b it appeared that the availability of 'bus services was of at least as great (and perhaps slightly greater) importance than the actual distance to be travelled to a library and no doubt this factor would have been greatly accentuated if the sample had included fewer city dwellers and more residents in widespread rural areas. It is interesting to compare the number of users who had no need of a 'bus service (i.e. books delivered, own transport or library within easy walking distance) with the number of similarly situated non-users when the 35† referred to under Table 33 are extracted. Again there were the stalwarts who managed without a convenient 'bus service, the elderly non-users who were unable to do so* and those who had the facilities but who did not use them. In this question there was initially the problem of defining the word 'conven-

ient'. A door-to-door service of twenty 'buses per hour was not convenient for people whose knees would not bend, who found the steps
difficult, had wheel-chairs, walking frames or replacement hips,
whereas at least one able-bodied user considered a two-hourly 'bus
service convenient; respondents' own personal definitions of convenience were therefore accepted.

One might expect that the majority of elderly people and a signif-
cant proportion of visually handicapped people would be living without the private transport which is so common today in our motor-
ized community and this fact is confirmed by Table 34; furthermore
four times as many of the car owners in these groups used their
libraries as failed to use them, which is especially significant when
considering the use of books which are larger and heavier than
average. Only approximately half of those dependent on public
transport or dependent on a lift in someone else's car used their
libraries and *only 29.5%* of the people dependent on a messenger
or delivery service were library users. Please note that this is not
29.5% among society as a whole, where presumably the figure would
be much lower, but among the respondents in a survey on reading
where library users were over-represented — another pointer for the
planners of future housebound and bulk loan services. (See†)

Clearly, most respondents had to walk to their libraries and
carry home their books* and this was often mentioned as a limiting
factor in the amount of reading done, particularly of large print
books. 'It takes me all my time to get there' and 'I do walk there
with a stick, but it's difficult' were comments from users and 'I
can't manage hills' — 'it's all uphill' and 'I'd have to be accompanied' were typical comments from non-users. Again the major
variations were between the young and the old, rather than between
the sighted and the partially sighted; young visually handicapped
people seemed less deterred by riding on 'buses than were old people
and private transport was available to more of them — either their
own cars or those of their families and/or friends in similar
age-groups.

Finally, from Table 35 it can be seen that more than half of the
respondents (271) stated that they had to (or would have had to)
cross main roads which they considered to be difficult on their
route to the library. In spite of the 35 Home residents previously
mentioned (o) the non-user totals as a whole and the user totals for
the elderly groups only show that this factor was another positive
deterrent, particularly to the old and infirm. Quoting a small selec-

TABLE 34

MODE OF TRAVEL USED BY ELDERLY AND VISUALLY HANDICAPPED GROUPS —
ANSWERS TO THE QUESTION 'HOW DO YOU (OR WOULD YOU HAVE TO) TRAVEL
THERE?' [THE LIBRARY]

Travel methods	Users	Non-users	510 respondents
	16	24	A = Elderly in community, including VH
	2	7	B = Elderly in OAP Homes, including VH
	3	9	C = VH interviewed, including elderly
	97*	45*	D = VH questionnaires, including the elderly
Walk	118	85	
	9	22	A
	1	—	B
	10	9	C
	44	29	D
Public transport	64	60	
	2	1	A
	—	—	B
	1	3	C
	25	3	D
Own transport	28	7	
	1	3	A
	—	—	B
	2	7	C
	16	7	D
Dependent on lift	19	17	
	—	48†	A
	18	39	B
	1	7	C
	25	11	D

Travel methods	Users	Non-users	510 respondents
Impossible/messenger delivered	44	105	
	—	7	A
	—	—	B
	—	1◊	C
	—	—	D
Unknown	—	8	

*   Note the number who walked and † the number of non-users who would have needed delivery

◊   The non-user whose home library had 'been knocked down'

NB The 510 respondents to this question have been allocated extra places in the table; this is because some users and non-users had to (or would have had to) use more than one method, or gave two alternative methods likely to be used with equal regularity, usually 'walk' and/or 'public transport'

tion of their many comments underlines this: 'I'm scared, that's the trouble' — 'it's a terrible one!' — 'I'm very afraid of them' — 'they're always being killed there' — 'I've got a heart condition and I'm frightened of crossing' — 'the roads are difficult, owing to the speed of the traffic' — 'people are frightened to cross there' — 'it's a very nasty one' and 'they're *all* difficult'. (Incidentally a few people made adverse comments regarding access to the library itself, some of them disliking the fuss of having to ring for the special admission of a wheel-chair and one said 'there's a set of very steep steps into the library, with a revolving door at the top and a brass rail dividing the stairs into channels too narrow for a wheel-chair'.) However, the user totals for the postal respondents† show that many in a library-orientated group did manage to overcome the disadvantage of having to cross difficult main roads.

Awareness about large print books

Having investigated various factors likely to influence reading in general and the use of the public libraries where large print books are available, we finally reached the section on the large print books

TABLE 35

REPLIES BY THE ELDERLY AND VISUALLY HANDICAPPED TO THE QUESTION
'DO YOU (OR WOULD YOU HAVE TO) CROSS ANY DIFFICULT MAIN ROADS?'

| Groups | Users | | Non-Users | | | Totals |
	A Yes	B No	A Yes	B No	C Unknown	
Elderly in community (incl. VH)	10	18	64*	22	19	133
Elderly in OAP Homes (incl. VH)	1	20	11	35°	—	67
VH interviewed (incl. elderly)	10	7	11	14	11$^\Diamond$	53
VH questionnaires (incl. elderly)	106†	72	58	17	5	258
Totals	127	117	144*	88	35	511

$\Diamond$ including the non-user whose home library had 'been knocked down', again

o our 35 Home residents again

†   the library-orientated group

*   demonstrating the deterrent effect of difficult roads

themselves. All respondents were asked one vital question 'Have you ever read, seen or heard of large print books?' and upon their answers to this key question depended the direction of the following questions to be answered, as the forms were then classified into four separate groups. It must be admitted here that this proved a very complex procedure for postal respondents completing a form intended for personal use by an experienced interviewer, and consequently many of them completed irrelevant sections which had to be disregarded.

From the replies to this question it became immediately apparent that the majority of the visually handicapped people interviewed, and, as might have been expected, the great majority of the visually handicapped people replying by questionnaire *had* read large print books at some time and to some extent. (A few of the people interviewed referred at first to paperbacks or chance purchases in bookshops however, which *happened* to be in larger print than average and not the specially produced series in libraries; it was possible, therefore — though unlikely among such a library-orientated group — that some of the postal respondents were referring to the same material.)

Only among the two groups of elderly people interviewed were the numbers who had never read, seen nor heard of large print books larger than the number of readers. It is most important to bear in mind again here that the group of postal respondents consisted of a higher than average proportion of readers in general and it seemed likely that many of these were motivated to reply in order to express their appreciation or their need for a wider range; nevertheless these results did show that some forms of publicity to visually handicapped groups had probably been more effective than was considered likely as a result of the earlier surveys. The random sample interviewed had to be considered as more reliable here and was likely to give a much more typical picture of the situation as a whole, however — yet even in that sample (because for speed and convenience it was obtained in or via group situations) no information about people living in *complete* isolation was obtained. Everyone interviewed was at least in touch with others at the one centre where contacted and in view of the percentages shown in Table 36a at † it was likely that the inclusion of a representative proportion of the 'unclubables' would have added considerably to this group that remained absolutely unaware of the existence of large print books. Even among the elderly groups contacted in Homes and at clubs and centres the publicity situation was not good, when one considers that 57 of the 110 'visually handicapped' people interviewed were located there and that those of the remainder who were readers at all could be considered potential large print users.

Having at this stage already isolated 132 potential users who had never read, seen nor heard of large print books, we had found yet another very obvious and expected reason why *some* people did not read them (probably in many cases overlapping an earlier reason — the non-use of public libraries.) 'Information to help old, disabled or blind people is not very easy to find — no help is ever suggested by any of the usual contacts and one finds out by chance or luck. Once

TABLE 36(a)

515 ANSWERS FROM THE ELDERLY AND VISUALLY HANDICAPPED COMMUNITIES
TO THE VITAL QUESTION 'HAVE YOU EVER READ, SEEN OR HEARD OF LARGE
PRINT BOOKS?'

Groups	Read	Seen	Heard of	None	Unknown	Total
Elderly in community (incl. VH)	35	20	15	62 (c.47%)†	1	133
Elderly in OAP Homes (incl. VH)	19	16	2	30 (c.45%)†	—	67
VH interviewed (incl. elderly)	28	8	5	12 (c.23%)†	—	53
VH questionnaires (incl. elderly)	170*	38	24	28 (c.11%)*	2	262
Totals	252	82	46	132	3	515

† Showing the greater awareness among the visually handicapped groups than
among the elderly groups

* Note the anticipated imbalance of the postal respondents

in touch with the correct people help is given, but the initial search
is a lot for an old person — they just can't try and they give in; would
a scheme of an 'alert' by the doctor or some other person in touch
be possible, to let the disabled know just what help can be obtained?'
It was not possible at this present stage of the investigation to estimate what proportion of the 132 would read the books once this
barrier of unawareness had been removed, however.

The 252 who read or had ever read large print books at some time
were asked how regularly they read them *at that time* and their
replies subdivided them with very interesting results, as shown in the

TABLE 36(b)

THE 252 IN COLUMN 1 OF TABLE 36a WHO READ OR HAD EVER READ LARGE PRINT BOOKS, FURTHER SUBDIVIDED

Groups	A Regularly- no others read	B Regularly plus normal print	Total Regular Users now	C Sometimes	D Rarely — less than 1 per month	Total users to any extent now	E Not at all now	Total who 'read or had read'
Elderly in community (incl. VH)	4	3	7	10	4	21	14	35
Elderly in OAP Homes (incl. VH)	2	3	5	3	3	11	8	19
VH inter- viewed (incl. elderly)	2	2	4	3	5	12	16	28
VH question- naires (incl. elderly)	56	42	98	14	27	139	31	170
Totals	64	50	114	30	39	183	69	252

lower half of the same table (36b). This subdivision quickly changed the impression given in the upper part of the table, in spite of the motivation of the postal group shown along the lower line — there were almost as many people who *rarely* read large print, i.e. less than one per month, as read it regularly together with normal print and there were more of its 'readers' *not reading it* at all then than were reading it exclusively. In all but the postal group the present non-readers easily outnumbered the two groups of regular readers — and among the visually handicapped people interviewed the present *non*-readers formed more than half of this group which 'read or had ever read large print'. This led to the question at the crux of Survey C — *why* didn't some potential readers read large print?

Reasons for non-use

Most of the 64 in column A who read large print regularly and exclu-sively were elderly people (for example 47 of the 56 visually handi-capped postal respondents.) The 50 in column B who read large print regularly but also read normal print and the 30 in column C who replied 'sometimes' were almost equally divided between the two age-groups selected (20 elderly and 22 younger respondents for column B; six elderly and eight younger respondents for column C, among those replying by post.) This very noticeable trend was con-tinued evenly for columns D and E, where the postal respondents numbered only four elderly to 23 younger people reading large print 'rarely — less than one per month' and nine elderly to 22 younger people not reading large print at all then. This showed clearly that although about the same number of younger people as older ones had at *some* time read large print books, they were very much less likely to do so exclusively or regularly and much more likely to have given them up or to read them only on rare occasions. It had been strongly suspected during the course of the earlier surveys that the existing books were more attractive to older people than to younger ones and often to the less severely visually handicapped, and the re-searcher was reasonably satisfied that these responses proved the fact. 'It is an unfortunate but all too common fact that in our society, family, friends and public and private organizations that provide educational, vocational, social and other services to the visually impaired fail to recognize that they are dealing with a visually heterogeneous population' (Genensky, 1973.)

The reasons given for then reading *few or none* at all (sometimes more than one reason per person) were as follows:

1	Insufficient books/range	31
2	Vision problem/deterioration	29

3 Preference for normal print/with LVA   22
4 Difficulty in getting to library   14
5 Slow speed/poor reading ability   12
6 Braille/Moon/talking books/alternatives or   10
    range preferred
7 Books too heavy/bulky*   8
    Discomfort/tiredness   8
9 Shortage of time   5
10 Unattractive covers   3
    Concentration failure   3
12 Lack of interest   2

*One reader said 'my hands stick in the shape I've been holding them — I couldn't finish the last one because I couldn't hold it'. In spite of the fact that many mentioned arthritis, the use of book-rests and stands was almost non-existent. 'I'd never heard of book-rests' — 'I have a very limited income, so I just read resting the book on the table'.

The older people mainly comprised the group dissatisfied with the number of books available and the younger people mainly comprised the group dissatisfied with the range, often preferring to read normal print whenever possible (usually with the help of a low vision aid) and a few of them read braille *because* the range was wider. Reasons 1 and 3 were obviously closely linked and a selection of typical quotes from both old and young helps to illustrate these very important points: 'they need more titles kept at the library' 'there should be half for people who like the literature you offer and half for those who like to use their minds!' — 'there are too many Westerns and mysteries on the shelves' — 'the *print* is good, that's all!' — 'the great failing is that they do not publish in large print the very books which are normally printed in the smallest print — e.g. Dickens and a lot more' — 'the range is patronizing' — 'progress was usually due to members of minority groups, so why not provide books for the minority as well?'— 'less ill-written, novelettish types' — 'twenty times more' — 'I think large print books are a noble effort but the publishers obviously appeal to the lowest common denominator; I realize it is probably a fact of economic life' — 'less rubbish' — 'I can read the same as everyone else with spectacles and an aid, though it's tiring if kept up for long periods' — 'it's less embarrassing reading normal print with a lens' — 'I can read anything and everything in small print with an LVA, a little at a time' and finally two very significant quotes typical particularly of those more recently educated in special schools — 'I can read normal print with my LVA and I'd still need it for large print, so there's nothing to gain' and 'I manage well enough with normal print for it to be just not worthwhile!' The older people mostly formed the groups which had given up reluctantly because of vision problems (especially deterioration), difficulty in getting to the library and the weight of the books.

TABLE 37

THE SAME RESPONSES TO THE QUESTION 'HAVE YOU EVER READ, SEEN OR HEARD OF LARGE PRINT BOOKS?' CLASSIFIED BY THE TWO SIGNIFICANT AGE FACTORS

| | Under retiring age | | | | | Retiring age and over | | | | | |
Method	Read	Seen	Heard of	None	Totals	Read	Seen	Heard of	None	Totals	Overall Totals
Elderly in community (incl. VH)	—	—	—	—	—	35	20	15	62	132	132*
Elderly in OAP Homes (incl. VH)	—	—	—	—	—	19	16	2	30	67	67
VH interviewed (incl. elderly	21	8	3	7	39	7	—	2	5	14	53
questionnaires (incl. elderly)	83	34	16	13	146	87	4	8	15	114	260*
Total	104	42	19	20	185	148	40	27	112	327	512*

NB The heavily outlined squares draw attention to the fact that when older visually handicapped people saw or heard of the books they were more likely to become readers than the younger people

* The three in the 'unknown' column of Table 36(a) are omitted here

Table 37 shows the same responses to the question 'have you ever read, seen or heard of large print books?' as does Table 36a, but here they are classified by the two age groups which have already been shown to be the most significant divisions.

Note the heavily outlined squares. When compared, these confirm the popularity of the existing books among retired people; they show that when older visually handicapped people saw or heard of large print books, most of them became readers ('one needs books much more as one gets older and has to stay in more') whereas a considerable number of younger visually handicapped people saw or heard of them but did not start to read them.

The 82 people who had *seen* the books were asked why they had never tried to read them and the reasons which were given (often more than one reason per person, especially from the younger respondents) are shown in Table 38a; it is interesting to compare these with the list above and with the lower figures on the same page (Table 38b) which shows the replies given when all 515 elderly and/or visually handicapped respondents were asked how they thought of themselves as readers. Six categories were suggested and an extra one for 'none at all' proved to be necessary. Incidentally, the postal respondents showed a greater tendency to classify themselves in writing as 'average' than the people interviewed, who probably gave the questions more consideration before answering; we have already seen from Survey B that different people meant different things by what they considered to be 'average' † and this particular reply was the least helpful in that respect.

TABLE 38(a)

REASONS GIVEN BY 82 ELDERLY AND/OR VISUALLY HANDICAPPED PEOPLE WHO HAD SEEN LARGE PRINT BOOKS FOR NOT READING THEM:

Reasons given	Elderly community (incl. VH)	Elderly in OAP Homes (incl. VH)	VH interviewed (incl. elderly)	VH question- naires (incl. elderly)	Total
1 Can read/prefer to read normal print	12	5	5	26	48
2 Not interested in range/insufficient titles	–	2	3	12	17
3 Vision problems	1	3	3	5	12
4 Discomfort/lack pleasure/slowness	–	–	4	6	10
5 Books too heavy/bulky	4	–	1	3	8
Lack of interest in reading	3	4	–	1	8
7 Unattractive covers	–	–	–	3	3
Braille talking books now	1	–	1	1	3
9 Words too long with LVA	–	–	2	–	2
Lack of time	2	–	–	–	2

NB Other reasons named once each were: lost concentration, lost spectacles (1), needing
   spectacles changed and leaving the books for those in greater need

   The groups were not entirely exclusive — there was a close link between the ubiquitous groups 1 and 2 and another between groups 3, 4, 7b and 9a

   More than one reason per person was given especially by the younger respondents

TABLE 38(b)

REPLIES GIVEN BY 515 ELDERLY AND/OR VISUALLY HANDICAPPED PEOPLE
WHEN ASKED HOW THEY THOUGHT OF THEMSELVES AS READERS

Groups	Intellec-tual	Profess-ional	Serious	Average	Light	Magazines	None at all	Total Nos of respon-dents
	1	2	3	4	5	6	7	
Elderly in community (incl. VH)	—	1	7	16	55	49	21	133
Elderly in OAP Homes (incl. VH)	—	—	4	9	25	29	20	67
Elderly Totals	—	1	11	25	80	78	41	200
VH inter-viewed (incl. elderly)	2	18	11	20	26	19	11	53
VH question-naires (incl. elderly)	26	17	41	114†	68	69	40	262
Overall Totals	28	36	63	159	174	166	92	515

† Different people meant different things by 'average'

Among the normal print readers in group 1 (38a) it was almost
entirely the pre-retirement respondents who did so with prescribed
LVAs ('I can read normal print with very powerful magnification
and I can't read large print without — so there's no advantage *and* the
disadvantage of the limited material') and the retired people who
read normal print with spectacles only, though many did use
'popular' magnifying glasses. Almost all the respondents in their
teens and 20s who had recently attended special schools used LVAs
and also some 'young middle-aged' respondents like the one who had
used braille all his life and was very happy with his LVA — 'I don't

need large print now and when I did need it I hadn't heard of it!' Obviously, there was very little incentive for low vision aid users to limit themselves to a specific set of leisure reading if the entire world of literature was available to them.

Although some young LVA users disliked using their aids publicly, there were indications that these same young people often felt self-conscious about being seen using large print books — 'people don't like to be singled out' — 'I feel that people are looking at me' — 'I'd prefer illustrated jackets — they're embarrassing and they stand out in a library'. As there was an optimum word size for convenience and some people using a high magnification found that the words in large print were too long, there seemed to be little likelihood and no evidence that reading years were being extended by the combined use of LVAs and large print (though some slightly younger readers did in fact use LVAs with normal print and read large print as well.) A chicken and egg situation had resulted in the production of a set of leisure reading more suitable for older people than for younger ones and those young readers who *were* keen to read large print were in any case faced with a dearth of suitable subject matter; for some there was nothing at all — in particular the less academic teenagers with adult interests, who were too old to read children's books and unable to cope with an adult text in small print.

To a certain extent it seemed that the changeover in readership was more regular than among the libraries' readership in general, with some readers at the first stage 'just ready for large print now' and others at the final stage who 'can't see even the big print any more'. There were cases of regular readership throughout the entire fifteen years that the books had been in existence, however, and these readers obviously found it desperately difficult or impossible to find a book of any kind that was unread, so librarians ought not to be unduly influenced by this rotation factor when deciding on the extent of provision.

Effective publicity among the visually handicapped

The smaller group of 46 people who had *heard* of the books were asked to name the source of the information and asked whether or not they had made any further enquiries about them. Nine people had heard about the books at a special school or college and seven people had been told of their existence at a class, club or association for the blind or partially sighted. Four had been told by librarians or library assistants and 'In Touch' or the radio was the source of the information in four cases. Parents and doctors had each mentioned them in three cases; relatives, clergymen, friends, fellow OAP club members, social workers and visiting hymn singers were each responsible in two cases and other sources of information named once each were a relative working in a library, a newspaper, a braille publication and 'professional knowledge' (an ex-librarian).

Only five of this group who had heard of the books without seeing them had ever made any further enquiries (underlining a point made earlier about the books themselves being their own best advertisement.) Three of these were teenagers who had approached their libraries but found that books for their age group were not available, one had written to a 'supplier' and one had eventually decided that they would probably not be suitable for her condition. Most of those who did not make any further enquiries failed to do so because they were either able to read normal print (11) or unable to read print at all (7). Six were not interested in reading, two did not know where the books could be obtained and two felt that it would be too slow or difficult. Other reasons given were 'can't get to the library', 'don't need them', 'don't read fiction', 'too old', 'only heard about them last week', 'wasn't ready to need them until now' and 'had read large print magazine (Oculus) but lacked the time and patience to persevere with it'. (Not everyone replied.) It seemed, therefore, that merely *telling* people about the books did not result in a high take-up, for it was possible that some of those 'able to read normal print' might have preferred large print if they had seen it and a few of those 'unable to read print at all' might have discovered that they were able to do so.

We come next to the group of 132 people who had *never* read, seen nor heard of large print books — and it is important to remember again here that this proportion (c. 26%) would have been much higher if isolated people had been interviewed in their homes and if the motivated postal respondents had been excluded. How many of *them* were potential readers? The people interviewed were shown specimens of 'standard' print and Ulverscroft print and asked to read them wearing spectacles if normally worn; those completing questionnaire forms could not be thus monitored and could only be shown a reproduction of each, however; although the quality of duplication was mostly excellent and two readers remarked that 'your own large print typescript is ideal' and 'all ordinary books are not as clear as this' [normal print] , a few copies fell below standard and two elicited the comments 'I found it difficult to read your letter' and 'this print is Hell, I must say!'

Thirty-seven people could read the *'standard'* print comfortably (if slowly in many cases) but 29 of them were elderly people interviewed in Homes and in the community; only one was among the visually handicapped sample interviewed and seven were among the postal respondents. Thirteen of the elderly groups and five of the visually handicapped groups were able to read the print but found it tiring; 23 in the elderly groups and seven in the latter read it only with difficulty and 47 people were unable to read it at all — 27 of these were found in establishments for the elderly and 20 via establishments for the blind and partially sighted. (Here one reader took the opportunity to add 'I expect I could read large print books if I could get them!') When they knew nothing whatsoever about the existence of large print books all 132 people could be considered as potential readers and after they had seen a speciment of large print only 29 of the elderly people and some of the seven postal correspondents were likely to be eliminated; in other words about 100 people who were *unable* to read standard print comfortably did not know of the existence of an alternative.

An overwhelming majority could read the Ulverscroft print more easily than the 'standard' print — 24 of 31 elderly people in OAP Homes, 48 of 62 elderly people in the community, five of 12 visually handicapped people interviewed and 19 of 28 postal respondents (96 of 132, or over 72% overall.) The 96 people who read or said they could read the large print more easily included *18 who had not been able to read the 'standard' print at all* and 29 who had read it only with difficulty — a very significant finding. Only 36 of the 96 people were considered likely to become regular readers of large print books even when they did know about them, however. The remaining 60 either lacked interest in reading (42 — a few very young, but mostly very old) — suffered discomfort, dazzle or mistiness in doing so (9) — would continue to read normal print with a low vision aid (5 — all younger people) — considered their reading to be too difficult or slow (4) — could not get to the library (3) — 'did not consider that they needed large print yet' (2) and 'was saving her sight' (1). Some people gave more than one reason).

Four of the 132 people could read the large print less easily than the 'standard' print, six considered that they could read each size equally well and five people were unable to read either size owing to non-visual problems such as illiteracy and mental state. Twenty-two of the 132 people 'tested' at this stage of the survey were unable to read either print — four of the elderly in OAP Homes, four of the elderly in the community, seven of the visually handicapped interviewed and seven of the postal respondents; these were of course in addition to respondents sifted out at earlier stages, like those who had read large print in the past but were unable to do so then and those who had seen it but could not read it.

By this stage in the study, the researcher shared with many others the exasperated feeling that the quality of so many lives could be improved, so much discomfort (and embarrassment) could be avoided, so much difficult publicity and so many other complications could be eliminated if only *all* printers were obliged to use larger and clearer print.

Use and non-use of aids

The respondents were using a variety of aids for reading, but contact lenses were not mentioned and could not be detected and some of the information about spectacles was unreliable. It was obvious that few of the people who filled in questionnaire forms thought of including 'ordinary' spectacles in the section about the use of vision aids and many of the old people interviewed had glasses 'somewhere' which they did not wear or were wearing the wrong spectacles for the task; several were very critical of recently prescribed lenses, such as the old lady who said that her new ones were 'hopeless' and shrewdly pointed out that her optician did not now 'plaster his name proudly on the case' since she stopped buying her spectacles from him as a private patient! Table 39a shows the situation regarding the use of spectacles among the people interviewed only, and 39b shows the use of other reading aids; *all* visually handicapped respondents were asked about these.

In the section of the questionnaire on the wearing of spectacles, statistics for the OAP Homes visited were rendered practically useless because so many residents who owned or had owned spectacles were either not wearing them, not wearing the correct spectacles for the task, had not had the lenses changed, had lost or broken them or were awaiting new spectacles. Several residents were unaware that they were entitled to free eye tests, several were unaware that the cost of National Health spectacles was heavily subsidized and some who *were* aware of the fact still considered the charge made to them

TABLE 39(a)

THE USE OF SPECTACLES AMONG THE PEOPLE INTERVIEWED

	No spectacles	Reading spectacles	Bi-focals	o 'Special' spectacles	Other	Totals
Elderly in community (incl. VH)	49* (37%)	58 (+ 1 pad)	18	7	1 (eye shade)	133
Elderly in OAP Homes (incl. VH)	23* (34%)	30	7	6	1 (intra-ocular lens)	67
VH inter-viewed (incl. elderly)	28† (53%)	6	8	11	—	53
Totals	100	94	33	24	2	253

† Librarians please note how few of the visually handicapped conformed to the stereotype

* Unreliable figures, as the spectacle situation among the elderly was fairly chaotic

o Where mentioned or used in the interviewer's presence

to be prohibitive; some expressed the wish to visit an optician but found the journey impossible or extremely difficult. However, the researcher's visit to one Home immediately followed that of a visiting optician and here it was found that residents had not always made the same complaints to the optician; in one case the lady had not 'remembered' to tell him that she found it impossible to read in her new reading glasses! This paragraph has been included without reliable statistics because it was felt that the information in itself provided a useful thumbnail sketch of the vision aid situation and the difficulties inherent in attempting to deal with it, together with evidence of yet another disincentive to reading.

Of the 26 visually handicapped Home residents by the study definition, ten did not possess any aids whatsoever. Nine used mag-

TABLE 39(b)

AND THE USE OF OTHER READING AIDS – BY <u>ALL</u> VISUALLY HANDICAPPED
RESPONDENTS

	Magnifying glasses	Telescopic spectacles	Supplementary lenses	Monocular	Binocular	Other	Totals of aids used
The 31 VH elderly in community	24	1	–	1	1	–	27
21 (of 26) VH elderly in OAP Homes	11	–	1	–	–	–	12
The 53 VH interviewed (incl. elderly)	32	12	15	12	4	7*	82
190 (of 262) VH questionnaires (incl. elderly)	108	31	24	16	12	17**	208
Totals	175	44	40	29	17	24	329

*   Two special typewriters, two CCTV, one cataract spectacles, one 'LVA spectacles' and
      one 'illuminated reader'

**   Five 'LVAs', three 'special spectacles', three undefined, two CCTV, one
      special typewriter, one anglepoise lamp, one old opera glasses, one
      'Opsec cataract glass'

NB No mention was made of the Optacon, though this was seen in one of the establishments visited

nifying glasses (by far the most common LVA among all groups).
Three wore dark glasses (which might or might not have aided close
vision), two used a combination of magnifier and supplementary
lens, one wore cataract spectacles and one an intra-ocular lens.
Among all of the visually handicapped groups there were many
people who seemed to have a poor opinion of their aids: 'they gave
me the lot but they never worked' – 'everything blurs as it magnifies'
– 'most of them aren't strong enough' – 'I can manage better without' and 'the binocular lens was too small' were a few of the
comments made. Some referred to LVAs that had been tried but
found unsatisfactory and two people named *six* different types of

aid. Some said that they hated wearing their telescopic spectacles, one middle-aged woman even used a magnifier 'only in private', another said that she felt sick after a page or two and many referred to the amount of effort involved. The users of such aids as telescopic spectacles, supplementary lenses, monocular and binocular aids tended to be young or middle-aged — those interviewed were mostly in special schools or colleges or in professional employment; the old ladies mostly used only magnifiers or no aids at all — some would have liked to use magnifying glasses but did not know how to obtain them, and this situation would probably have been worse among the isolated people not contacted.

Negative attitudes to print reading

The majority of respondents (the more severely visually handicapped respondents in particular) had never been encouraged to use their vision for ink-print and this question more than any other brought forth a flood of responses such as: 'I taught *myself* to read when I was about five but I've only just been taught to write properly' — I was *dis*couraged — they wanted me to learn braille' — 'the feeling was if you're blind you read braille and that's that!' — 'very much the opposite' — 'I just learned to read and write at eighteen' — 'they didn't want me to read print at all in my junior school but things have changed since my day' — 'you must *feel* — you mustn't *see!*' — 'the teachers haven't been trained to teach print reading' — 'they wanted me to learn braille when I was young, but actually my sight hasn't got much worse for reading' — 'you *must* fit conveniently into their category and learn braille with the rest of the class' and I'm always being encouraged to read braille, but I can't feel it and was using my eyes, so I was determined to read print instead'. One young LVA user replied, 'frankly, I think it'll be years before everyone in my position gets the chance I've had — it's far too convenient to teach braille to the whole class and besides that the teachers haven't been trained to teach print reading'. Another was very disillusioned about a registration system that classified people who could read print with an LVA into a group forced to use braille and felt that there should be a very carefully defined scale with many very narrow divisions. One answered 'not until I came here and that meant I was years behind! I was made to learn braille and they didn't want me to read print at all at my junior school — I found I was reading the braille by sight, which is ridiculous, so my sister helped me, but I really taught myself to read. They're marvellous here, though — I was immediately given this LVA and encouraged to please myself'. A blind social worker commented wryly 'blindness is more emotive and better for fundraising than partial sight and people seeing with thick glasses; they want you to stay 'blind' and stagger about'. Though unable to estimate in what proportion of the cases this apparent rigidity was justified on grounds not appreciated by the respondents, the lay researcher was nevertheless obliged to record the amount of dis- satisfaction expressed, and in doing so to underline yet another reason why large print books were not read by some of the visually handicapped.

One hundred and ninety respondents had never been encouraged to use their vision for ink print, six replied that it would not have been possible, nine did not reply to the question and 62 people replied in the affirmative — 52 of them below retiring age and only ten above, which must surely be an indication that 'things *are* changing in recent years' Several college students interviewed were included in the group which had been encouraged, but some quali- fied their replies by adding 'but not before I came here' and 'only very, very recently'. Incidentally, an oculist had advised one old gentleman that 'large print encouraged lazy eyes' and this ambiguous statement had —rightly or wrongly — been taken as a criticism.

Alternatives to reading large print

Table 40 shows what kinds of print or other reading were being done at the time of the study by those of the 372 visually handicapped respondents who replied to the question — i.e. all those interviewed and most of the postal respondents. (Many in the younger groups were reading two or more kinds simultaneously but this did not apply to the elderly groups interviewed, as can be seen by their total responses.)

The reading being done currently by the twenty-six visually handicapped people in OAP Homes ranged from none at all to 'any- thing I've a mind to!' Ten of them were not by then reading anything at all, including one lady taught Moon but unable to feel the shapes because of lack of quiet in the Home. Ten were occasionally reading and 'skipping' extracts of newspapers in short spells, one the head- lines only and two the Births, Marriages and Deaths. Five were read- ing only large print books: one of these restricted her reading to the Bible and hymn book; one replied 'very littel! I wish I could get out to the optician and carry on reading!' — one replied 'books, papers and magazines, but it's very painful — I wish I could have that cataract operation' — and the lady with only one eye (her weaker one, by then also failing) replied, 'anything I've a mind to!' though it later emerged that this referred only to large print.

TABLE 40

ALTERNATIVES TO READING LARGE PRINT — THE KINDS OF READING BEING DONE AT THE TIME OF THE STUDY, BY THOSE OF THE 372 VISUALLY HANDICAPPED RESPONDENTS WHO REPLIED TO THE QUESTION

Kinds of reading at the time of the study	VH elderly in community	VH elderly in Homes	VH interviewed (incl. elderly)	VH questionnaires (incl. elderly)	Totals
1 Large print	2	5	4	70†	81†
2 None at all	9	10	12	49	80
3 Normal print with LVA	—	—	10	41	51
4 Normal print	—	—	—	43*	43
Braille	1	—	17	25	43□
6 Newspapers only or parts of newspapers 'in spells'	12	10	7	8	37°
7 Large print, plus news and magazines with a magnifier	3	1	3	17	24
8 Textbooks or professional material, in normal print with LVA	—	—	9	14	23
9 Magazines and newspapers with LVA, with difficulty or 'when eyes fresh'	4	—	1	15	20
10 'Very little!'	1	—	9	5	15
11 Talking books	—	—	2	12	14
12 Section not completed and unable to estimate from other replies	—	—	—	11	11
13 Moon	—	—	4	1	5
14 Irrelevant replies	—	—	—	2	2
Totals	32	26	78	313	449

† Note the imbalance of the postal sample

* The 43 included students in special schools, some of whom were likely to be using LVAs though they failed to complete the section on them — and some sufferers of progressive diseases such as those in the early stages of *retinitis pigmentosa*

○ This group consisted of 16 who read the entire paper in this manner, 16 who read the headlines only, 4 who only completed the crosswords, 2 who consulted only the horoscopes and 1 only the births, marriages and deaths. (One gentleman in his 90s, registered blind, was an expert on the ink quality of *all* the leading dailies.)

▢Many others could read braille but were not doing so — 'I prefer print reading with an LVA to braille' — 'I *can* read braille but don't do so' — 'braille when it can't be avoided and normal print with an LVA for short periods'. Some read it because they were unable to obtain large print that they wanted to read or had not read — 'I've joined a braille library now because my library hasn't got many large print books'.

The balance was upset by the large print readers among the postal respondents and lack of exclusivity in the categories resulted in considerable overlap between Groups 1 and 7; 6 and 9; 3, 4a and 8. It should also be remembered that frequently two or more kinds of reading were being undertaken, such as large print plus normal print with an LVA and large print or normal print with talking books or braille. One reader was using large print, normal print with a low vision aid, braille and Moon, in order to increase the range available. It would be impossible to interpret the replies with absolute accuracy in any other way, therefore, and the table makes interesting and enlightening reading. Note also the amounts and kinds of reading being done by the readers among the 53 (mostly younger) people interviewed via the organizations for the visually handicapped.

Seventy-three respondents had talking books and three others had them on order at the time of the survey. (One family which included three visually handicapped people had cancelled membership because 'the tapes were in poor shape when they were received and there was no-one near to service it'; this is apparently common among elderly inexperienced users.) All age groups were represented, though there were more in the 60s and 70s than in the other groups. Eighty per cent of these also read some kind of print or alternative material, over half of them used their libraries and about half of them read large print books, so it seemed safe to conclude that talking books were not a significant disincentive to the reading of large print among those who were able to do so. Only in three cases where large print readers did not then read the books or read them rarely was the stated reason 'because I have talking books' or 'a talking book machine'; obviously these often complemented reading, increased the range available and took over when print reading was no longer possible.

Radio and — to a lesser extent — TV might have seemed likely to be greater deterrents to reading than talking books, being popular with both the readers *and* non-readers 'by inclination' as we saw earlier, yet there was little evidence that readers 'by inclination' discontinued reading by one method or another because they heard or saw radio or television plays, stories or features instead. Like the talking books this seemed to be a complement to some kind of reading for the *real* readers and to take over only when reading became impossible.

Only 37 people had readers on occasions and most of these were the more severely handicapped respondents, often unable to read large print and also using talking books. Many respondents stated that there was 'no need' or that they 'did not like a fuss' and 58 people did not reply at all. Some enthusiastically volunteered the information that they had or enjoyed Talking Newspapers, although no specific question had been asked about these.

The BBC's Radio 4 programme 'In Touch' had been heard by 106 of the visually handicapped respondents; several commented that they found it useful and enjoyable and one listener made the point that it should be longer than 15 minutes. Even though some young respondents considered it to be a programme for older people, the wide range of age groups sampled were all well represented among these listeners, though the highest numbers were again in their 60s and 70s. Sixty-seven people did not reply to the question and 199 did not listen to the programme. The non-listeners included 21 of 26 visually handicapped OAP Home residents and 25 of 31 elderly visually handicapped people interviewed in OAP clubs and centres — in many cases these had either never heard of the programme, had the communal radio permanently tuned into a different channel, 'observed Sundays' or the programme coincided with tea-time in the Home and/or visitors at home. As some did not regard themselves as handicapped the possible relevance of the programme had not occurred to them; a few did not possess a radio and among other comments volunteered by non-listeners were 'it's all piffle — fancy telling a blind person how to prepare lettuce! How would you see the worms?' and 'I found it had virtually no relevance to the partially sighted.'

A perceptive student (optic atrophy, retinobulbar neuropathy and papillitis) came to the conclusion that 'no matter what lengths you go to you will not succeed — despite a highly commendable effort — in reprinting every textbook in large print and therefore the partially sighted person should be encouraged to read normal print books with either a lens, telescopic spectacles or his own eyesight (providing he undergoes no strain) until he has achieved a practical speed' and probably those people contacted in visual handicap circles who disapproved of the use of large print would agree with him. It did seem likely that prescribed low vision aids and other technical developments would completely obviate the need for large print textbooks and professional material long before these would be likely to become available, but it seemed extremely *unlikely* that such aids would ever supersede large print books for home and leisure reading, however, particularly by the older and/or less seriously handicapped readers — and such leisure reading would include a large number of biographies, a large collection of books linked to a wide range of leisure activities, some travel and history and such authors as Voltaire, Proust, Shakespeare and Balzac if they were available. (One elderly RP sufferer was, for example, struggling through *'Sam Johnson and His World'* in standard print with a magnifier, and several made a plea for large print crosswords.) With increased publicity, more books and many more retired people in the community the demand for large print books seems certain to increase in the near future and it is to be hoped that librarians will begin to purchase them in sufficient quantities to encourage a more adventurous approach on the publishers' part.

SUMMARY,
CONCLUSIONS AND RECOMMENDATIONS

Summary

This study has been concerned with large print books and their users, with the inter-related problems of publicizing the available material, public relations and liaison with other services, and with the needs of the non-users. Its main purpose has been to supply reliable data and information by a variety of methods for librarians, publishers and workers with the visually handicapped and the elderly, upon which the Library Association's Panel on Reading for the Visually Handicapped could base some of its future activities. Four separate surveys formed the basis of the study — with librarians and libraries, with large print readers, with the community and with the link-men. It was hoped that such evaluation would enable us to match our service and resources to the real needs of our readers and potential readers.

The librarians were not complacent about the existing large print provision and many expressed a wish for standards; *not one* suggested that the need had already been met and the demand was estimated as moderate to heavy. Separate statistics of purchases, stock or issues were rarely kept and those asked to record them were surprised by the extent of use. The trend (where known) was for increasing expenditure on large print books to meet increasing demand, though there were tremendous variations in sums spent, proportions of bookfunds and total stocks; changing methods of ordering, the emergence of new publishers in the field, the lack of statistics and recent financial cuts tended to mask this trend. Many librarians failed to appreciate the viability aspect from the publishers' point of view and wanted a vastly increased range without being able to guarantee to purchase a larger total at the present time; some books were not bought because of price, print or unawareness of their existence.

Mobile library visits were regarded as important for communication with users and potential users; many hospitals were without
libraries for patients or without many large print books; a wide range
of large print provision was found in Homes, clubs and centres for
the elderly, though there was a very significant number of large print
books in the majority. The provision of housebound services in the
area under scrutiny was extremely patchy and the large print in these
ranged from 0 to 100%, though many librarians thought of the
housebound service as the basis of their large print provision. Not all
members of staff were convinced that such time-consuming minority
services were a legitimate activity for library staffs and because of a
great deal of internal movement due to the 'freezing' of posts some
were doing work in which they had little or no interest. Few NLB
Austin books were borrowed, mostly because of unawareness but
also because these were often thought to be the province of the
Social Services Department together with the Talking Book Service
and braille, and probably also because of increased postal costs; few
examples of close liaison with Social Services Departments were
encountered. It was not usual for large print reference materials,
information or alternative materials to be stocked and there was little
liaison with organizations for the visually handicapped, but it was
encouraging to find that concessions such as the waiving of fines for
the elderly and the visually handicapped were widespread, that some
libraries were already beginning to build up reserve stocks of large
print and store complete sets of Talking Newspapers, and that
librarians would be willing to help with the distribution of a large
print newspaper if one were produced free of charge.

Librarians were more critical about typefaces than the readers
and they considered size of print as being only fourth in the order
of importance in making something easy to read, whereas the readers
placed it first. With so many eye conditions no print could be perfect
for all but the present large print suited the vast majority of its
readers. Many of the elderly or visually handicapped respondents
who were unable to read normal print or to read it comfortably were
unaware of the existence of an alternative; the majority could read
the large print more easily, including several who were unable to
read normal print at all and even more who were able to do so only
with difficulty.

Readers would read many more books if the publishers would
publish them and the librarians would buy them; every group
contacted was dissatisfied with the range but very pleased with the

books themselves. The number of books available (of the existing types) was the main complaint from the elderly, and a much wider range was the main demand from younger visually handicapped users — a tremendous range of non-fiction would be required even if the young and middle-aged readers were to be able to read only about their hobbies. Among the present users overall, romances were the most popular category, though mysteries came closely second (which had not been recognized by most librarians) and biographies were also popular and in demand. Non-fiction would be more popular if more were available — what was required for the disadvantaged reader in theory was the same element of choice available to others, yet in view of the present reading trends it might seem extravagant to provide it. The weight of the books was still the main complaint among frail, arthritic and bed-ridden readers, few of whom used or knew of book-rests; this factor also restricted the number carried home by the elderly in general and many found them tiring to hold. Some readers had never seen octavo format books and many had never seen the older quarto size, but those who had seen both un-animously preferred the smaller ones. More than half of the readers interviewed had seen only Ulverscroft books, and of those who had seen other publishers' large print three-quarters preferred the Ulver-scroft books and a quarter preferred the newer ones; most readers found jacket colours helpful but a significant number had not noticed them. Several people observed searching for a large print book failed to borrow one and more than half were men.

People of 60 plus comprised just over 64% of those seen at the shelves and 84½% of the actual readers; 18% of the readers were esti-mated to be in their 80s but this only applied to 1% seen at the shelves; many readers were using messengers for one reason or another. Females outnumbered males among the actual readers by 70% to 30% and many read more books; many of the females lived alone. The librarians' picture of the existing readers was unanimously one of mainly elderly people, almost 100% indigenous, of both sexes but with a female bias; there followed a wide division of opinion about reading levels, though all were probably equally accurate. Characteristics revealed during interviews with the group were that many were reading lighter material now than when younger, most were on fixed incomes and few could afford to buy books, the majority left school early (a characteristic which will change), many were in unskilled employment and the group was extremely home-orientated. They spent little time at the shelves, made little use of

other departments of the library, made little use of catalogues, in the
main had never seen lists and did not like to trouble the staff. Librarians named a long list of readers other than the elderly and the
visually handicapped; of these, the group making most use of large
print had been the literacy students and teachers and the group
making least use had been the immigrants and people learning
English as a second language.

One of the most significant findings of the study was that most
librarians regarded the books as books for elderly readers, meaning
readers out of preference rather than necessity, and they underestimated the degree of visual handicap among the group. This was
understandable, as it was often not possible to estimate from appearances whether or not readers would be able to read normal print —
the use or non-use of spectacles gave little indication and few were
visibly visually handicapped. In fact one in three were unable to
read normal print; several who said that they could do so experienced considerable difficulty and had serious eye problems, and had
the question been extended to include the words 'without undue difficulty' the number would have been extended from one third to
a half; 12% said that they could never manage to read even important
documents. in normal print under any circumstances. The main
reason for reading large print by those who *could* read normal print
was that it was more restful.

Difficulties encountered during the study underlined the state of
confusion which existed about registration, statistics of visual handicap and where the lines between 'blindness', partial sight, visual
handicap and failing sight should be drawn — if, in fact, they should;
it was estimated that for every partially sighted person there were
about 20 with poor sight. The majority of the responding link-men
now encouraged the use of residual vision, but there was little general
awareness about low vision aids and not only the elderly among the
visually handicapped complained that they had been discouraged
from reading print — while many of the elderly in general had been
discouraged from reading when they were young and expected to use
their time 'more productively'. Early attitudes to reading seemed to
be the most significant factor isolated in connection with the reading
habit in general. Many non-library users among the general public
were unaware of the address or whereabouts of their local library so
it was hardly surprising that some of the visually handicapped were
unaware.

Attempts to link non-reading in general among the elderly and visually handicapped communities to the isolation factor, to a lack of higher education or to the existence of a high degree of alternative leisure activity or competing interests proved inconclusive. The main reasons for the non-reading of large print books by the *pre-retirement* group were found to be the nature and extent of the visual handicap itself (resulting in discomfort or lack of pleasure in reading); the fact that the existing books were more attractive to the elderly, and that almost all those recently educated in special schools for the partially sighted and others with low vision aids preferred to read normal print; the dearth of material for young people and for those newly reading print; unawareness of its existence; non-use of libraries because the expectation of suitability was low; the use of alternative materials such as braille, Moon and talking books specifically because of the greater range available; slowness of speed; the fact that large print words exceeded the optimum size for convenience for some users of high magnification, and lack of incentive in cases where normal print could be read with very powerful magnification and large print could not be read without. In the case of the *elderly* non-users (and it must be remembered that the elderly form the major part of the visually handicapped group) the same reasons connected with the visual handicap itself applied, together with unawareness and the non-use of libraries. In their case, however, additional reasons connected with travel, accessibility and the lack of messengers were at least equally important as were early family attitudes to reading, deterioration of vision and a fairly chaotic situation regarding spectacles. There was little likelihood and no evidence to suggest that reading years were being extended by the combined use of LVAs and large print, though often two or more methods of reading were used at different times by the same person. Among the groups contacted in the Community Survey, in addition to non-users there were almost as many large print readers who rarely read large print (less than one per month) as read it together with normal print and there were more of its 'readers' not then reading it at all than were reading it exclusively.

The elderly were unaccustomed to tape recorders, but these were growing in popularity in some housebound services and some non-library users would use their libraries if tapes and records were available. Potential use of CCTV or technical reading machines was not likely to be high among today's old people, but it would be higher among the younger and more seriously visually handicapped; it might

already justify provision at some selected points in well-used libraries with easy access, following adequate and appropriate publicity,
and such potential use would be likely to increase in the future. A
few imaginative schemes came to light but on the whole there was
little evidence of efforts made to attract the group and they had less
than average contact with public libraries, though about one third of
the social workers' and the health visitors' visually handicapped
contacts were known to read large print books. It seemed probable
that there was a fairly isolated group living at home and not coming
into contact with any of the groups of link-men, and that the need
for housebound services was much greater in general than was being
met. Age was more significant than visual ability when it came to
leisure activities — there was a much great difference between the
leisure activities of different age groups than between the elderly and
the elderly visually handicapped. The elderly in residential care had
extremely few interests and the elderly in the community had few;
the young and middle-aged visually handicapped groups had very
many more interests, and 37 people named 100 *different* hobbies
among them.

Librarians did recognize the need to increase or improve publicity but thought that personal contact by staff was the most effective method of communicating with the elderly and/or visually
handicapped, whereas in the West Midlands there was little contact
with readers' advisers or with other staff. Providing and displaying
lists was the second most popular suggestion nationally but there
were few lists on display; most of the actual readers suggested lists
in the library as the best method of informing them and their peers,
followed by lists in Homes and talks in clubs, and some of the
middle-management librarians would have preferred lists from the
newer publishers instead of books on approval, which were not
always seen by the group. An impressive list of publicity methods
was produced but many of the methods were passive and most were
only rarely undertaken. To reach potential users in the community
liaison with OAP Homes, clubs and centres was the most popular
suggestion followed by close liaison with Social Services Departments, and another very interesting list was produced. The publicity situation in Homes, clubs and centres was not good, however,
even though the librarians knew that liaison with wardens, book
deposits and talks had important publicity potential; few Homes
received publicity material, though they housed significant numbers
of potential readers with visual handicap and failing sight.

30% of the general public had at least seen large print books — the friends, relatives and neighbours who were expected to pass on information to potential users — but 70% had not seen them, and this group included most of the older respondents and the visually handicapped, many of whom would have used their libraries if they had known of the existence of large print. The response rate and the replies from link-men suggested that 'word of mouth' publicity from link-men would not be as frequent as expected, though most of those who replied had seen large print, especially Ulverscroft books. Most link-men who had never received publicity material would welcome it and many would be willing to display or distribute it. There were large pools of untapped resources, with so many workers in the significant Groups 2 and 3 (social workers, health visitors, district nurses, doctors, ophthalmologists and opticians) never having received any lists, etc — not one responding GP had ever been contacted, yet most would be willing to display a poster and/or to distribute lists as would most of the uncontacted opticians, health visitors and social workers. The link-men with the highest number of visually handicapped contacts were the LVA clinics, ophthalmologists, opticians and the voluntary agencies and associations. The books were their own best advertisement, however; merely telling people about them did not result in a high take-up — some people able to read normal print might have preferred large print if they had seen it and some people 'unable to read' might have discovered that they were able to do so.

Conclusions

The various methods used to collect this information have been fully described in Chapter 2, but if we are to draw general conclusions and to apply the results on a national scale it might be useful to summarize here some of their known strengths and weaknesses. 'It is rare to find a piece of statistical information that is 'perfect' in the double sense of being observed without error and being precisely suited to its purpose' (Carter and Roy, 1954) and indeed one postal respondent described himself as 'librarian in charge of lies, damned lies and statistics'.

In general, not all respondents interpreted every question exactly as intended and there was the usual difficulty of comparing the dour man's 'satisfied' with the effusive woman's 'delighted'. Interviewing was (as always) an unnatural intrusion into the various situations being measured and particularly in the case of the librarians this was likely to have had some unknown degree of effect upon some of the attitudes being assessed. Not all of the characteristics of all of the samples selected could be considered as proportionate to the characteristics in the populations being represented; for example, people in their career years were under-represented in the visually handicapped sample, and in the sample of elderly respondents both the extremely isolated and those who were fit, active and independent were under-represented. Estimates from Chief Librarians were accepted gratefully in place of firm statistics when these were unobtainable, and in the survey of link-men we do not know whether the 71% of non-respondents had little information or little time, had little time for libraries or had little time for large print! The timing of the study during a period of financial constraint was possibly a little unfortunate.

The most important strengths of the study were that so many avenues were explored by so many different methods, though consistency was ensured by the fact that all were undertaken by the same experienced researcher. No method was ever used alone; estimates were from informed people and their inclusion in tables or findings has always been mentioned; whenever these or responses from groups whose motivation was thought to be suspect were considered likely to be misleading they were excluded. Questions were as carefully prepared and tested as was practicable in the available time, samples were carefully selected to be as balanced as possible, and the study was built on an excellent foundation when statistics were supplied and/or opinions were expressed by 90% of the library authorities in Britain.

The researcher's task was basically a) to discover whether there was insufficient large print material for the needs of its users and potential users, or whether there was sufficient bearing in mind new developments to help partially sighted readers to use ordinary print, and b) whether or not the existing stock was being sufficiently well-publicized and used. The conclusions reached come under seven main headings, 1) large print books 2) services 3) publicity 4) liaison 5) 5) present users 6) non-users and 7) demand:

1) LARGE PRINT BOOKS
Libraries on the whole do not carry a sufficiently large stock of the titles that are available, either to make reasonable provision for their readers or to encourage diversity on the part of the publishers, and

the existing range is too restricted; it is not attractive to the majority of younger readers and to some older ones. Most readers are much less aware of the finer points of book production than are trained librarians, and whereas it was only fourth in order of importance to librarians the size of print was considered the most important factor in making something easy to read in its present readers' opinions. Readers are very pleased with the books, though a very small number (mostly of young people) are embarrassed to be seen reading books which are conspicuously different from the others; there is a dearth of material for young people. Preference for the smaller octavo format books is unanimous and if publishers could find an acceptable way of further reducing the weight of the books, frail, arthritic and bed-bound readers would find them more convenient to hold and those who carry them to and from a library would be enabled to borrow more. Opinions are fairly evenly divided regarding the attractions of book jackets with illustrations and the usefulness of colour-coded jackets; presumably jackets combining both features would satisfy everyone and a synopsis on the back of the cover is popular.

2) SERVICES

Many special services are patchy at present and reference services for the visually handicapped are rare, but one which it *is* within the librarians' ability to improve when staff and money are available is the housebound service, which is extremely patchy in availability, quality, methods, publicity, staffing and financing. Poor vision can no longer sensibly be considered in isolation among the elderly, many of whom suffer additional disabilities; a large proportion of visually handicapped people are elderly, and many live alone without transport and are unable to use 'buses. Frail old people are unable to carry the books home, and unless bulk loans to Homes, clubs and centres are increased and services to the housebound are provided and publicized more generously there will continue to be potential users who do not use the books at all and others who will read less than they would like to read.

3) PUBLICITY

In spite of the fact that the publicizing of available services is now a mandatory requirement, publicity about large print is totally inadequate. This applies particularly to the librarians in their failure to reach those non-library users who could benefit. Very few of the existing users came into libraries specifically to find large print books; most people now choosing them in library buildings were already library users beforehand and there must be a considerable number of potential users living isolated lives who do not use their libraries, are totally unaware of the existence of large print and who are not being reached by any form of publicity. The statement also applies to most publishers' unsuccessful attempts to contact middle management and branch librarians (probably owing to requests that all mail should be centralized) though the publishers have been responsible for more than their fair share of effective publicity to the link-men. There is massive unawareness of the availability of Austin books, reading aids, talking books and the Partially-Sighted Register, and librarians could do a great deal more in the way of advertising the availability of magnifying glasses and booklists close to the large print books; many could improve the signposting to the books themselves. There is little evidence of the use of local radio, of displays, of exhibitions outside of libraries, and the monitoring of effectiveness of publicity methods is rare. The importance of staff contact and 'word of mouth' as publicity methods is exaggerated, for the group is not easy to contact. The books themselves proved to be their own best advertisement, used with talks or displayed in such places as Homes, clubs and centres; of mere mentions in print, those in free civic newspapers are probably the most effective.

4) LIAISON

Links between Libraries Departments and Social Services Departments vary between extremes but in general they are at informal worker level, if existent, and consequently there is probably an assumption of knowledge and awareness on the part of each other's workers which is not always accurate, together with a heavy dependence on printed statistics which has led in some cases to the under-provision of large print. There is very little evidence of liaison with special schools and colleges, researchers, societies and agencies for the blind and partially sighted, and this lack has resulted in low expectations among the group about the potential of library services for the visually handicapped and initial suspicion about the librarians' role in this present study. Opportunities for liaison with such important links as doctors, opticians, ophthalmologists and health visitors are being missed and liaison with the book trade is rare.

5) PRESENT USERS

Librarians are right to consider most of the books which have been published as books for elderly people and right in their assessment that the majority of the readers are indigenous retired people, with more females than males. The stereotype of a groping figure in dark glasses does a disservice to the visually handicapped, however, for there is a serious but understandable tendency for librarians to underestimate the numbers of these elderly readers with visual handicaps which are not visible. One in three of the existing large print readers (including people without any visible eye defect and some even without spectacles) is unable to read books in normal-size print, and this proportion is increased to about half by the inclusion of a further group which should also be catered for because such difficulty is experienced that they have no wish to read normal print. Librarians in general have probably never been as aware of and as concerned about disadvantaged groups as they are today, but this awareness and concern rarely extends to the partially sighted simply because the group is thought to be rarely encountered. The majority of this existing user group is home orientated, spends little time at the shelves and none at all using other library facilities, is now reading for leisure and would make little use of technical equipment or CCTV in libraries, though a small minority group might be likely to do so. The group is unlikely to be able to afford to buy reading material and is therefore more dependent than most on libraries to make adequate provision. The books are occasionally also used by literacy students and teachers but this use is merely peripheral and likely to decrease.

6) NON-USERS

The non-users include a significant number of elderly and visually handicapped people who do not at present use libraries (for various reasons, including inaccessibility) and others who are also unaware of the existence of large print. The non-user group also includes a number of younger people and some older ones who are not interested in the existing range available but who could and would be readers if and when this is considerably extended; therefore both of these groups can be considered by librarians as potential users. The remainder are likely to *remain* non-users of large print for the following reasons: 1) this predominantly elderly group includes a considerable number of people who have little interest in hobbies or leisure activities in general and reading in particular; this is accentuated at present by the presence of a group of very old people who left school early and were discouraged from reading when they were young 2) the group obviously includes some people who are unable to read even large print and who are using such alternatives as radio, television, braille, talking books and Moon 3) many visually handicapped people do not find reading a pleasure and suffer varying degrees of discomfort and tiredness; they are unlikely to read anything which is unnecessary and are certainly unlikely to read a collection of leisure reading 4) some people educated to read braille and others with poor reading or visual ability are deterred from reading print by slow speed and difficulty in sustaining interest and 5) many younger readers and some older ones are always likely to require access to all the literature which exists in normal print, and if low vision aids can make this possible for them there is no advantage to be gained by reading large print.

7) DEMAND

Librarians are correct in estimating that the existing demand for large print is not yet being met, though purchases are unlikely to be greatly increased until the financial situation improves. They are aware that more light biographies and many more romances are needed but many have not recognized the almost equal need for mysteries; no category of book achieved as high a rating as 'average frequency' for its uncomplaining readers' ability to find one! Most libraries need more of the existing books in addition to the wider range which does not yet exist, though many younger librarians do not appreciate that the first provision would lead to the second. Some non-readers consider the range patronizing and they would prefer non-fiction books; many readers have never seen non-fiction books and are less likely than expected to discriminate against them if there were more. Choice is dictated to some extent by what librarians will buy (what they think their readers require or what they approve of supplying) and to a large extent by what publishers will produce (what they can sell to librarians with certainty). The message is loud and clear: the publishers are in business and they have done their homework; they know that most of the group is elderly and they are understandably catering for the largest market in what is already a minority area. If librarians fully appreciate the value of large print books in extending or bringing back the enjoyment of reading for the elderly and visually handicapped and they also want to satisfy their younger readers and the non-readers who require a wider or a different range, then as almost the sole customers they must buy large print in sufficient quantities to make such production viable, encourage a more adventurous approach on the publishers' part and make full use of their training to reach the potential users. In an area where there has been little research or guidance, many would appreciate standards. The degree of use of the large print books at present in libraries depends more upon the need in the area, the location of the library and the knowledge of their availability than on librarians' housekeeping methods, though good guiding and lighting, convenience and facilities such as chairs and booklists are appreciated. Most collections are receiving good or adequate use, and no section in the library can have given more pleasure.

Low vision aids are unlikely to supersede large print books for home and leisure reading in the future, particularly by the older and less seriously visually handicapped readers of whom there will be increasing numbers in our society; even at the present time at least 12% of the people encountered among the general public out walking in the daytime are unlikely or unable to read normal print for visual reasons. Talking books are not a significant disincentive to the reading of large print among readers able to do so — they often complement reading for the real readers, increase the range and take over when print reading is no longer possible. Both large print and reading aids will be needed even after the technological revolution of the next 20 years which might possibly make everything in print available to the visually handicapped — there will still be occasions for reading large print on 'buses and trains, at home, in crowded rooms and in bed; there will still be people prejudiced against 'technical things' and people who read large print because it is more restful, and many more visually handicapped people will by then have been taught to read by means of print.

Recommendations

According to 'The Libraries' Choice' (DES, 1978) librarians should be thinking of the disadvantaged as those who are barred from the normal use of their services physically or psychologically — either because they need to have the service specially delivered or they need materials or equipment which the library does not traditionally provide or they need help or encouragement to use the library or they are offered a deficient service. Judging by the findings of the study it would not be an exaggeration to state that *all* of these restrictions apply to some of the visually handicapped and that some of the restrictions apply to them all. In an attempt to show some of the ways in which the situation might be improved and the readers and potential readers in the group might become less disadvantaged, the following recommendations are made, though no doubt the interested reader of the findings will think of others. The recommendations to emerge from the study fall automatically into five sections, 1) policies 2) training 3) administration 4) publicity and 5) liaison:

1) *Policies*
In view of the very varied stocks and expenditure across the country, the formulation of standards for provision would be helpful and welcomed by many librarians in what is an area of uncertainty, though differing situations must be carefully defined so that those already providing an above-average service do not become complacent. As inadequate provision for the housebound was often found to be linked to the non-reading of large print and seemed to be the most erratic provision of all, the preparation of formal standards is also suggested in this area, though further research into this aspect peripheral to the Large Print User Study would probably be necessary before undertaking the task. In addition to arranging for the two sets of standards to be prepared, the Library Association might provide information and speakers for library schools and ensure that the study of reading by the visually handicapped forms part of the education of *all* librarians. It is assumed that the Library Association intends to continue collecting and publishing information on visual handicap, organizing and participating in appropriate conferences and working with other interested agencies and organizations in the field, and it is suggested that a representative should attend all meetings of the organization recently set up to unite and rationalize the work of the various existing voluntary associations and to provide a forum for all disciplines working within the field of visual handicap. Funds should be sought in order to finance such activities as the making of a short film about the reading needs of the visually handicapped, some suggested basic scripts for radio interviews, a competition to devise an appropriate sign for large print and the widespread distribution of unsolicited copies of its excellent leaflet 'Reading for the Visually Handicapped' via the various workers and agencies regarded as link-men for the purposes of this study. (On a lighter

note, Jimmy Savile's help might be invited, or a felt-tip pen manu-
facturer might be persuaded to finance publicity.) It is also hoped
that regardless of (or perhaps because of) the restricted level of
circulation of the earlier, very specialized report and regardless of
the form of publication of this report of less specialized but more
general interest, positive steps will be taken to publicize its existence
alongside all forms of large print publicity where possible, in library,
OAP welfare, optical health and social worker journals, and in
particular to draw its conclusions and recommendations to the
attention of those busy senior librarians who will pass on the full
report to their special services librarians. Some form of action should
be taken to ensure the publication of large print material which is
not profitable for the publishers though the researcher is uncertain
about the way in which this should be approached. The majority of
the librarians interviewed approved of the idea that the publication
of *all* large print should be a non-profit-making social service likened
to the literacy campaign, and a fascinating list of potential providers
was produced, with the Social Services, the Library Association, the
Ulverscroft Foundation and the National Library for the Blind heading the list in that order. Perhaps a Government subsidy should be
sought, together with financial aid for the establishment and running
of small libraries in Homes, and an adventurous publisher might also
be persuaded to produce a potentially popular series in large print
only, so that libraries had to stock large print in order to obtain
the series?

2) *Training*
Whereas on the whole conferences and short courses tend to preach
to the converted, it is suggested that library school courses and staff
training schemes should always include training in work with the
partially sighted, helping handicapped people, understanding visual
problems, information about reading aids and reminders to changing
library staffs about the NLB's large print collection. Library orienta-
tion courses should ideally include basic information about the work
of other library departments and other relevant departments of local
authorities, such as Social Services and Special Education; this latter
would be most beneficial if arranged on a reciprocal basis, with the
other departments' workers learning about the potential of the
library service in general and large print in particular, while the library staffs learned more about the communities they serve and the
other services available to them. Libraries should also provide

speakers, booklists and large print books for the various link-men's own training courses, including help for the newly retired to enable them to assist in turn with pre-retirement courses, and help for welfare workers with old people to enable them to give basic advice about reading.

3) *Administration*

Librarians can best serve the existing large print readers by making adequate provision at service points situated close to post offices, local shops and housing for the elderly. The section is best located in a prominent position with adequate guiding both *to* and *at* the large print bookshelves — if in any doubt librarians should try to put themselves in the position of their most severely visually handicapped users. The books should not be at too high or too low a level, the nearby chairs should not be too soft or low and the lighting in the area should be good. The books should not be constantly moved and they should *not* be integrated with normal stock (no matter how well-meaning the motive) though all groups who could benefit in any way should be encouraged to make maximum use of them and so provide a wider market and eventually a wider range. As most collections were unanimously considered to be inadequate in number and/or too restricted in range there is little scope yet for skilful selection and an attempt should be made to stock all that is published somewhere in the system, avoiding duplication of all but the most popular types in small libraries and allowing for regular changes in order to keep the users. In large print book purchase there needs to be a marked emphasis as at present on romances, coupled with a similar emphasis on light biographies and mysteries and the gradual acquisition of *all* the less popular titles available; ideally publishers should be able to publicize their material to branch librarians direct, in order to increase awareness and satisfy local needs. Where reserve stocks are available there should be notices nearby to that effect, together with mention of the NLB's Austin series, booklists and magnifiers. More reader guidance by outgoing personalities is needed to develop tastes and make elderly people feel at home in libraries, and an effort should be made to collect information that will be of special interest to the elderly and the visually handicapped — information on such topics as income, health care, nutrition, home, reading aids, transport, organizations and retirement. The lending of records, cassettes and pictures free of charge in libraries, housebound services and OAP Homes would be a welcome service where it does not already exist, as would the circulation of periodicals to elderly readers who lack the ability to concentrate for long periods. Ideally this is a field of work which should be staffed only by people who have an interest in it, and they should seek guidance from local agencies and find out about the community for themselves (with the aid of simple surveys where necessary) rather than being dependent upon printed assessments of the people and the numbers already identified as being in need of help.

4) *Publicity*
A positive effort needs to be made if non-users in the visually handicapped community and the younger members in particular are to be attracted to libraries. An effective public relations exercise is needed to let the group know what is available, and in addition to liaison with the link-men some of the following methods might be used:- insertions into large print books already reaching some of the group, leaflets at supermarket check-outs, publicity through schoolchildren to parents and grandparents, the regular use of local radio where it exists, publicity to press officers and local associations, advertisement on 'bus and car stickers, bookmarks (which might be presented to OAP Homes at Christmas), recorded information at the end of the RNIB's records and cassettes which already reach some of the blind with residual vision, posters in opticians' and GPs' waiting rooms and hospitals, and, in fact, any or all of the ideas provided by librarians. These would be worded 'if you can read this' — (or 'please tell your friends and neighbours that if they can read this') — 'there are books in your local library . . . etc.' The use of a spare room for pre-retirement courses might ensure that reading plays an important part in enriching the lives of many more of the elderly, including those with failing vision, and the imaginative provision in this of a general information centre could provide one means of co-operation between all the fields of welfare (including some of the 250 different voluntary organizations for the blind) and help to solve the problem of communication common in all fields of social service.

5) *Liaison*
In addition to existing links between libraries, making direct exchanges and borrowed large print collections possible, local government reorganization has linked libraries with a variety of other departments, and as it is an accepted fact that all need more effective channels of communication with the general public, all should

benefit from co-operative efforts and librarians ought to insist that library services are given equal publicity with other community services in information leaflets, guides and civic newspapers. They should try to liaise particularly closely with Social Services Departments at official levels, in addition to encouraging informal relationships at worker level by arranging exchange visits and mutual help in staff training. This might make both services and facilities more widely known to the other's clients (with particular reference to housebound reader services and the availability of reading aids) and produce ways of sharing, financing, publicizing, increasing and standardizing the housebound services. Such liaison would also include contact with the senior officers of OAP Homes, hopefully resulting in the exchange of information about books and readers, and the establishment of visiting library services or bulk loans with little onus on the warden. (This uneconomic service to Homes and centres is of inestimable value, as inability to get to a library was a major reason for non-use of large print among the elderly.) Librarians might also attempt to liaise (or liaise more closely) with some of the organizations for visual handicap operating in the area, perhaps by establishing panels or working parties with visually handicapped representatives to encourage consumer participation and self-help, and they should try to establish links (or closer links) with special schools and colleges, researchers and societies; not all of them approve of large print, but they can explain the special problems of the visually handicapped and would be able to advise on requirements and raise the expectations of the group about the potential of library services for the visually handicapped, where this is justified. Liaison with the local community could be extended to include liaison with local volunteer groups who might distribute surplus large print to opticians and GPs, with art colleges which could be invited to produce large print posters, with Age Concern and similar organizations which sometimes deliver books to housebound readers, and with health visitors — now more difficult to contact because of the autonomous structure of the health services yet almost entirely dependent on librarians for large print publicity, in common with the Citizens' Advice Bureaux and the OAP Homes and centres. Finally, in view of the amount of contact such people have with the elderly and the visually handicapped and the amount of goodwill demonstrated by these busy respondents, doctors, ophthalmologists and opticians should have their attention drawn specifically to the entire range of large print books now available, and should be invited to display posters and/or specimen volumes and to distribute lists to potential users.

Clearly, no library would have the time and money available to implement every one of these recommendations even if the librarian wished to do so, and hopefully no library exists which would still need to implement every recommendation; however, if the majority of these procedures were followed in some libraries and a few of them were followed in others an improved service to the visually handicapped would undoubtedly result.

Research

In the researcher's own opinion the Large Print User Study has to varying degrees fulfilled most of its stated aims, but inevitably such studies leave some questions only partly answered and other questions raised. Now we need to discover the extent of use of a really superb reference service for the visually handicapped, when well situated and publicized; we need to measure the need for large print among the multi-handicapped; we need to know the extent of the demand for *simple,* illustrated large print and short stories, among new readers, literacy students, hospital patients and elderly people lacking in concentration, and we need to monitor the effectiveness of different kinds of large print display and publicity (including its effects upon visually handicapped teenagers and new readers) without incurring stock moves because of the inconvenience caused to some of the group.

It would be interesting — if a little indulgent — to measure the lasting effects of the study (if any) upon West Midlands areas in two years' time by comparison with areas which produced similar statistics and were not researched. It would be interesting to investigate the ideas about the blind and partially sighted found among library workers and users, and to compare the reading habits of the visually handicapped in areas with and without LVA clinics. Five areas for further research could be considered more important than just 'interesting', however:

A further extension in depth into the usefulness of large print in relation to different visual problems and different degrees of visual handicap would be useful and would ideally result in definitive statements. If this could be combined with an investigation into the psychological effects of various kinds and degrees of visual handicap and of registration as blind upon attitudes, interest, efficiency and willingness to read print, then it would be even more useful. As laymen are unable to reliably assess levels of vision and have no means of identifying or classifying eye conditions, the work would need to be undertaken by a researcher with optical training, qualifications and experience – someone coming into regular professional contact with the visually handicapped, who could collect a large sample without undue inconvenience to the subjects and who would be able to identify and measure the disability, infer behavioural consequences and assess reading performance.

As the Large Print User Study has suggested that blind and more seriously visually handicapped people of all ages make little use of public libraries either as a source of leisure reading material or as an information centre, this issue could usefully be researched either by a librarian or by a member of the group in order to establish the reasons, to consider whether it is advisable or desirable for public libraries to fulfil this role, and if so, how this could be achieved most effectively. In conjunction with this piece of research the method of flooding or making bulk loans of attractive selections of the smaller format large print books by all publishers could be used in special colleges, schools, centres and club premises where the more visually handicapped groups are gathered, or a comparison could be made between the use made of two similar branch libraries, one of which had introduced an experimental service.

The whole question of large print for young people (including the teenagers for whom there is at present such a dearth of material) needs looking into, and since professional opinion among teachers is divided on the issue of whether or not large print should be provided for partially sighted schoolchildren who will grow up in a world of small print, it might be appropriate if – without the restriction of detailed terms of reference – a controlled experiment were to be carried out in schools with differing views and a fact-finding study were to be undertaken by an unbiased teacher or teachers at a special school, who would presumably have reasonable access to other special schools, to ex-pupils and to libraries and who would be able to ascertain the value of large print to these readers.

In addition to the senile people and old people lacking in concentration span encountered during the present study, many elderly readers were interviewed who referred to the reading being done at that time as 'lighter' than the reading done in the past. Research in this area about the effects of retirement on reading habits would certainly have important implications for librarians and could be helpful in maintaining mental resilience into the old age of an ageing population. Such a piece of research would presumably best be undertaken (perhaps by one of the organizations for old people) both on the 'Costa Geriatrica' where many who can afford to do so retire at the end of their working lives and also among people in their 60s in an area of heavy industry, perhaps studying the effects of retirement on the reading habits and interests of a group of teachers and a group of factory workers before and after retirement.

Finally we come to what is now probably the most urgent piece of research needed from the librarians' point of view — research into methods (other than the obvious one of cash injection) of improving library services to the elderly. Research into housebound reader services is needed most of all, with particular reference to the percentages of elderly populations served in different areas and the degree of tolerance and flexibility exercised in the interpretation of the term 'housebound', since so many who are sometimes obliged to leave the house to visit nearby shops are physically unable to get as far as the library. This, hopefully, would lead to the formulation of standards if these are then considered to be necessary. The effects upon readers in OAP Homes of differing kinds of library service could also be studied to advantage, since there *seemed* to be more borrowers in Homes where a trolley service operated deposit collections on different floors or in separate lounges were often not known about or remembered. The latter could take the simple form of dividing 20 Homes into four sections and, after pre-testing, to have a book flood in one quarter (including large print), to introduce a trolley service in another quarter, to have service on an individual basis with reading aloud and the loan of aids in the third group and to leave the fourth group as a control group with no new services added. These, then, are the directions in which further work is suggested.

REFERENCES

Bier, N
Optical management of partial sight *in The problems of the visually handicapped: transactions of a symposium held at the University of Aston in Birmingham, 3 May 1972;* edited by M. Wolffe, Birmingham, Department of Ophthalmic Optics, University of Aston in Birmingham, 1973. p.33-39.

British Broadcasting Corporation
In Touch: aids and services for blind and partially sighted people. London, BBC, 1973, 11

Cameron, A T
Bibliography of published material (including large print) concerning partially sighted people; compiled by Agnes T. Cameron. London, Disabled Living Foundation, 1977. 97p.

Carter, C F
British economic statistics: a report; by C.F. Carter and A.D. Roy. Cambridge, Cambridge U.P., 1954. 186p. (National Institute of Economics and Social Research. Economic and social studies series no. 14)

Childers, T
The information-poor in America; edited by T. Childers and J.A. Post. Metuchen, NJ, Scarecrow Press, 1975. 182p.

Community Relations Commission
Ethnic minorities in Britain: statistical data. 6th ed. London, Community Relations Commission, 1976.

Craddock, P R
Talking newspapers and library and information needs of the visually handicapped. *Leabharlann,* 7 (2), Summer 1978, p.54-65.

Cullinan, T R
The epidemiology of visual disability: studies of visually disabled people in the community. Canterbury, Health Services Research Unit, University of Kent at Canterbury, 1977. 148p. (HSRU report no. 28)

Cullinan, T R
Studies of visually disabled people in the community. *Regional Review,* 63, Spring 1978, p.21-25

Cullinan, T R, *and others*
Visual disability and home lighting *Lancet,* 24th March 1979, p.642-644.

Department of Education and Science.
The libraries' choice: London, HMSO, 1978. 54p. *(Library Information Series no. 10) (Chairman:* Mrs. A. Corbett).

Department of Health and Social Security
Blindness & partial sight in England, 1969-1976. London, HMSO, 1979. 31p. (Reports on public health and medical subjects; no. 129).

Genesky, S M
Binoculars: a long-ignored aid for the partially sighted. Santa Monica, California, The Rand Corporation, November 1973. 48p. (R-1402 HEW).

Going, M E
The pattern of care in old age *in Hospital libraries and work with the disabled;* compiled and edited by Mona E. Going. 2nd ed. London, Library Association, 1973, p.207-210.

Gray, P G
Mobility and reading habits of the blind; by P.G. Gray and J.E. Todd. London, HMSO, [1968]. 119p.

Greenhalgh, R
Who are the partially sighted? Who are the blind? *Oculus,* July/August 1978

Harris, A I
Social welfare for the elderly: a study in thirteen local authority areas in England, Wales and Scotland. London, HMSO, 1968. 2 vols.

Home Office — Prison Department. *Library facilities for people in custody.* London, HMSO, 1978. 20p. (Policy statement 7)

Hopkins, H — *The numbers game.* London, Secker and Warburg, 1973. 310p.

Hunt, A — *The elderly at home: a study of people aged sixty five and over living in the community in England in 1976.* Office of Population Censuses and Surveys. Social Survey Division, HMSO, 1978.

IFLA/FIAB Libraries in Hospitals Sub-Section — IFLA standards for libraries in hospitals (general service). *Unesco Bulletin for Libraries, 23* (2), March 1969, p.70-76

Large type books in print, 1978: subject index, title index, author index. London, Bowker, 1978. 674p.

Lewis, M J — *The elderly reader: a study of the reading needs of, and the scope for library services to, the elderly.* 1974. 300p. (Library Association Fellowship thesis).

Lewis, M J — Equipment in *Hospital libraries and work with the disabled;* compiled and edited by Mona E. Going. 2nd ed. London, Library Association, 1973, p.157-172.

Library Association — *Hospital libraries: recommended standards for libraries in hospitals.* [Revised ed.] London, Library Association, 1972. 18p.

Library Association — *Reading for the visually handicapped.* 3rd ed. London, Library Association, 1978.

Library Association — *West Midlands Branch. Report on library services to hospitals and handicapped people.* Birmingham, Library Association West Midlands Branch, 1970.

London Borough of Hillingdon. — Social Services Department. *Survey of the visually impaired in private households.* London Borough of Hillingdon Social Services Department, 1973 (Unpublished)

Marshall, M — *Seeing clear: books suitable for the partially seeing child.* London, School Library Association, 1977. 24p.

Ministry of Health — *The incidence and causes of blindness in England and Wales 1948-1962;* by A. Sorsby. London, HMSO, 1966. 80p. (Reports on Public Health and Medical Subjects No. 114).

Morris, A — *No feet to drag: report on the disabled;* by Alfred Morris and Arthur Butler. London Sidgwick and Jackson, 1972. 190p.

Munford, W A — Books for the partially sighted. *British Book News,* April 1976, p.245-247.

Optical Information Council. — *So you're partially sighted. . . a summary of the help available, and the use of low vision aids.* London, Optical Information Council, [1977]. 4p. (Optical Information Council Fact Sheet).

Pearson, A — Libraries and educational facilities in prisons. *Book Trolley,* 3 (7), September 1972, p.3-12.

Public library services. *In Touch,* 14, January 1979, p.5.

Richards, M — Spending cuts pushed up prices of technical books — publishers. *Times Higher Educational Supplement,* February 10 1978, 4.

Sanders, B M   *Library services in hospitals.* London, Library Association,
                           1966. 45p. (Library Association pamphlet, no. 27).

Shaw, A   *Print for partial sight: a report to the Library Association
                           Sub-Committee on Books for Readers with Defective Sight.*
                           London, Library Association, 1969. 92p.

Shaw A   Typographical factors for partially sighted, *in The Louis
                           Braille British conference on research into reading and
                           listening by the visually handicapped.* London, Southern
                           Regional Association for the Blind, 1975, p.58-73.

Silver, J   The use of low vision aids, *Regional Review,* 63, Spring 1978,
                           p.9-16.

                           Social trends, *1*, 1970, 52

Sturt, R   Help the blind, *Library Association Record, 79* (11),
                           November 1977, 654.

Armstrong, D J   Open forum: the future roles of voluntary associations.
                           Regional Review, 63, Spring 1978, 4-8.

                           Survey of public library service to hospitals, the housebound
                           and prisons. *Library & Information Bulletin, 1* (4), 1967,
                           p.113-118.

Thorpe, F A   Large print: an assessment of its development and potential.
                           Library Association Record, 74 (3), March 1972, p.42-43

Warren, M D   *The Canterbury survey of handicapped people.* Canterbury,
                           Health Services Research Unit, University of Kent at Canter-
                           bury, 1974.

Wolffe, M   The scope and application of visual aids *in Proceedings of the
                           Symposium on Light for Low Vision held at University
                           College, London on 4 April, 1978.* Hove, Partially Sighted
                           Society, 1980. p.39-43.

Yelland, M   Large print — difficulties and opportunities *in Proceedings of
                           the Symposium on Light for Low Vision held at University
                           College, London on 4 April 1978.* Hove, Partially Sighted
                           Society, 1980. p. 47-51.

USEFUL ADDRESSES

Age Concern, Bernard Sunley House, 60, Pitcairn Road, Mitcham, Surrey CR4 3LL

Association for the Education and Welfare of the Visually Handicapped, 'Highbury', 9, Yarmouth Road, Lowestoft NR32 4AW

Austin books (on loan only) — (*see* National Library for the Blind)

Blind Mobility Research Unit (maps) Nottingham University, Nottingham NG7 2RD

Bowker Publishing Co Ltd, PO Box 5, High Street, Epping, Essex CM16 4BU

British and Foreign Bible Society, 146, Queen Victoria Street, London EC4 4BX

British Association of Workers with the Visually Handicapped, 89, Park Hill, London SW4

British Broadcasting Corporation Publications, (In Touch) 35, Marylebone High Street, London W1M 4AA

British Diabetic Association, 3—6, Alfred Place, London WC1E 7EE

British Library of Tape Recordings for Hospital Patients, 12, Lant Street, London SE1 1QR

British Talking Book Service for the Blind, Mount Pleasant, Alperton, Wembley, Middlesex HAO 1RR

Chest, Heart and Stroke Association, St Martins, Grimms Hill, Great Missenden, Bucks HP16 9BG

Chivers, Cedric Ltd, 93-100 Locksbrook Road, Bath BA1 3HB

Contact magazine, 20, Middleton Hall Road, Kings Norton, Birmingham B30 1B7

Curley, John (*See* Magna Print Books)

DHSS Library, (Social Service Abstracts) Alexander Fleming House, Elephant and Castle, London SE1 6BY

Disabled Living Foundation, 346, Kensington High Street, London W14 8NS

Eyre and Spottiswoode Publishers Ltd., (Bible), 11 New Fetter Lane, London EC4P 4EE

Firecrest Publishing Ltd, Combe Park, Bath BA1 3NF

Foundation for Audio Research, 12, Netley Dell, Letchworth, Herts S96 2TF

Hall, G K (*See* Prior, George)

Harrap, George G and Co Ltd, 182, High Holborn, London WC1

In Touch (1p) bulletin, G Marshall, Exhall Grange School, Wheelwright Lane, Coventry CV7 9HP

Lloyds Bank PR publications, B Ousey, Lloyds Bank, 71, Lombard Street, London EC3

Look Forward (1p) *see* Chest, Heart and Stroke Association

Lythway Large Print Series, Lythway Press Ltd, Combe Park, Bath BA1 3NF

Magna Print Books, Bolton-by-Bowland, Nr Clitheroe, Lancs BB7 4NZ

Moon Society, Holmesdale Road, Reigate, Surrey

Multiple Sclerosis Society, 4, Tachbrook Street, London SW1V 1SJ

National Library for the Blind, Cromwell Road, Bredbury, Stockport SK6 2SG

National Listening Library, 49, Great Cumberland Place, London W1H 7LH

National Talking Magazines, Melbourne House, Melbourne Road, Wallington, Surrey SM6 8SD

New Beacon monthly (*See* Royal National Institute for the Blind)

New Portway Reprints (*See* Chivers, Cedric)

Northern Regional Association for the Blind, Headingley Castle, Headingley Lane, Leeds

Oculus magazine (*See* Partially Sighted Society)

Partially Sighted Society, 40, Wordsworth Street, Hove, East Sussex BN3 5BH

Prior, George, Publishers, Rugby Chambers, 2, Rugby Street, London WC1N 3QU

Reader's Digest (1p) enquiries, P K Robins, Hunter Publishing, 1, May Road, Twickenham, Middlesex

Research Centre for the Education of the Visually Handicapped, Birmingham University Faculty of Education, Selly Wick House, Selly Wick Road, Birmingham B29 7JF

Retinitis Pigmentosa Society, 24 Palmer Close, Redhill, Surrey

Royal National Institute for the Blind, 224, Great Portland Street, London W1N 6AA

Scottish Braille Press, Craigmillar Park, Edinburgh EH16 5NB

Scripture Gift Mission, Radstock House, Eccleston Street, London SW1W 9LZ

Southern and Western Regional Association for the Blind, 32, Old Queen Street, London SW1H 9HP

Students' Library, RNIB, 338 Goswell Road, London EC1

Students' Tape Library, Braille House, 338—346, Goswell Road, London EC1

Talking Newspaper Association of the United Kingdom, 4 Southgate Street, Winchester, Hants.

Tape Recording Service for the Blind, 48, Fairfax Road, Grange Estate, Farnborough, Hants GU14 8JP

Torch Trust for the Blind, Hallaton, Market Harborough, Leics LE16 8UJ

Trinitarian Bible Society, 217, Kingston Road, London SW19 3NN

Ulverscroft Large Print Books Ltd, The Green, Bradgate Road, Anstey, Leicester LE7 7FW

Warwick Research Unit for the Blind (1p and BR info, maps) Dr J Gill, University of Warwick, Coventry

World Contact magazine, Red Cross House, 100, Brook Green, London W6